Sweet Sugar

A symbol of the ancients returns to fight for the justice of the society

EMIL LOUSTAU

A catalogue record for this book is available from the National Library of Australia

Publisher:
ASPG (Australian Self-Publishing Group)
P.O. Box 159, Calwell, ACT Australia 2905
Email: publishaspg@gmail.com
http://www.inspiringpublishers.com

National Library of Australia Cataloguing-in-Publication entry

Author: Emil Loustau

Title: **Sweet Sugar**

ISBN: 978-1-922920-35-5 (Pbk)
ISBN: 978-1-922920-36-2 (eBook)

Foreword

Many people were involved in the formulation of this story and the actual facts that it is based upon. Tannen Heights certainly does exist, but under a different name, as a suburb of the metropolitan area of Perth, Western Australia; only the residents – past and present – will be able to identify it. The Australian Security Intelligence Organisation did have a building, called ASIO House, in view of the Barracks Arch at the western end of St. George's Terrace, in the 1970s. In the 1980s, this organisation relocated – for security reasons – and the address remains classified. The original building, however, still exists to this day.

Many thanks go to the proofreaders: Devon, James and Robin, Ian, and Daniel. Our ASIO liaison, who has reviewed this novel, is known, only to me, as 'Cherub'.

Table of Contents

Prologue 9

1: Who Needs A Bodyguard? 19

2: The Last Ensign 33

3: The Expensive Magazine 46

4: The Gorgons' Conference 57

5: A Kiss to Past Dangers 75

6: Two Halves Make A Golf Ball 98

7: Non-Police Brutality 116

8: Mr. Simos Reports 134

9: The Body In The Bushes 148

10: The Battle of Tannen Heights High 167

11: Flunked? 193

12: Two Minus One Leaves None 208

13: *Ç'est La Guerre!* 231

14: The Pavement Artists 249

15: The Liquidator, Liquidated 268

16: The Farm Of Death .... .285

17: Pain Will Not Stop Them 304

Epilogue 316

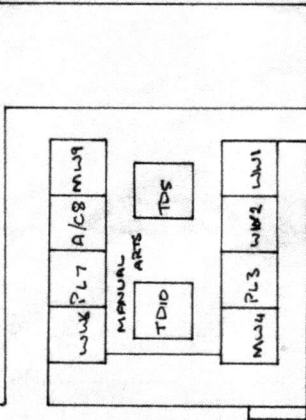
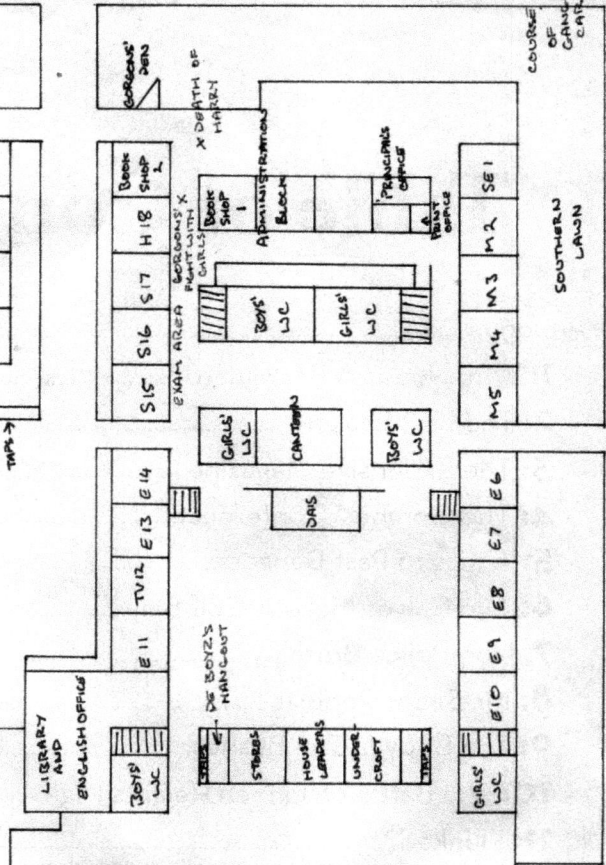
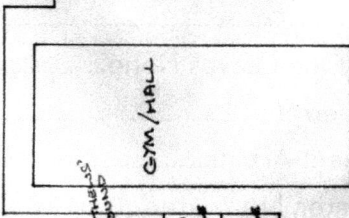
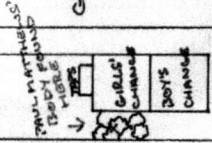
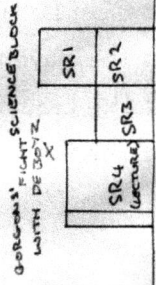
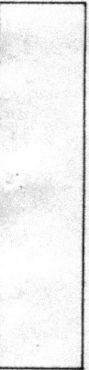
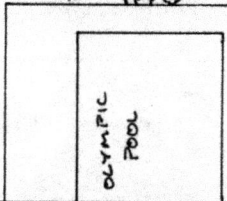
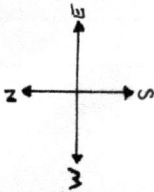

TANNEN HEIGHTS
SENIOR HIGH
SCHOOL
UPPER FLOOR
PLAN

U
T
S
STAFF ROOM
2
M
L
K

STORE
V
SCIENCE OFFICE
W
GUIDANCE OFFICE
SOCIAL STUDIES OFFICE

Q
HANK'S MEDICAL ROOM
CARETAKERS' LOCKERS
CLEANERS' LUNCH ROOM
X
Y
A
B
C
D
E DANCING
MUSIC STORE
F

BOYS' WC
MATHS OFFICE
O
STAFF WC

I
H
G

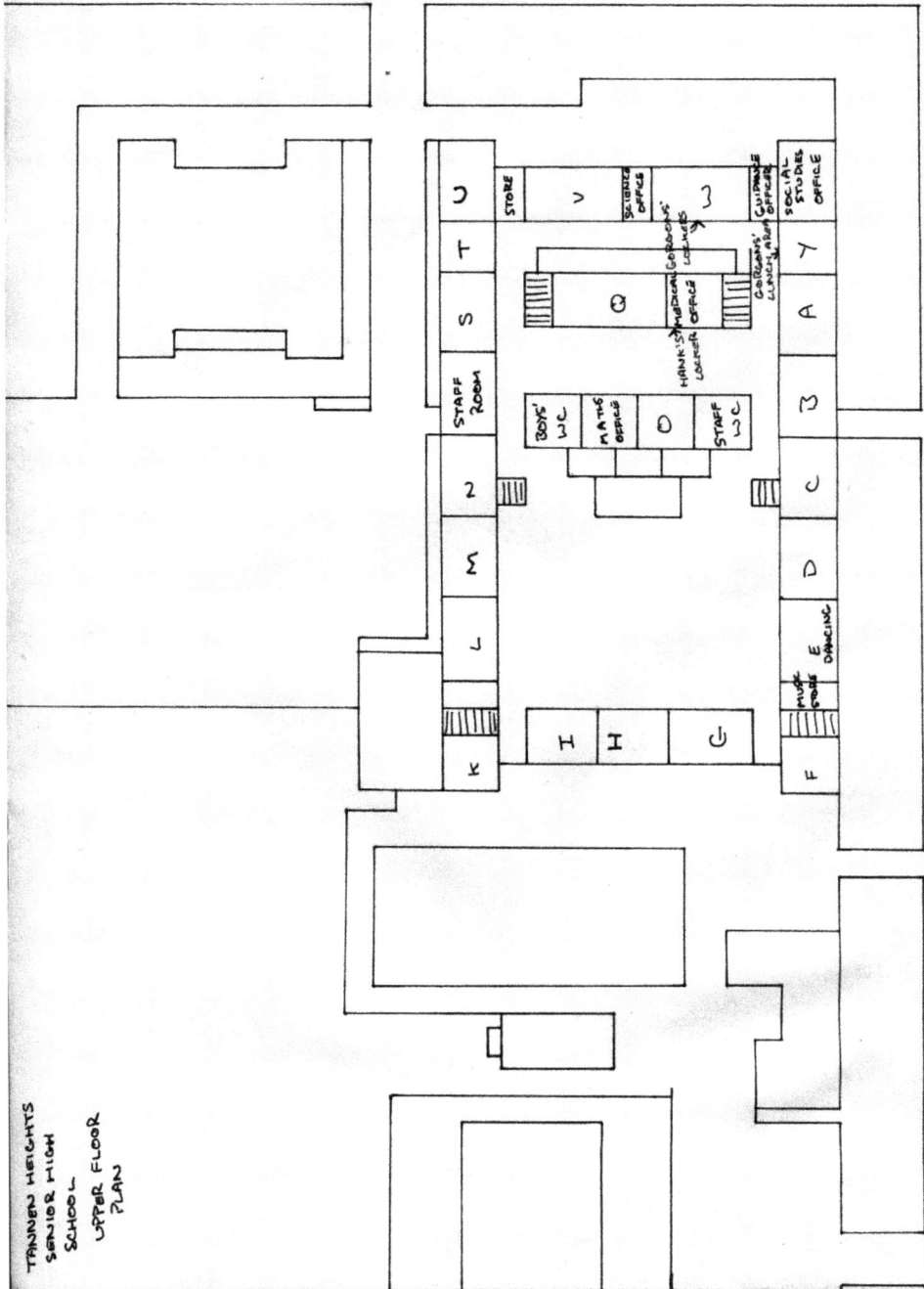

Prologue

The Geraldton Highway was dark, the July sun had disappeared behind the low hills in the west, leaving a magnificent sea of red in its wake. The vast expanse of low scrub and the occasional tree, which stretched from the distant horizon to the road edge, was changing colour from the natural darkish greens and sunburnt beige to blackish greens and darkish brown.

Only a Mack was using this stretch of road as it went on its way south to the state capital, Perth. In the cab, Graeme Chesston's mind wandered back to the events in Geraldton earlier that day. The job had been easier than he'd anticipated; the warehouse – a long, A-frame structure – was not difficult to find. A 'hawk-faced' man, with the habit of rubbing an extra-large knuckle against his lips when in thought, shut the roller door as Chesston had guided the eighteen-wheeler into the warehouse, where a team of storemen waited beside a fork-lift to load his rig.

While the storemen got on with their work, 'Hawk-face' took Chesston aside. The verbal business was short and to the point: 'Drive straight to Perth. Don't stop anywhere. You're expected in Osborne Park at half-past seven at the latest.'

His accent had confirmed Chesston's suspicions. As the Interpol files had informed him, he was American, and 'Hawk-face' had

9

once been involved with the Mob in Las Vegas. But now, here in Australia, he was a transport manager of a respectable sporting company ... or was it?

The pangs of hunger brought Chesston's thoughts back to the present and, as the lights of the petrol station/roadhouse at Cataby brightened, he turned the rig into the semi-trailer parking area. Despite the darkening sky, the lights of the roadhouse caused the surrounding bush to appear as ominous, towering shapes that threatened to engulf this small, isolated representative of civilisation in this small corner of the vast island continent. He parked the truck near the antique – and probably disused – petrol bowsers, set off to one side of the main bowsers, and lit by reflected lights from the awning. Another rig was parked beyond the brightness of the lights and visible only by the ambient light. Chesston squinted and could make out the logo of SMAU ENTERPRISES, emblazoned on the side of the trailer in large gold letters. Further still was another rig with no sign at all.

'A private ute,' he mused, climbing down from the cab. The gravel crunched beneath his feet, as he approached the door. With the sun a memory behind the hills, the easterly wind was growing steadily colder; he zipped up his parka.

A dog distrustfully watched Chesston from the shadows of the roadhouse but made no move, consolidating his position. He had been skulking in the shadows of these buildings for many nights, spending the daylight out deep in the bush. In his dim memory, he remembered the comforting rumble of these large vehicles, but from the inside of one, and with his master who had driven it. Then one day, he barked and barked and barked until his master stopped the truck and let him out. He had run out into the bush, as he had been trained to, and wet a tree ... but when he returned, the truck had gone! For days and nights, he had sat by the side of the road, watching vehicles speed by; some had even swerved off to try to run him down, just for the fun of it. He began to stay just off the side of the road, just out of sight, and await his master's return from the edge of the bush. Eventually, his hunger forced did not know how to find food ... food had always been given to him! He began to walk, following an instinctual urge to go home, eating wherever he could smell out carrion and keeping close to the road, but staying out of sight of it. The dog was confused about why he had been left behind but, somehow, he believed that all would be normal again when he reached home.

It took him many days before he sniffed out the odours of the cooked food, diesel, oil, and hot rubber. As he got closer, the odours intensified and now he could smell the presence of man; he slowed down and approached, warily. The closer he got, the more compelling the smells; before long, he was running through the bush, his tongue lolling out the side of his open mouth. Then, suddenly, he was in the open! In his excitement, he had burst out of the bush and into the gravelled parking area at Cataby Roadhouse. Quickly, he ducked back into the security of the bush and lay down to watch the comings and goings of trucks, vans, cars, and cars pulling caravans or trailers. Once the safety of darkness had arrived, the dog emerged from the scrub and kept to the shadows, skirting the open area, and headed for the strongest odours of food. This was found towards the rear of the main building, from large metal receptacles. The odours were strong, despite the covers on the receptacles, and his empty stomach began to growl painfully. His first attempt to remove the lid failed. The second attempt had been noisy and had attracted the attention of one of the people inside, who came to investigate. His third try had succeeded, and the lid had fallen with a large crashing sound, which had startled him, and he retreated to the bush, his tail between his legs. A person came out and scanned the area with a torch but failed to see the dog. The person gave up and returned inside without replacing the fallen lid. He had eaten well, that night, and had slept well afterward. By the next morning, he was back in the bush, but his stomach, the odours, and – more importantly – his short-term memory of near-starvation caused him to linger there.

JULY 28. 7:15PM, WESTERN AUSTRALIA TIME

The interior of the roadhouse was brightly lit, and the attendant followed Chesston's move to the counter with a glass and watery eye. Chesston was aware that the other truckies eyed him with disdain and suspicion through the thick cigarette smoke. Two rough-looking characters shouted to him, in a series of curses and four-letter words, to close the door which had refused to shut. He ordered some food and a coffee and glared, menacingly, at the other truckies, while he waited. Chesston didn't have to wait long.

Ignoring the swear words, he closed the door behind him, taking himself and his food back to the truck. The dog, hiding in the shadows, would provide better company, he told himself. He went back to the rig, facing the cold and darkness, rather than confront those dissolute truckies.

Across the distance of the road, a maroon Holden Commodore was devoid of its passengers. A man focused a pair of binoculars on the truck driver, with some difficulty from the lack of light, but caught his silhouette in all its stillness. He exchanged a glance with the Commodore driver who stood next to him, and with an evil grin that resolved him, he raised his right hand and rubbed the large knuckle of his index finger against his lower lip ...

JULY 28. 7:25PM, WESTERN AUSTRALIA TIME

Chesston looked at the food with distaste, a serving of greasy French fries, a quarter piece of salty chicken, and a cup of weak and milky coffee. He carried it back to the cab of his truck. With food like this, it was no wonder that the truckies were usually bad-tempered. The one thing Chesston couldn't understand was why most truckies were overweight when this was the low-quality rubbish served up at roadhouses. He had taken a bite out of the chicken, nibbled a chip, and sipped at the coffee. That had been enough. One did not have to be a food connoisseur to realise that he had purchased food unfit for human consumption. Chesston looked across the lit area to the shadows, where he could just see the dog's nose. He knew that the dog was watching him.

Chesston pitched a chip toward the dog. It landed on the far edge of the lit area. Warily, the dog's head emerged from the shadows and, slowly, he approached the chip. Chesston watched the animal swallow it whole and then sniff around for more, so Chesston threw another one and watched the dog gobble it up. The next one landed further into the lit area and closer to Chesston's truck. At first, the dog just moved back and forth, pacing along the edge of the lit area, weighing up the feasibility of getting the food safely and making a quick getaway. Then he bolted for the food but, by then, Chesston had thrown a piece of chicken closer to his truck. The dog threw caution to the wind and went for the white meat, and the next piece of white meat, and the next one, and the next. Chesston peeled the chicken flesh off the bone, making sure that there were no small bones anywhere. He knew chicken bones were bad for dogs.

Chesston climbed down from the cab of his truck and the dog fled to a safe distance, but he made a small pile of chips beside the truck, before heading for the nearest bin. The pile was gone, by the time he returned, and the dog was sitting, expectantly, beside the truck. Its tail was sweeping the gravel. He looked at the dog and the dog looked at him. Chesston reached into the cab and grabbed the last of the chips. He showed the dog how much was left and threw them back into the cab. One dropped at his feet and the dog leapt forward and devoured it, then made an incredible jump into the cab. Chesston climbed in, settled, and started the truck.

As the truck rumbled to life, the dog sat up in the passenger's seat, already assuming the role of the permanent fixture; in fact, the dog appeared to be enjoying his new position, and sat high in the cab, eagerly waiting to leave the roadhouse.

The occupants of the Commodore watched the receding taillights of the rig reduce in size with distance. Hawk-face nodded slightly, and the driver brought the car onto the road. He made a stop, Hawk-face told himself, and disciplinary measures were required.

The country music on the radio faded into a news brief with the leading story being of the search for terrorists that had murdered a *ding*[1] politician that they had kidnapped. *Why bother about other people's problems when we have enough of our own?* Chesston asked himself. If the law didn't knuckle down soon, Australia would develop into a society of fear, crime, and psychotics ... very much like America. Chesston smiled as he regarded the bitzer[2] sitting beside him. The dog looked like a cross between a cocker spaniel and a kelpie. The coat looked the same colour as that of a cocker spaniel, but the kelpie traits were more than visible. Anyway, whatever he was, with his belly full, he laid down contentedly and slept. Chesston smiled inwardly; it was going to be interesting having this creature around.

Something flashed in the rear-view mirror and Chesston's eye wandered there. A pair of lights were approaching rapidly. As the lights neared, they slowed and Chesston realised it was a car and not a truck, as he had first thought. The car swerved from side to side, the driver obviously trying to pass the rig, but unsure of his chances of survival.

'Like a mouse creeping past a sleeping cat,' Chesston remarked to the dog.

The driver, with confidence bubbling over, eased his all-white car into the other lane and prepared to pass.

Chesston applied pressure to the accelerator; no mouse would pass this cat, sleeping or otherwise. As the car driver, only slightly perturbed, slid alongside the cab, Chesston looked down

---

[1] Derogatory term for an Italian (West Australian slang).

[2] A mongrel (Australian slang).

only to discover that the vehicle was a police car. The passenger signalled for him to pull over. He obeyed immediately; the last thing he wanted was trouble with the law.

But then again, who was he kidding? He suddenly realised he was in hot water if they searched the rig and discovered his real cargo. But then, it wasn't common practice to search the trucks on the Geraldton to Perth run. He indicated and guided the left wheels onto the highway shoulder. The truck came to a standstill with the loud wheeze of hydraulic brakes.

The police car stopped a short distance ahead of the Mack on the highway shoulder.

Having climbed from the cab, Chesston watched as the two patrolmen left their car and approached him with slow, deliberate steps. One – the passenger – produced a piece of paper, and when in reach, handed it to the truck driver.

'Can I help you two gentlemen?' he said cheerfully, whilst glancing at the sheet of paper and discovering it was a search warrant, stamped and signed in Geraldton. Chesston felt his stomach drop thirty metres.

'We're going to search your rig … mate!' the officer, who had given him the warrant, said curtly. He seemed to be the spokesman, while the other stuck his nose into every nook and cranny of the truck.

Refolding the warrant, he handed it back to the officer. 'What're you looking for?'

'We'll tell you … when we find it,' the officer said smartly, pushing past Chesston and climbing up into the cab. The dog, noticing an invader in his new domain, jumped up and growled – loudly, menacingly – at the policeman. The officer froze and then turning, retreated from the cab with feigned dignity. Clearing his throat, he turned to Chesston. 'Nothing in there.' He moved off towards the rear doors of the trailer, where his companion had already broken the seals and had them open.

Chesston grinned and glanced into the cab where the dog had settled back into his previous position on the passenger's seat. He winked: 'Good on ya, mate. That's one problem solved, and one I owe ya.' He then closed the door and joined the two officers.

One of them had opened the nearest crate and now, six or seven cartons of golf balls were sitting on the other crates. A crowbar lay at one of the officers' feet and Chesston picked it up, to put it back. The spokesman glared at him suspiciously, until it had left Chesston's hands.

He smiled sweetly at the officer. 'Only putting it away.' Looking at the open crate, he asked with genuine interest: 'Found anything?'

The policeman ignored Chesston and when he had walked away, went back to his search. 'That bloke's a shit-house,' he told his partner. 'He's full of himself!' The other laughed.

Fifteen minutes later they weren't laughing, having opened nine other crates which had produced nothing but more golf balls.

Chesston looked up from the paperback he held, and which also rested against the steering wheel, to see the two police officers glaring at him through the windscreen. 'What now?' he asked the dog, as he closed the book and climbed out. 'Can I help you, gentlemen, now?'

The spokesman didn't answer immediately. Instead, he produced a citation booklet and hurriedly filled in the details, moving about casually to check the registration and plates. 'Your tyres are going bald,' he finally said, 'when you get to Perth, grace them with your presence and pay this fine, as well as have the truck checked out.'

Taking the citation, Chesston gave it the once-over. 'Okay.' He moved to the rear of the trailer. Good thing he had, as those bloody bastards didn't even close and lock the doors. Looking inside, he saw that the crates had been left open, spewing out their contents of golf balls. He stuffed the cartons back into their place and, eventually, closed the doors. When he got back into the cab, he noticed that the police car had gone.

Chesston let the truck idle while he fished in his pocket for the citation. Having given it a second once-over, he screwed it up and threw it out the open window. The dog's ears shot up as the ball of paper hit the macadam.

'Don't worry, dog,' he said, 'it's nothing.' Glancing at the ball of paper, he continued: 'Nothing at all.'

Guiding the stick into gear and releasing the clutch, the Mack left the shoulder.

Shortly after, a maroon Holden Commodore pulled up near where the paper ball had rolled to. The passenger got out and strolled over, casually. Soon, the paper was straightened out in his hands, and, as he watched the receding lights of the Mack, his right hand rose, and he began rubbing the much-loved knuckle against his lower lip.

Chapter One
Who Needs A Bodyguard?

Jim Saston sat sideways in his chair, facing the bearded English teacher, who was perched against his desk. Behind the façade of interest, the boy was silently counting the seconds – which would lead to the end of the period and the dismissal of school for another day – while Mr. Ross, the English teacher, droned on and attempted to draw his visibly bored class into the one-sided discussion about the English reader: a copy, of which, lay unopened on Jim's desk.

Mr. Ross paused and looked forlornly at his class before letting out a long sigh. To say he had one of the most interest-filled classes at Tannen Heights Senior High School, he believed, would either be called a lie or a gross understatement. Since he had started discussing the novel, less than ten percent of the class had participated in the one-and-a-half hours of the two periods. Thinking about it he began feeling uneasy; having some twenty-odd pairs of bored eyes watching you constantly was not comforting.

Jim regarded the dog-eared paperback with distaste. *The Last Ensign*, he read silently. A cheap, smelly spy book. Its author, Bernard Everett Brown, knew as much about the work of spies as Moses knew about the theory of relativity.

The teacher's eyes found their way to his watch and Jim referred to his own, neither one trusting the display of the Education Department-issued wall clock. Twenty-five minutes past three. Five more minutes to go, and then it's goodbye to school for another day. Mr. Ross's eyes returned to his class. 'The siren'll be going soon,' he announced. 'So instead of waiting for it, you're all dismissed – on the condition that all the chairs are on the desks before you leave.'

The students obeyed, mumbling things about unfair conditions, and soon E7 was empty. While Mr. Ross, with a file in hand, marched across the main quadrangle to the library and English faculty office, his students were on their way to their lockers ... or home.

Jim and a friend headed towards their lockers, situated on the upper floor of the nearly thirty-year-old building. 'Exams start on Friday,' he said, 'you ready for them?' When no answer came, he noticed that the boy was busy eyeing one of the few girls in Year 11 to have a figure worth boasting about. Jim snapped his fingers in front of his friend's nose. 'Fab, your entire future's on the line!'

Fabrizio Arterro's smile slowly disappeared as his head turned to face Jim. 'My future's on the line? Speak for yourself, mate. At least, I didn't fail physics last term – or English, this term.'

'Just because I refuse to read that dilapidated piece of rubbish doesn't mean I'll fail English,' Jim said sternly. 'As far as I'm concerned, that book's a lot of *kak*[3]! Super—'

Fab shot up a hand, interrupting Jim's diatribe. 'You're in Australia now,' he reminded Jim, 'so cut out the Afrikaans.'

---

[3]Shit (Afrikaans).

'Oh, excuse me,' Jim replied sarcastically, giving a slight mock humbled bow. 'That book's a lot of shit! Super-secret agent, Burt Hammond, can destroy an army while supposedly unarmed – only because the US scientists have given him shoes that automatically become hand grenades by removing the heels, or some other idiotic idea. We shouldn't be reading trash like that. What we should be reading are the selected books of Charles Dickens, George Eliot, Thomas Hardy ... or even ... William Shakespeare.'

Fab sighed. They had had this argument before. 'Everybody's entitled to their opinion. But to pass the exams at the end of the term it's better to read what they give you. I don't like the book either, Jim, but I'll worship it till it gives me high marks in the English exam on Monday.'

Fab was a little taller than Jim, with light brown hair that curled at the nape and his forehead. He possessed the handsome features that are born of most Italian males. Jim, on the other hand, had pitch-black hair that tended to curl more than Fab's and for that reason, his hair was always trimmed short and neatly combed.

Their lockers were outside Room W, directly above the Administration Office. A dark-haired boy was sitting near Fab's. As they approached, he looked up from the book he was reading and, seeing nothing of interest, returned his full attention to it. 'Wagging class again?' Fab asked him, placing the extra-large grey school bag on the bench beside the reader.

The boy's eyes rose distractedly from the paperback and regarded the speaker matter-of-factly. 'Actually, Mr. Flood was away today, as I told you at lunchtime – but as usual, nobody listened. Anyway, our replacement – Miss Turner – got tired of trying to keep us quiet and dismissed us ... early.' He glanced into the open bag as Fab searched his pockets for his locker key. 'You're reading *The Last Ensign*, too?'

Fab nodded. 'Yeah. Not much of a story, though.'

'Oh, I don't know,' he replied, 'I liked it.'

Jim turned towards the seated boy in disbelief. Mike Daniels always seemed so ... level-headed. Oh well, Jim wasn't perfect, he could've been wrong about him. 'You've read that *kak*? Since when have you been interested in spy stories, Mike? I thought you were a sci-fi buff.'

'I am,' Mike replied defensively. 'But these Burt Hammond stories are interesting ... and easy to read.'

'Easy to read?' Jim mocked. 'How many of these scraps have you read?'

'Just the one, but I'm reading this one now,' and he handed Jim the copy he held.

'*The Leper's Curse*, featuring Burt Hammond.' Jim gave Fab a queer look. 'Our friend has finally flipped.'

'These books are okay. What could possibly be wrong with them?'

Fab felt like he would love to be able to crawl into his locker and shut the door. But unfortunately, Mike's question had opened the floodgates for a full Jim Saston rant.

'For one thing, they're pulp literature; they're badly written and constructed; they lack detail and credibility ... Need I continue?'

Mike looked at Jim for a moment before answering, the words forming a sentence in his head. 'If they were badly written, then the Education Department wouldn't've chosen them as English readers.'

Jim shrugged. 'Oh well, it just proves that the hallways of the Education Department are filled with illiterates!'

'That's your opinion,' Fab stated, shutting his locker. 'But then, the opinion of a sixteen-year-old doesn't mean much.'

Mike turned to Fab. 'What do you think of *The Last Ensign*?'

'It's so-so,' Fab replied with an accompanying hand gesture. 'But I have to admit that it's better than the rubbish we had to read last term.' He checked the books in his bag once more and asked, 'When do your exams start?'

'Middle of next term,' Mike said and after a slight pause added, 'At the moment we're sitting through a few tests to close the term.'

'I wish it was the same for us,' Jim remarked, squeezing the last textbook into his own grey bag, leaving his locker practically empty. 'Unfortunately, our exams start on Friday. Thank the gods there's a half-day tomorrow. I can dedicate the whole afternoon to studying physics.'

'What're you complaining about?' Mike demanded. 'At least you have the holidays free from upcoming exams.'

'Yeah,' Fab agreed, 'but we still spend those holidays worrying about the marks we haven't seen yet.'

Tired of the conversation, Jim consulted his watch and found that the siren should've sounded seven minutes ago. 'The siren'll be going any minute,' he announced uncertainly, 'and then we'll have to fight our way out of here.' Even before the words had left his mouth, the siren whined across the grounds like an air raid siren warning of an enemy air attack. What had once been a quiet and peaceful seat of learning exploded into a hubbub of chaos and activity, as students rushed from their classes to their lockers. 'Well,' Jim sighed, putting down his bag, 'now we wait.'

'Did you hear about Trevor Jameson's brother?' Mike asked them.

'Isn't that the one that goes to the "special school"?' Fab inquired, seating himself next to Mike.

Jim leaned against the iron railing and watched a pretty blonde making her way to her locker, outside SE1, on the lower level. 'I heard that he was in the hospital,' he said, without looking away.

'"Was" is the right word,' Mike replied. 'He died yesterday still in a coma. He never woke up.'

'How come he was in the hospital, anyway?' Jim asked.

'Overdose, I heard,' Fab answered.

'Yeah, sugar ... heroin,' Mike said.

'We know what sugar is,' Jim replied, looking away from the blonde for a few seconds to regard his black-haired friend. Eventually, his attention returned to her, and his eyes surveyed the contours of her body.

'It's amazing how he got his hands on that shit,' Fab said, half to himself. 'Especially in a school like that.'

'What's so amazing about it?' Jim's eyes left the blonde, momentarily, to glance at Fab. 'Drugs are now a part of life. It's easy to get your hands on what you want – providing you have the contacts.'

'Well, it doesn't go on here. At least, I've never seen anything of the sort.'

'That's your trouble, Fab,' Jim said, the blonde temporarily forgotten. 'You look, but you don't see. It goes on around you all the time. Right under your nose ... and that's quite a feat, considering the size of yours.'

'How do you know?' he challenged. The size of Fab's nose was always a sore subject.

'Because I've seen ... and haven't seen. If you know what I mean.'

'I never know what you mean!' Fab retorted, still stinging about his nose, 'and no, we don't know.'

'I've noticed things being passed. But that doesn't necessarily mean the items were narcotics. And besides, the people didn't look like drug addicts.'

'How would you know what they're supposed to look like?'

Jim smiled confidently in the face of Fab's challenge. 'Because I know the signs. I know what to look for,' he lied.

'Like?' Mike queried.

The smile slowly disappeared and was replaced by a vacant expression. His confident smile always worked; why not now? They had him, but they didn't know it – he hoped. Come on, Saston, think of something, he urged himself.

'We're waiting," Fab baited. It was Jim's time to be the focus of ridicule.

What had he read once about heroin? Didn't the users develop a jaundiced complexion? Too bad, he told himself, these twerps wouldn't know too much about it. 'The addicts have a yellowish complexion—'

'So do Asians!' Mike said. The two listeners burst out laughing.

Jim glared at both of them. 'Their features are also drawn.'

'So, they're not photographed,' Fab offered.

'Shut up!' Jim snapped. 'As for the pushers, they normally seem to be loners and, also, you'll find that they are addicted to their own merchandise as well.'

Fab leaned forward and picked up his bag. 'That was interesting,' he said. 'I must admit that I don't know much about it, so I can't say if you're bullshitting or not.'

Jim smirked in the face of his little victory and turned back to admire the blonde, but she had already gone.

'Chris left while you were lecturing,' Fab commented. 'If it's any consolation, she did look up here and smiled at the back of your head.'

Jim glared at him and retrieved his bag. 'It's late,' he said and headed for the stairs, not waiting for them.

'He's angry with you, Fab,' Mike said, loud enough for Jim to hear. 'You know he doesn't like Christine Porter; he just has wet dreams about her.'

'He's horny, like the rest of us,' Fab admitted fatalistically.

'Very funny,' Jim replied without turning. 'There are two ways of getting downstairs: you can use the stairs, or I can throw you both over the railing ... if you keep making jokes.'

The two laughed and trotted down the stairs behind Jim. At the bottom, the three split up and went their separate ways home: Fab, out the front breezeway and up the street to the bus stop on Wanneroo Road; Mike, across the oval and two more roads to the three-bedroom, weatherboard house he shared with his parents and eight siblings; and Jim, off across the quad to the opposite breezeway which gave access to the gymnasium and science block. As usual, he cut across the science block instead of using the closest exit to the outside world. Going this way, he would pass the school's Olympic-sized swimming pool and the change rooms, which were commonly used at recess as students' illicit smoking rooms.

Voices, emerging from the alley separating these change rooms from the gym, attracted Jim's attention. One of the voices was familiar, and, noting the menacing tone in which it was uttered, Jim decided to listen in on the conversation.

'The price's gone up,' the voice said. 'Inflation!'

'But I need it,' the other voice said. The desperation of the owner made the voice higher than normal. 'I need it, bad. I'll pay what you want tomorrow … just let me have it now!'

'Get outta've it! What ya take me for?' The voice paused for a reply, almost inviting one. But when none came, it continued. 'First ya give me the money … then ya get this.'

Andrews! Hank Andrews! Those 'ya's' were unmistakable. That voice belonged to Hank Andrews! To confirm his suspicions, Jim risked a glance around the corner and discovered that he was right.

Hank Andrews had long black hair that had probably felt a comb twice in his sixteen years. His thin cheeks and aquiline nose were covered in pimples. His grey eyes betrayed his hatred for the society that had refused to understand him.

The other boy was also familiar, although Jim couldn't recall his name. But for some unknown reason, he was certain that this boy was a Year 10 student. It was because of this that Hank was displaying his alien tough-guy routine to him.

The boy suddenly lashed out at Hank, as he began to head for the oval and away from where Jim stood. The blow to Hank's arm was answered by a vicious jab to the boy's throat and, as he fell, Hank's steel-capped shoes were waiting to kick him into the gym wall. Without a second glance or expression of concern, Hank left him wheezing for air.

'Are you okay?' Jim asked him when Hank was out of earshot.

Not having the strength to say anything, he nodded painfully and attempted to rise. Jim grabbed his arm and helped the boy to his feet.

Jim took a stab in the dark. 'He put the price up, hey?'

The boy shot round and stared, fear awash on his face. 'You saw?'

'A little,' Jim said and noticed the boy's hand, subconsciously, go to his left arm, just above the elbow.

Like that, is it? he asked himself. Hank Andrews: the tall, wiry, black-haired ex-member of De Boyz – a gang of toughies, whose only enjoyment, apart from smoking marijuana, was to gang up on any lone student from the Catholic school up the road – was selling drugs in the school. There had always been rumours floating around Tannen Heights connecting Hank with the local drug flow. But never had anything been proven and everyone just took it as vicious gossip started by an unknown. And now, Jim Saston had discovered the truth of the rumour. Old Hank was a pusher – a small one, but a pusher, nonetheless.

Suddenly realising where his right hand was, the boy began rubbing it and made excuses about injuring his elbow in the fall but cowered back when Jim offered to examine the affected area.

'How long have you been addicted to narcotics?' he queried out of the blue.

The boy's mouth fell open in surprise to the directness of the question, and the calmness in Jim's voice. 'What?' he finally managed to croak.

'Come on. You know quite well what I'm talking about. The marks on your arm are caused by a hypodermic – and don't try telling me they're mosquito bites, or I'll thump you harder than Hank did!'

'You're crazy,' he cried before running away.

'Mate,' Jim murmured, watching him sprint across the oval, 'you're in a lot of trouble.' He picked up his bag and continued his way home.

The Alsatian was stretched out on the garage floor, dozing. Attracted by a sound, his eyes lifted lazily, and his ears flicked while his tail began to brush the cool concrete upon seeing his master – dressed in faded blue jeans and the blue and gold windcheater that passed as the official colours for Tannen Heights Senior High School – enter the yard.

'Hello, Shaka,' Jim said pleasantly, passing him on the way to the front door.

Tail beating empty air, Shaka followed his master inside. The two cats curled up on Jim's bed and regarded him lazily as he deposited his grey school bag beside the student desk. Shaka sniffed at the felines, contemplating whether to join them or not.

Sensing the German shepherd's supposed thoughts, Jim said without looking up from his open bag: 'I wouldn't try it if I were you, boy.' With all his homework on the desk, the empty bag collapsed on itself, Jim decided to have a snack before starting work.

Sitting at the breakfast bar, casually paging through a large gourmet cookbook full of colour pictures was Julianne Peterson – his guardian's wife. She was tall and seductively slim with long blonde hair and jade-green eyes. Though she spoke perfect English, her Swedish accent was more than noticeable and, when angry, the accent would become dominant, making her words unintelligible. She looked up, as Jim entered, and asked about his day at school.

Jim opened the fridge and removed a packet of sliced ham. 'Rather interesting,' he said and disappeared into the pantry for a moment, reappearing with two slices of bread. 'I discovered a pusher at school today.'

Julianne closed the book. His last sentence meant trouble. 'And what do you intend to do about it?' But before he answered, she already knew what he had decided.

He halved the sandwich with meticulous care. 'There's nothing I can do ... for the moment. But when I've gathered the proper evidence, I'll serve it to Sam on a silver platter.'

Julianne sighed. Poor Sam, she told herself. The last time Jim had played policeman, Senior-Detective Sergeant Samuel O'Reilly had ended up hooked on aspirins because of this boy's unorthodox means of acquiring proof for his well-meant investigations.

'Somehow, I don't think Sam will be overwhelmingly excited about your help,' she said.

Jim looked hurt. 'It's not my fault Sam's a sore loser.'

Julianne refrained from commenting and reopened the cookbook, thinking how similar Jim was to his deceased father. In the brief period that she had known John Saston, she had found him to be a very stubborn, self-centred man who suffered greatly from over-confidence. It was this over-confidence, she believed, that finally got ASIO's number one trouble-shooter killed.

'What are you thinking about?' Jim asked.

'Just comparing you to your dad,' she said.

'Do I pass?'

Julianne nodded slowly, sadly. 'If that Russian hadn't killed him, he would have been so proud of you ... you're just like him.'

Jim nodded, not fully understanding what she meant.

'But, in a way, it's a good thing that Mark put you through that training,' Julianne said, 'otherwise you wouldn't have Department 9 and Callobar to protect you when playing detective.'

Jim scowled. 'I don't need Callobar to protect me,' he retorted, and taking the remnants of the sandwich, returned to his room. 'Callobar to protect me – ha!' he said to himself, placing the plate on the desk.

Smelling food, the two tabbies jumped from his bed and began flirting around his legs. Jim gave each a pat and tore one of the two slices, in his sandwich, in thirds, and fed the cats and Shaka.

On one corner of the desk was a black and white photo, in a simple wooden frame, of a typical wedding scene. There were four people: the bride and bridegroom, and the bridesmaid and best man. As Jim studied his parents' wedding photo, tears welled up in his eyes. His mother was beautiful, a bit shorter than his father's five-foot-nine height and dark coloured hair. He never knew her. From what his father had told him, she died a few hours after giving him life, from irreversible complications.

Jim's eyes rested on the face of the only parent he'd ever known. 'What do you think, Dad? Do I need protecting?' Wiping the tears from his face, Jim decided he didn't. He did not need protection from anyone, having been raised in a suburb of Pretoria. Being an English-speaking child in an Afrikaans-dominated society had had its drawbacks. Every day Jim would return home from school looking like he'd been put through a grinder – always the victim of a group of Afrikaans boys.

Weeks of his father talking to the school principal having resulted in no change to the situation, John Saston, finally, decided to teach his son basic karate, emphasising that he expected Jim to: 'put all of them in one of two places: hospital or the cemetery!' The boy corrupted the blows, kicks, and blocks into his own pattern of fighting, and by the end of the week, the two top Afrikaner bullies were in hospital both suffering from broken bones, and Jim, having lived up to his father's advice, was in serious trouble. By the time the Service recalled John Saston to Australia, Jim had changed schools nine times.

Moving over to the pine wardrobe, he opened the top drawer and removed a small object, wrapped in newspaper, which had been taped behind it. He unwrapped the parcel to reveal a black-handled switchblade and a small leather pouch. Julie and Mark were unaware of this item's existence, and that, though it resembled an ordinary switchblade, it didn't function as one. After buying it, he had pulled it apart and replaced the spring with a stronger one and placed it so that the blade no longer flicked out but was catapulted from the handle and flew straight as an arrow until hitting its target. The pouch carried seven spare blades.

Holding the switchblade, he studied it diligently. 'Bodyguard ... ha!'

Chapter Two
The Last Ensign

AUGUST 3. 10:30 AM, WESTERN AUSTRALIA TIME

Gangs exist in all schools. A few are liked by the teachers; others detested. Some are feared by the younger students and the not-so-brave older ones, while others are totally ignored or merely tolerated. Tannen Heights Senior High School was no different and full of gangs fitting all categories. One of the gangs liked by the teachers – and tolerated by the students – was the League of the Gorgon Five. There were nine members in this group; the original number having been five, as suggested by the latter – and original – part of the name. As the membership grew, however, 'the League' prefix was added. Their favourite hangout was a small, paved triangular area at the front of the school and not too far from the principal's office. The teachers had dubbed it *The Gorgons' Den*, while the general student population was not aware of it.

Leaving his bag at the history class, Jim descended the stairs and made his way to the Gorgons' Den where Fab, Mike, and the other six members would meet during morning recess. Two more periods and then home for the rest of the day to study physics for tomorrow's exam. He wondered what the exam would be like. What diabolical trick questions had old man Radke sneaked into it? Jim shrugged. Oh well if you fail – you fail! You can only do your best, not better than that.

Passing through the breezeway, near the bookshop that sold study aids and textbooks for senior school, which the Gorgons used to reach their den, Jim could hear Fab's voice above the usual din of the school. A deep, placid voice answered, and Jim recognised it as that of Danny Fletcher. Danny was a new member of the group and was still surprising the other Gorgons. His voice always remained calm and betrayed very little, if no emotion at all, and made it difficult to determine just what sort of mood he was in. Danny was no taller than Fab, with straight dark-brown hair and blue eyes hidden behind thin wire-rimmed, photochromatic, prescription glasses. Unlike Fab, he wore blue jeans instead of dark grey school trousers but retained the grey shirt.

Fab caught sight of Jim and refrained from completing the sentence long enough to greet his friend, then returned his attention to Danny. 'Where was I? Oh yeah ... the book was written at the height of the Cold War and gives a basic idea of what the Communist Bloc was up to during the fifties and sixties.'

Jim rolled his eyes. 'The Cold War centred mainly in Europe,' interrupted Jim, leaning against the wooden railing. It creaked under his weight. 'But occasionally, it stretched as far as Cuba ... or Australia.'

'We've never had trouble with the Russians,' Fab challenged.

'Oh, really? Ever heard of the Petrov Affair?' Jim replied, with a twinkle in his eye. 'It's about a Soviet spy who defected over when he was working at the embassy in Canberra, sometime in the fifties. The actual operation was to get his wife from the two KGB guards who were taking her back to Moscow to be executed.

ASIO removed her from the plane when it stopped in Darwin for refuelling. The Kremlin wasn't too happy.'

Fab exchanged looks with Danny. At times, Jim also managed to surprise the other Gorgons. Where Jim got his information on espionage operations, Fab wanted to know. But if Jim could get it so could he and intended to check up on it. For the moment, Fab decided, it was time to change the subject. 'The English exam's on Monday,' he announced. 'How do you expect to pass it without reading the book?'

'I have read it,' Jim replied matter-of-factly.

'Oh, yeah,' Fab said, glancing momentarily at Danny, in triumph. 'When?'

'Last night.'

'You read the whole book last night?' Danny asked.

Jim regarded him innocently and smiled. 'If you don't believe me, I'm happy to recite the story to you.'

'What story?' asked one of the four newcomers who had just rounded the corner.

'*The Last Ensign*,' Fab replied.

Larry Mitchell looked at Jim in disbelief, then remembered the carton of choc milk he held and opened it. He was short, with a weasel-like build and shaggy dark brown hair. With one gulp he emptied the carton. The tall and well-rounded boy standing near him regarded Larry with disgust. This was Harry Callahan: good-looking and well-dressed in expensive clothes and Italian-made shoes and a two-hundred-dollar watch wrapped around his left wrist. Tony Waters and the Japanese boy, Tetsuro Shomira, were dressed like Jim, in grey jeans and a light-coloured body shirt. Mike Daniels's and Jack Talbot's late arrival interrupted Jim's recital and he started again:

'Burt Hammond is the hero of the book and one, in the never-ending long line, of America's super-spy heroes. He gets orders to report to CIA headquarters and there, Murdoch briefs him on his latest assignment. Top secret plans of advanced weaponry are disappearing from the Pentagon and the Soviets and Red Chinese are manufacturing identical weapons without the necessary research and experimentation. CIA agents in the USSR and China report that the missing plans are being purchased from a wealthy West German industrialist and a thorough examination of the flight manifests for the past year turns up the name of the Baron von Hemann. Nothing can be done about the plans already sold – except sabotage the projects and destroy the plans – but coinciding with the Baron's last trip to the USA plans for a sophisticated heat-sensing ground-to-air missile – the last in its series – are missing. Hammond's assignment: stop the Baron's nefarious activities and recover, or destroy, those plans.

'So, tall, dark, and handsome Hammond flies to West Germany. The Baron lives in the country in a mansion surrounded by a large expanse of land into which Hammond sneaks one night, and after a hair-raising experience with two fierce Alsatians, he gains entrance to the house. The dogs' barking fails to warn the Baron, and Hammond overhears him talking to his manservant and bodyguard, Boris, about their proposed trip to Switzerland in the Mercedes Benz. He waits until the two Germans are out of the room before he helps himself to the mahogany desk. In it, our favourite spy finds the Baron's financial records – consisting of three sheets of paper. Public Enemy Number One is making more money than his antique business – one of his many interests – can account for.

'Before he leaves, Hammond places a small tracking device on the Mercedes – I forget where – and he picks up the signals on a little receiver disguised as a transistor radio. The next day, he follows Boris and the Baron in a hired Ferrari. Boris finally brings the Mercedes to a halt in a tiny Swiss village near the border. Here, Hammond meets Sarah Williams, an American tourist … or so she seems. He asks her to have dinner with him and at dinner, I don't remember how, but he finds himself with her handbag, and – quite shamelessly – searches through it and discovers her passport containing visas for France, Great Britain, Spain, East and West Germany, Italy, Greece, the USSR, China, and, naturally, Switzerland. Also, in her handbag, under a pile of make-up, he finds an automatic. Quite a well-equipped tourist!' He stopped and thought for a moment: Had he forgotten anything? Oh yeah … 'The Baron knows that there's someone on his trail and the world's favourite spy notices that he's gained an extra shadow.'

'But that doesn't deter our hero, who, after numerous escapades in bed with Sarah, discovers that she is after the Baron's blood because he had her father killed; her dad was also a CIA agent.' Jim stopped his narration and looked at his friends. 'This is why this type of story is stupid,' he said. 'If it was that easy to get sex from a girl, we would've lost our virginities long ago!'

The rest of the Gorgons just looked back sheepishly, saying nothing.

'Anyway, in the village, the Baron contacts two men at a sidewalk café. Hammond recognises one of them as a member of the *Komitet Gosudarstvennoi Bezopasnosti*—'

'What?' Larry asked.

'The KGB,' Jim replied. '*Monsieur le Baron*[4] has a second appointment, but in another village. Instead of leaving straight away, he stays another night and lays a trap. After another session with the sensuous, long-legged, sexy Sarah, Hammond dresses and goes down to the carpark. But Boris is lying in wait down there, and what results must be one of the best duels since the Flynn-Rathbone swordfights – from the old movies. In the end, Hammond gives Boris a stiff kick … in the throat and returns his attention to the Baron's Mercedes. This time, quite undaunted, he breaks into the car, and on the floor he finds a screwed-up piece of paper. Though he thought it an insignificant scrap discarded quite unthinkingly, it turned out to be a puzzle. On it were three words – at least, part of the third: ENSIGN, CORD, and SANT–. The rest of the word having been torn off.

'Next morning, Sarah and Hammond are awakened by the Swiss police, and Hammond is arrested when they find in his holster the forty-five-calibre gun that killed the manservant of Baron von Hemann. But. The US ambassador somehow gets him freed. Having lost his quarry, Hammond returns to Bonn; the Baron must come home sometime. The next day, a man arrives at the Baron's mansion, and he leaves a short time later without the briefcase he'd been carrying before. That night, Hammond plays cat burglar again and this time his brief career as one comes to an end with a knock on the head.

'When he comes to, he discovers that he's strapped to a bunk in a cramped cabin; the smell of salt and seawater drifting in through an open porthole.' Again, Jim paused his narrative. 'You

---

[4]Mister the Baron (French)

know, it's amazing how the crook waits until the hero is conscious before arriving to gloat.'

'It wouldn't help if the hero was unconscious,' Fab remarked.

'No, what I mean is, that a few seconds after the hero has awakened, the villain makes an appearance – as if he knew, by a sixth sense that his victim had awakened. Instead, the author should be a bit more realistic; the hero should be awake for some hours before the villain's gloating session.

'Well, anyway, the Baron comes stalking in pushing Sarah before him. He tells them that they're on their way to Red China with the plans for the missile that had been stolen. He couldn't hand over the plans when he met his contacts in Switzerland, as he didn't have them then, hence the visit of the guy with the briefcase. As for the Baron's prisoners, well, they're a bonus for his customers.

'He locks the cabin door leaving Sarah in there. She frees Hammond and, from the heel of his shoe, produces one of those little gadgets used to pick locks. The guard, posted outside, is swiftly disposed of. Now armed, the two go around shooting anybody they come across while in search of the Baron. They soon find him in the parlour, but Hammond is rendered unarmed due to some skilful handling of a whip by the Baron. But the tables are turned when Hammond ends up with the whip in his possession. The Baron runs and Hammond finally catches up with him in the galley and ends the Baron's miserable life by – would you believe? – baking his head in an oven!'

'What about the words Hammond found?' Larry asked, intrigued. Being a Diploma student meant not reading the kind of books the TAE students did, and he was more than interested in this story. 'What'd they mean?'

'Well,' Jim said, counting each point on his fingers. 'ENSIGN was the series name of the missile – hence the name of the book; Alex CORD was the man stealing everything for the Baron, and the SANTinovich was the name of the Baron's yacht.'

'What happened to Cord in the end?' Mike asked.

'He was arrested by CIA agents,' Fab put in. Turning to Jim, he asked: 'What made you read it – and don't say the exam, because I won't believe you!'

The moment Jim had been waiting for had arrived. Moving to a position where his view of each Gorgon was unobstructed, he told them of the incident he had spied upon the previous afternoon between Hank Andrews and the Year 10 boy. 'This morning I had the opportunity of identifying him as Paul Matthews,' he said.

'How'd you do that?' Tet asked.

Jim smiled. 'Trade secret.' Better to be secretive than to tell them that he had gone through Paul's bag when that boy had left it on the bag rack at the library, before school. 'Remember the rumours about our friend Hank?'

Fab raised his hands. 'Oh no, not again,' he said. 'About Hank being a drug pusher? It doesn't hold water – and you know it. How many times have we tried to prove it? Year 9, Year 10 – and last time we nearly had trouble with De Boyz! At least we managed to talk our way out of it, but they warned us that if we tried that again, they'd castrate us! I'm a virgin, Jim. I'd like to use it at least once!' The others laughed.

When the laughter had stopped, Tet moved between Fab and Jim. 'That was strange,' he said. 'They throw him out of their gang, yet every time we tried to find out about him, they stepped in.'

'Well, it's about the same with us,' Larry stated. 'Just because Wally's back in Los Angeles, doesn't mean he's out of the Gorgon Five. But we can't help him out of any trouble over there.'

'Don't you believe it,' Jim murmured.

'How are we going to get to America to help him?' Mike wanted to know.

'Is Wally in some sort of trouble?' Larry suddenly asked, concerned for their American friend.

The rest of the Gorgons looked at him.

'You're a drongo,' Mike stated and turned back to Jim. 'Well?'

Jim smiled. 'Trade secret,' he said.

Tet turned to Mike. 'I had a feeling he was going to say that.'

'Anyway, we're getting off the track here. We may still be able to prove Hank yet. From what I learnt yesterday, our friend, Matthews, isn't happy over the price rise of the goods he so desperately craves. So much so that Hank did him over.'

Suddenly interested, Tet asked: 'What's the merchandise?'

'Ten to one it's sugar,' Jim replied. 'The way he was carrying on it just couldn't be grass. But there's always the possibility that it's coke or acid. There's only one way to find out and that's to question Matthews. Do any of you know him?'

Mike nodded. 'I do. He lives up the road from me.'

'Good,' Jim said. 'Tet'll go with you. Bring him back here – and don't let Hank see you with him.'

'Yes, *Bwana*[5],' Tet replied, saluting.

As they left on their errand, Fab turned to Jim. 'You expect him to tell you everything about Hank?'

---

[5]Sir (Swahili).

Jim thought for a moment and then regarded his friend solemnly. 'Yes.'

Fab simply shrugged and leaned back on the railing. 'He's going to spill his guts because he loves truth, justice, and the American way, I suppose?'

'No,' Jim replied, calmly. Fab's attitude was beginning to annoy him. He thought for a moment and when he spoke, his voice was low and menacing. 'I don't expect him to simply "spill his guts" – but he will talk even if I have to knock the living hell out of him!'

The uncomfortable silence that resulted from Jim's statement was broken by Paul Matthews's curse-filled protests as Mike and Tet pushed him towards the waiting Gorgons.

There were two exits from the Gorgons' Den: one was through the breezeway into the main building – from which he'd just been dragged; and the second was around the corner of the bookshop, leading to the teachers' carpark and the oval. Fab, Mike, Tet, and Harry blocked the two exits while the rest of them stood along the railing.

Paul looked at the ring of boys surrounding him, and his eyes fell upon the boy who had helped him yesterday afternoon. 'Oh, shit!' was all he said.

Standing between Danny and Jack, looking like an enraged Zeus about to hurl a thunderbolt, Jim said: 'You've got a good memory. Not very many people have, these days.' Fear kept Paul quiet. 'My friends and I want to know about Hank Andrews and your connection with him.'

Paul's eyes widened in surprise, then quickly surveyed his surroundings once more. Was there an escape route? No, these wankers were too close together.

'I'm either going deaf or he's not talking,' Tet said innocently.

Fab gulped loudly. He wished Tet hadn't said that.

'Paul,' Jim said in a friendly tone, 'why don't you tell us, and maybe we'll let you leave with your teeth intact.' A pair of shocked eyes fell upon Jim. Slowly, the Gorgon was losing control of his temper. Taking two steps towards Paul, Jim grabbed the boy's shirt. Again, his voice was low and menacing. 'You're trying my patience, f**kwit! You better talk and you better talk now, because you're going to find it hard through torn gums.'

Paul checked around him again. No hope. Face it, you're dead. Don't kill yourself, act dumb – he doesn't know anything. Regaining his composure, Paul said: 'I don't know what you're talking about.'

'Don't spin me that *kak*, man!' Jim countered and tore the long cotton sleeve from Paul's shirt. His left arm was not tanned at all and around the crook of his elbow was covered in tiny black marks. 'These marks were either made by a hypodermic or a vampire with incredibly skinny teeth and a terrible sense of direction. These are a passport to a detention facility. Now – do you talk?' Paul glared at Jim and, quite obstinately, remained quiet. 'Well?' Jim persisted, shaking his victim violently.

Paul's arms shot up knocking Jim's hands away. 'Okay, okay! Quit shaking me! You know it's sugar, I know it's sugar, so let me bloody go!'

'Where do you get it?' Jim demanded.

'Greenways,' was the only answer.

Jim sighed and grabbed Paul by the collar. 'Don't get smart, you can't afford it!'

'Get your mits offa me! I told you I get it from Greenways, but you don't believe me. Then, stuff it!'

'You get heroin from a shopping centre?' Fab asked incredulously. Paul nodded.

Jim knew Fab hadn't caught on. Though no names had been mentioned, Jim and Paul were both talking about Hank Andrews. 'How do you know?'

He turned to face Jim before answering. 'Because I needed some bad and followed him there, once. He must've known, went to a newsagent instead, and bought something.'

'Do you know when he's going to Greenways, next?'

Paul shrugged; he didn't care anymore. What was the use? He'd already signed his death warrant. 'Sometime this arvo, I suppose.' He looked at the other Gorgons in turn. 'Can I go now?' He began to move away.

Jim's eyes narrowed in distrust. Something was not kosher. Suddenly he's happy to tell all. He stood firm in front of Paul and stopped him from going. 'How do you know?'

'What?'

Jim answered him with a backhand. 'Try again,' he said.

Paul's hand went to a burning cheek. He glared at his antagonist. 'I ... I went to get some, this morning. Doesn't have any ... not till this arvo. I'm going now!'

'Before you go,' Jim said, grabbing Paul's bare upper arm. 'You caught your arm on something – didn't you?'

Paul regarded the amputated sleeve he now held and nodded. 'Thanks for the funeral,' he said contemptuously, 'don't forget to send a wreath.' With that comment fresh in the air, he left and, when the Gorgons let him pass, all but ran towards the nearest breezeway.

'I'm coming with you,' Fab stated.

Jim regarded his friend with surprise. He wanted to get involved. Jim nodded his agreement. 'The rest of you just act normal and don't play bodyguard. Okay?'

They exchanged glances and one by one they agreed.

Checking his watch, Jim announced: 'The siren'll be going soon ... let's go.'

Before they started moving, the air raid siren sounded the end of recess and the disgruntled school population grudgingly shuffled towards their classes.

Chapter Three
The Expensive Magazine

AUGUST 3. 12:15 PM, WESTERN AUSTRALIA TIME

In the three years he had attended Tannen Heights High, Jim never knew why the second last Thursday of second term was a half-day. Every year the reason was different, but then which student cared as long as there was one? He removed the maths and biol textbooks from his locker and placed them neatly in his bag, then regarded the files. Hell, there were a lot! All six wouldn't fit into the bag, not with the biol manual in there. With three files crammed in his bag, Jim closed the locker and waited for Fab.

At that very moment, Fabrizio was talking to a friend of the Gorgons. He would be a few minutes and then arrive at his locker to do what Jim had just completed. A grin spread on Jim's face as he remembered the first time, he ever met his friend. It had been in Year 8 on a Friday morning in music class. Both were new students to the school with no friends and were very cautious. The teacher was late, and the other students were talking among themselves – all but Fab and Jim. Suddenly, Fab turned to Jim waving a ballpoint pen as if it were a cigar, and said:

'Penfields, mate. You can smoke it, suck it, twirl it, wave it, and – would you believe it? – even write with it!'

Jim had just stared at him in utter surprise for a few moments, then muttered something about him being an idiot *scaapa*[6] and returned to the book he'd been reading. But that unorthodox introduction was later to become the symbol of friendship and trust between them. Like Jim, Fab had been born in Melbourne but had been raised in Perth since his father insisted on moving west due to his weak chest. Three years ago, Fab's father had died and his older brother, Giovanni, had left school to support the family. But work wasn't easy to find, and he finally joined the army.

Fab appeared at the top of the stairs and was casually making his way to where his friend sat; pulling Jim out of the memory. He carried his bag in his right hand with his left arm held perpendicular to his body, for balance. 'Bremenh said he'd keep Hank busy for ten minutes,' he said, dropping his bag next to Jim and searching his pockets for the locker keys. 'Bloody hell, that Bremenh's nosy. He practically gave me the third degree about our interests in Hank.'

'Hurry up, then,' Jim said. 'We've got to dump our bags and get to Greenways before he does.'

'Then we can go,' Fab said, closing the locker after checking the contents of the bag. 'All I need for studying's here.' He patted the bag. 'We better leave them at the library.'

Greenways Shopping Centre was situated roughly half a kilometre north of the high school and covered two and a half residential blocks. When it had been built five years ago, Greenways had been regarded as the first of hundreds of space-age shopping centres. It was in a pentagram shape with a sunken

---

[6]Sheep (Afrikaans).

mall, beneath a gigantic glass-dome skylight at the heart of the entire structure.

'What do you hope to find?' Fab asked, breaking the beam of the electric eye which opened one of the centre's five doors.

'The illicit narcotics industry is like a ladder,' Jim explained in a low voice as they passed through the doors. 'Paul is the bottom rung; Hank is the next one. What we're going to do now is discover the third rung. That person's somewhere in here. Eventually, we trace all the rungs until we reach the top and discover who's making the fortune from all this.'

'Jesus!' Fab exclaimed shaking his head. 'You are one nosy parker!'

'I'm an Aussie – of course, I'm a nosy parker,' Jim replied. 'Besides, I was brought up in South Africa. That makes me doubly nosy.'

'How do you know Hank'll come?'

'Because Paul said,' he replied.

'You don't honestly believe him, do you?' Fab replied.

'He wouldn't dare lie,' Jim assured him. 'Because if he did, we'll give him to the cops.'

Fab jabbed his friend in the ribs with his elbow. 'Look.'

Jim cast his eyes towards the automatic doors. They were open and Hank walked in. Jim grabbed Fab and ducked into a shop. Unaware of the two spies, Hank Andrews passed the shop, his hands in his pockets, holding the wad of money he had collected from his customers during the week.

Removing his windcheater and handing it to Fab, Jim followed Hank as he crossed the mall. Experience had shown him that people subconsciously recorded how others were dressed. Remove a pullover or jacket, or even change shirts and one could practically become invisible. But just to be on the safe side, Jim remained about four metres behind his quarry. Fab was further back, guarding the windcheater and making sure that other people kept him covered from Hank's wandering eye.

Jim stopped halfway across the mall at the fountain, watching Hank as he entered the newsagency and stop at the magazine rack. Picking up a copy of *Playboy*, he thumbed through it waiting for the two other customers to leave. The first one, a man, took a newspaper only to stop in the doorway and return for a packet of cigarettes. The elderly lady that remained was a bit choosier and thumbed through numerous magazines. Finished with the *Playboy*, Hank returned it and took a copy of *Penthouse*. The woman eyed him with disgust, and he smiled at her and made an obscene sign with his middle finger. Shocked, the woman quickly returned the magazine to the rack, bought a newspaper, and left. Hank returned the *Penthouse* with a laugh and marched over to the counter.

Jim had witnessed what had passed between Hank and the woman and silently laughed. He glanced around the mall to see where Fab had deposited himself. The other Gorgon was sitting on a bench just outside the supermarket and from there was watching the newsagency. Jim's eyes returned there and saw that Hank and the proprietor were talking, though the latter was fishing for something beneath the counter. He straightened eventually, holding a ready-rolled magazine which he handed to Hank, who gave over what – to Jim – looked like a large wad of money.

Holding tightly onto the magazine, Hank began crossing the mall and glanced at the fountain. His eyes widened as he noticed Jim standing on the other side staring back at him. Surveying the mall frantically, he spotted Fab rising from the bench. Not wasting any time and tightening his grip on the precious magazine, Hank headed straight for the doors. Had they seen anything? The transaction? The money? Knowing Jim Saston too well, he knew better than to ask himself that. He glanced back; Fab and Jim were in front of the fountain, and both were looking in his direction. Those f**ken buggers never give up, he told himself, and this time they'd gotten too close. He'd have to ring Emilio later; De Boyz can practice on the bloody Gorgon f**ken Five!

'Was that money?' Fab asked, not believing what he'd just seen.

Jim slowly nodded. 'Yeah, that was money all right. Every cent of it; stolen, earned, or "found"!'

Fab chuckled. 'Hank just bought the world's most expensive magazine.'

'At least we discovered the third rung of the ladder.'

'What do we do now?' Fab had to admit it, this was getting exciting.

'It's about time we let the police in on it,' Jim said with a wink. 'But we'll leave the newsagent out of it for the moment.'

'His name's Craig St. James,' a deep Caribbean voice informed them from behind.

Jim turned slowly, knowing full well who was there.

The tall, dark West Indian gave a huge grin, showing off two rows of magnificent white teeth. 'I'm one jump ahead of you, man,' he said.

'What are you doing here, Callobar?' Jim asked, a little annoyed at seeing him.

Callobar regarded Fab and said, 'It's Julie's birthday tomorrow and I've only just remembered it.'

Jim glared at the West Indian in defiance of his lie. 'It's not Julie's birthday tomorrow,' he challenged.

50

Callobar's resolve didn't falter. 'Not Julie Peterson – my Julie!'

Feeling left out Fab, cleared his throat and Jim introduced them then turned back to Callobar. 'How do you know the newsagent's name?'

Callobar gave a knowing grin. 'I have sources,' he said. Jim knew what he meant and refrained from pursuing the subject. It could wait until Fab was gone.

Oh, well, Fab decided with a shrug, at least this guy didn't say 'trade secret'!

The West Indian's Saab was parked not far from the entrance and soon the boys were on their way back to the high school. Callobar brought his car to a halt at the east entrance and watched the boys as they walked up to the library, while his hand rested on the butt of the automatic in his shoulder holster.

Fab grabbed his bag and waited for Jim to do the same. 'That's a bloody nice car he's got,' he said, giving the Saab another once over. 'What does he do to afford something like that?'

'He's a lawyer,' Jim replied, referring to Callobar's cover.

'Jesus, divorces must pay well these days!'

'You want a lift home?' Jim offered. He knew Callobar wouldn't mind and besides, Fab was dying for another ride in the Saab.

'No,' replied Fab, 'I'll walk. Thanks, anyway.'

Jim shrugged, perplexed. 'Okay. See you tomorrow.' He had underestimated his friend. Oh well, you can't be right all the time, he told himself.

'Yeah … see you.' Fab turned and headed for Wanneroo Road.

Jim climbed back into the blue Saab 900 Turbo Automatic Sedan and dropped his bag on the token back seat. 'Now,' he demanded of Callobar, 'how did you find out about St. James?'

Starting the car, Callobar said, 'It's quite simple, really. My investigations have led me to him.'

'Investigations?' Jim queried. 'What investigations?'

'You should know better than to ask,' Callobar replied. 'Now tell me what you were doing following that little pusher.'

'Hank? We were just follo—Wait a minute, how'd you know Hank was a pusher? I didn't even know that until this morning. Did Mark tell you to follow me?'

'No,' Callobar answered. This was going to take a long time, he told himself and decided to drive around while explaining everything to the teenager. 'I'm working for the Narcotics Liaison Division now. Now they are working in conjunction with the Federal Police to destroy the distribution of heroin from Red China. The man they have decided to pick on is an American expat called James Slattery. Before they can touch him, they must hurt his state managers. I stumbled upon our friend the newsagent a few weeks ago, by mistake, and have been watching him since. That kid is a regular customer. The drugs are already in the rolled-up magazine. It's a pretty nifty operation. Meanwhile, here in Perth, an undercover cop infiltrated Slattery Transports and has been working as a truck driver for the last three months. A month ago, he called your friend, Sam O'Reilly, and said that the manager – one Paul Edmonds – had assigned him to pick up some stuff from the Slattery Sporting Goods warehouse in Geraldton.'

'Geraldton?' Jim regarded the West Indian questioningly. 'What are they doing with a warehouse up there?'

'Beats me,' Callobar said, bringing the car to a halt at a set of traffic lights. 'But here's something interesting ... that undercover cop, Graeme Chesston, he never came back from there. He's simply disappeared from the face of the Earth!'

'When was he due back?' Jim asked, watching a pretty brunette as she passed the car, giving it the once-over, and stopped on the corner at the lights. He shook his head. No, Christine was better, by far.

Noticing what Jim was admiring, Callobar smiled. That's what should occupy a teenager's mind, not catching drug pushers. 'He never said.'

The lights changed.

'Very smart of him,' Jim said sarcastically. 'Edmonds probably had him done in.'

'If you knew anything about Paul Edmonds and his state organisation, as well as the man pulling all the strings – James Slattery – you wouldn't have had to say that to know that that is exactly what happened.' Approaching the Peterson house, Callobar guided the Saab onto the verge and parked it under the large gum tree. The clouds which had been gathering all afternoon began dropping their load of rain.

Glancing up at the drops on the windscreen, Jim said, 'Well, I'm listening.'

Callobar sighed. 'Paul Edmonds – according to Criminal Records – was born and raised in Ottawa but changed his nationality after seven years' residency in the United States. He went to work for Rick Valentine as a hotel manager in Las Vegas and there he met James Slattery. The two became very good friends, so much so he followed Slattery here four years ago. Now he's the manager of the West Australian division of Slattery Sporting Goods and Slattery Transports.

'James Slattery came from New York where he met Rick Valentine. They grew up together and were the best of friends. When Valentine began to climb the ladder in the syndicate, he took Slattery with him. They went to Las Vegas and set up their own operation there. The records aren't clear about what exactly happened, but Slattery had to leave the States in a hurry, and he came here. But he didn't come alone. Apart from Edmonds, he brought over two thugs: one Jim Barton and a Steven Cruickshank.'

The rain was falling heavier now, and Jim noticed a black cat suddenly burst from under a bush in Christine's yard, and head towards the shelter of the red Holden Gemini parked in the driveway. Poor Licorice, Jim thought, then turned to face Callobar. 'Are you trying to scare me?'

Callobar regarded the boy. 'Heaven forbid, no,' he said after a while, 'I'm trying to discourage you. The guys you want to tackle are hardened criminals – professional killers. They're not petty crooks!'

Callobar had been in Australia for ten years and after being naturalised, joined the army. In the following three years, he'd gone through four promotions and, finally, he entered the intelligence service. Following two more promotions, he became an operative for ASIO and was assigned to Perth and Mark Peterson. Boredom had led him to frequent numerous hotels and nightclubs and eventually getting into fights. As a disciplinary measure, his one and only assignment was to act as bodyguard to Jim when the boy got involved in police work. In the past, Jim's escapades had been fun and this one, so far, was proving no less. But, just the same, it was his duty to at least try to discourage the boy from pursuing this caper – because, with this one, Callobar believed, he was going to be well over his head. 'Now, you tell me what you were up to?' Callobar asked.

'I'm going to get the drugs out of my school,' Jim replied after a few moments' contemplation. The rain had stopped, and he opened the car door, and then turned to the West Indian. 'Does Slattery Sporting Goods have a warehouse in Perth?' Callobar nodded. 'Where is it?'

'Why?' Callobar demanded.

'Because we should go and check it out,' Jim replied. 'We'll go there tomorrow night; tonight's study night.' He grabbed his bag and began to climb out. 'One more thing,' he said, holding the door open, 'try and get Marty to come.'

Callobar's eyes narrowed. 'Torino?' he asked suspiciously. 'What do you want him for?'

Ignoring the jealousy, Jim said, 'He happens to be the best "break and enter" man we have in the Department – and you can't deny it!'

Of course, he couldn't deny it. He'd love to be able to, though – but couldn't. Marty Torino was good; he was one of the best. What was worse was that Torino was South African-born and kept referring to Callobar as *kaffir* – and meant it!

'All right,' he finally conceded.

Jim smiled. 'Thanks. *Tot siens*[7].' He closed the door and headed towards the house.

Callobar lit a cigarette. Whether he liked it or not, he had just been adopted by a nosy partner. He sighed and drove off.

Julie was out at the animals' hospital where she worked part-time. Jim found the cats taking full advantage of it by sleeping on the kitchen table. 'Shaka,' he said to the Alsatian, standing beside him, 'you're supposed to keep the order here when nobody's home. How come Toby, next door, can?' Shaka just snorted in disgust, recognising the name of the dog next door, and went to lie down in Jim's room.

---

[7]Goodbye (Afrikaans).

Jim made himself a sandwich and with a glass of Coke in hand went to his room to study for the physics exam. Two and a half hours later, the peace and quiet in the house was shattered by a cat's high-pitched shriek. Not knowing what had happened, Jim rushed from his room and followed the sound to the bathroom where Ginger stood, back arched, and staring into the shower. Peering in, Jim discovered Licorice curled up in one corner trying to get some sleep.

'What are you doing here?' Jim asked, picking him up. 'I'm going to have to talk to your mistress about you. We can't have you walking into our house and give Ginger a heart attack.' He took the cat outside, Shaka following. 'Shaka, get lost. I know he looks delicious, but you can't eat him, Toby won't like it.' Placing Licorice on a tree whose branches hung over into the Porters' yard, Jim and Shaka returned to the house.

'Christine has some silly animals, doesn't she, Shaka? Imagine a cat that sleeps in the shower!' He closed the sliding door and returned to his studying. Occasionally, the thought of Slattery, Edmonds, and the drugs passed through his mind, temporarily interrupting his studies.

Chapter Four
The Gorgons' Conference

AUGUST 4. 8:20 AM, WESTERN AUSTRALIA TIME

Hank Andrews ran down the slope from the top oval towards the school. Once clear of the rise, he resumed his usual shuffling gait. He looked at the main building, which he was slowly approaching from the northwest, and imagined it as the cell block of a maximum-security prison, complete with rifle-bearing guards and barbed wire.

He imagined his hands were held together by the cuffs and guards flanked him on both sides as they led him through the gates and up a set of stairs. They marched along the balcony to where a cell had been made vacant for him; for Hank was a dangerous criminal who could only be trusted in solitary confinement. After all, hadn't he viciously killed another person … and eaten parts of the corpse? Hadn't he injected a deadly dose of dope into that addict's arm and sat there happily watching his victim slowly deteriorate and finally die? Also, wasn't he responsible for the untimely death of one Jim Saston? No, he wasn't cracked, as the judge had commented. He wasn't mad at all – just sadistic!

Hank's imaginings dissolved as he stopped in front of his locker. He dropped his bag on the floor; there was no bench here as everywhere else on the upper level.

From the shadows of the canteen breezeway, Tony Waters spied on Hank as he emptied the contents of his bag into the locker: the orange Biology textbook and the large blue journal, a white lunchbox, a black chemistry textbook, and three different coloured ring files.

From the corner of his eye, Tony noticed a guy approaching Hank. He was as tall as Hank, wiry with flaxen hair, and wore a pair of immaculate white slacks, a white cotton shirt, a white coat, and was carrying what looked like a briefcase! A few words passed between Hank and this guy, then the newcomer produced a set of keys and opened his locker, which was above Hank's. Tony wiped the tears away from his eyes. Because of the brilliance of the light bouncing off that twit's clothes, his eyes had begun to water. Oh well, he'd done what Jim had asked and had seen nothing unusual. Hank had not sneaked drugs into the school as Jim had believed he would. More students were starting to appear, and Tony knew it was only a matter of minutes before Jim and the rest of the League of the Gorgon Five arrived. A quick consultation of his digital watch told him the time was 8:23. The exams would start in another twenty minutes, he reminded himself and moved from the shadows.

Jim found Tony sitting at the lockers of The Gorgon Five, just outside Room W, with his face in his physics file. 'Well?' he asked expectantly, placing his bag on the bench, next to Tony, and began to search for his own keys.

'No hello?' Tony asked, not looking up from his file. 'No g'day, how are you? You need a lesson in manners.'

'All right,' Jim conceded. 'Hello, Tony, me old mate. How are you this very fine day? I hope you are well?'

Tony looked up from his file. 'That's better,' he said. 'I didn't see Hank put anything resembling a magazine into his locker.'

The smile slowly disappeared from Jim's face. He was so sure. What did he do with it, then? He frowned. 'Damn!' he swore, hitting Fab's locker. 'You watched him all the time?'

The tone of accusation made Tony look up from the file. He nodded silently and, noticing the new dent in Fab's locker, felt it. Hell, Jim can be destructive, he told himself, Fab will be so happy! 'Hank went straight to his locker, and, as far as I know, he's still there. Why is this so important?'

'Because!' Jim said, looking around to make sure no-one was near, 'I've arranged for the police to come and arrest Hank. I also promised to hand over the heroin he was going to sell.'

Now it all fell into place. If they didn't discover where Hank had hidden that rubbish before the cops arrived, there would be hell to pay. With the physics exam forgotten, Tony said: 'Boy, you're f**ked!'

'Not really,' Jim replied. 'All I have to do is find those drugs before the police arrive.'

'What if we don't find it at all?'

Jim inserted his key into the lock, then looked at Tony. 'We tell the police that Fab called them!'

Tony laughed. 'He won't like that.'

'You can say that again,' Fab said as he placed his bag on the bench and noticed the dent in the locker. 'What the f**k? Who the hell did this?'

Jim examined the dent and shrugged. 'I don't know,' he said and returned his attention to his own locker.

'If I ever find out, I'll kill them!'

Jim glanced at Tony, who was battling to keep a straight face, and shrugged.

'What's the latest on Hank and the sugar?' Fab asked, transferring his files and textbooks from his bag to the locker.

'We've temporarily lost the sugar and Jim's made promises he won't be able to keep,' Tony informed flippantly.

'The sugar must be in the school,' Jim insisted, closing his locker. 'We have to find it before noon.'

'How do you intend to do that?' Tony wanted to know.

'Hope he goes to get the sugar after the exam,' he replied.

'Talking about the exam,' Fab put in, closing his locker, and double-checking the lock – a habit he developed from Year 8, we'd better get down there.'

'There's still about ten minutes to go. I'll get my lunch first,' Jim said and headed for the stairs.

A line had already formed; students waiting for the canteen to open. Fab, Tony, and Jim joined the end. The canteen lady opened the window and began placing the different coloured lunch discs in their colour piles in front of her. Finishing her routine, she looked at the first student who ordered her lunch and moved away, with her coloured disc in her hand.

Jim glanced at his watch. Not that he wanted to know the time, but whenever something troubled him, he always looked at the little instrument strapped to his right wrist. Where had Hank hidden the stuff? Would they find it in time before the police arrived? Had he even brought it to school? Jim hoped he had.

'What would you like?'

'Hmm? Oh, a hamburger, please.' Jim handed her the money, and she returned the change and a blue metal disc. Pocketing it, he returned to his friends who were just discussing their tastes in cars and the girls who like riding in them. The three friends exited the canteen area and headed towards S15, where the Year 11 second-term exams were being held. Hank passed them on his way to the canteen and fell into the line. He exchanged glances with Jim. Jim shrugged. Strange, he told himself. They continued on their way to the examination area which was closed off by a line of benches upon which were displayed signs warning: EXAMS IN PROGRESS. QUIET!!!

The Gorgons jumped over the bench and dropped their bags outside S15 and removed a pencil case and rule, each. The examiner had not yet arrived, and the other Year 11 physics students just stood around, waiting, and chatting. Fab and Tony returned to their discussion on cars and girls while Jim wondered about Hank and his merchandise. He noticed Hank returning from the canteen, with a white disc in his hand. Putting it in his pocket, Hank leaped over the bench, glared at Jim as he passed, and joined his friends who were gathered not far from the Gorgon.

Standing beyond the barrier, away from the gathering Year 11s, was a pretty blonde girl. Her baby blue eyes searched the group for one person. There he was, standing near the door to S15 glaring at the greasy guy with the long black hair. For the last two days, he'd been sort of moody. Probably the exams, she mused silently. Normally they would chat late into the evenings, over the fence that divided their two properties.

Jim turned and spied Christine Porter standing near the back wall of the canteen. They moved towards each other. 'Ready for the exams?' she asked when they were close together.

'Yeah,' he replied and sat on the bench. 'As ready as I can be.'

She sat down next to him, and asked: 'Why didn't you come out and chat, last night?'

'Sorry, I really had to study and couldn't spare the time,' he replied, taking her hand in his. 'Were you waiting?' She nodded. 'I'm sorry.'

'It doesn't matter,' she said, giving his hand a squeeze. 'Are you worried about the exams?'

'Not really,' he admitted. 'There is something else on my mind. Unfortunately, I can't talk about it, now.' His eyes lowered to admire her figure which was accentuated by the tight blue jeans and sky-blue blouse she wore.

He had met her at the beginning of the year, a week after her family bought the house next door. She had admired Shaka one day when Jim was exercising him. They'd talked all that morning over the backyard fence and when the temperature had risen, he had invited her over for a swim in the Petersons' pool. She arrived in a pair of small, blue-and-white bikinis accompanied by her thirteen-year-old brother.

The examiner arrived and Fab called Jim back.

Christine glanced past him, and said: 'Good luck, Jim.'

'Thanks, Chris,' he replied, rising. They regarded each other for a moment. 'Thanks,' he said again and, reluctantly, let go of her hand. As he returned to the classroom, he quietly swore to himself. *You're an idiot, Saston. You had the girl there and you didn't even kiss her. You're a coward!*

The students had already filled S15 and the remainder, Hank included – who had been watching Jim as he talked to the blonde – were being herded into S16. Fab had saved a seat for Jim in S15. Two students walked between the desks, one distributing the exam papers and the other, the answer booklet, while the teacher explained the simple rules of an exam. Since they had heard it all the previous term, the students wrote their names on the cover of the answer booklet. When the examiner discovered that he was only wasting his breath, he glanced at his watch and officially started the exam. The siren sounded three minutes later, for the benefit of the rest of the school.

AUGUST 4. 9:05 AM, WESTERN AUSTRALIA TIME

Outside, Chris Porter walked to her science class in Room Q. She wondered why Jim hadn't kissed her, in fact, she'd been waiting for him, too, and had wanted him to do so. But the fool hadn't! 'My God,' she said aloud as she climbed the stairs, 'he's weird!'

AUGUST 4. 11:45 AM, WESTERN AUSTRALIA TIME

The door to S15 slid open and like a pride of lions stalking their prey, the physics students left the exam area, silently. Fab gave a sigh of relief and exchanged glances with Jim. Retrieving their bags, they headed up the stairs to their lockers.

'That was some exam,' Jim said, placing the key in the lock.

Fab nodded and asked, 'Do you think you passed?'

'Yeah, I passed ... but, just.'

'The trouble was they kept on about light all through the exam.'

'Yeah, that was good,' Jim replied. 'I spent more time studying Light than any other topic.' Discovering he had nothing to put in his locker, he shut it and slid his bag under the bench. Then waited for Fab. 'We have about twenty minutes before the police arrive to get Hank.'

Fab looked around before replying. 'I don't think we're going to find that dope.'

'Tony most probably will have to go through what he observed this morning, all over again.'

Fab closed his locker and felt the dent Jim had made earlier. 'I'd love to find the bastard who did this – I'd give him a dent!'

Jim ignored the comment and said, 'If you've finished, let's go to the Den and hear what Tony has to say.'

Leaving their bags under the bench, they headed for the stairs and Fab inquired about Chris Porter.

'She just wanted to wish me luck,' Jim replied nonchalantly.

'She has the hots for you,' Fab said.

'Good luck to her.'

'Don't you like her? She's a gorgeous girl.'

Jim shot his friend a glance, jealousy dancing in his eyes. 'Do you mind?'

Fab grinned and remained silent until reaching the Gorgons' Den. Three other Gorgons were there discussing the physics exam. Tony stopped his monologue until Fab and Jim had joined them.

'What about that exam, eh?' he asked the newcomers.

They exchanged looks, the silent message sent and received, and Fab said: 'It was quite easy.'

Tony's mouth fell open and when he spoke, he didn't realise he was shouting. 'Easy? Easy? If I passed, it was only by the skin of my teeth! Easy!'

Jim smiled. He enjoyed teasing Tony; he was the only member of the group who had an entertaining reaction to everything. 'Calm down, or you'll attract the principal – and we don't want him around here, just yet. What we do want is another rendition of Hank's movements this morning.'

'Again?' Tony said. 'But I already told you. He went straight to his locker. That's all he did!'

'Okay. Then tell us what he put into his locker.'

Tony shook his head. 'All right.' He fell silent for a moment as he tried to remember. Damn exam made him forget ... Oh, yeah ... 'Biol textbook and journal ... um ... Chem textbook, three or four files and something else ... um ... a lunch box.'

Danny Fletcher, the fourth member of the group, eyed Tony suspiciously. 'That can't be right,' he said. 'Hank bought his lunch this morning; he was in front of me in the line.'

'Are you sure?' Fab asked.

'No, of course not ... I just said so for the fun of it!' he replied sarcastically.

'Then the sugar's in the lunchbox,' Jim said excitedly. 'That's the only place it could be.'

'And what if he didn't bring the sugar to school today?'

'He must have.'

'Why?'

'He couldn't have two lunches.'

'Well, Larry does.'

'But not everybody is Larry Mitchell, thank God.'

Fab shrugged. I give up, he told himself, lifting his hands in a form of surrender. Arguing with Jim's worse than arguing with his mother.

The siren announced the beginning of lunchtime. What had been a quiet school had, in a matter of seconds, become as noisy as a market in Mauritius. Actually, a Mauritian marketplace was quieter. The Gorgons started for the breezeway and when Fab noticed that Jim hadn't followed, he returned to the Den.

'What's wrong?' he asked his friend

Jim looked at him. 'What?'

'What's wrong?' Fab repeated.

'I just thought of something … what if the sugar isn't in the lunchbox?'

Fab shrugged. 'I don't know. You won't get into trouble, will you?'

'No. But Sam O'Reilly won't be happy.'

'Too bad,' Fab replied. 'He's never happy, anyway. Come on, it's lunchtime.'

A large crowd had already gathered at the canteen waiting for their lunches and Jim joined one of the many lines. After what seemed an eternity, Jim reached the counter and exchanged the blue disc, he carried, for the hamburger he had ordered. The rest of the Gorgon Five were already at Room Y and Jim raced up the stairs to join them.

Waiting upstairs for him was Hank and another boy. He made to pass them, but the other boy held Jim back with a large, menacing hand.

'What're you after, Sas?' Hank asked.

Jim stepped back a little and looked puzzled. The hand went down by the boy's side. 'After? I'm not after anything. Why do you ask?'

Hank looked at the other boy. 'He's not after anything, Emilio.'

Emilio Meshattro turned his dark, Roman face and rested his small rat eyes on Jim. 'Why was Waters spying on my friend, here?'

'You'll have to ask Tony that – not me,' Jim replied and began to move away, but Emilio's strong grip on Jim's arm forced him to stop.

'I think you know something about it.'

Jim didn't answer but looked calmly at the hand holding his arm. In his ears he could hear his heart beat faster.

'Well?' Emilio demanded. 'What you say?'

'I say this,' Jim replied, his voice laced with lethal finality. 'I'll give you five seconds to let go of my arm. If by then you haven't, I'm going to tear your fingers right off your hand and shove them so far down your throat that they will stop your heart forever! Understood?'

Emilio hesitated a moment, but eventually, his fingers released their hold. Without a word, Jim walked off. 'We'll be watching you, Sas,' Emilio shouted after him. 'One wrong move and you're all f**ked!'

Jim smiled to himself and headed for Room Y. The League of the Gorgon Five were eating and talking as usual with one extra member: the boy dressed in white, from that morning.

Fab had reserved a space for his friend and removed his bag at Jim's approach. 'What took you so long?' Fab asked, removing a sandwich from the lunchbox somewhere in his overfull bag.

Jim always wondered how Fab could jam a lunchbox in a bag which was always choc-a-bloc full of textbooks, files, and such-like. Maybe he had found a bag like Mary Poppins' carpet bag! He chose not to answer Fab's question lest it frighten him from pursuing this little adventure. But as he began to unwrap his lunch, he wondered if it would. It would be better if he informed the group that Hank enlisted the backing of De Boyz, otherwise, he would be left standing alone when they did find out. He decided to take a chance. 'I ran into a welcoming committee on my way here,' he said.

'A welcoming committee?' Tony echoed from the new boy's right.

'Emilio Meshattro and Hank Andrews,' Jim replied when his mouth was empty. 'He's turned to De Boyz for protection, so be on your toes.'

'He knows that we're on to him, then?' Tet asked.

'Yeah,' Jim replied. 'Not only him - but De Boyz also know. While Tony was busy watching Hank, this morning, they were watching him.'

Tony shuddered. 'Sooner or later, we're going to clash with them,' he said.

'Preferably later than sooner,' Fab muttered.

All through the small discussion, the new boy had kept quiet, enthralled with what he was hearing. This was his first year at Tannen Heights High having just moved to Perth from Sydney. Since his arrival, he had heard quite a bit about the League of the Gorgon Five and decided that he would join that group by the end of the year.

But membership didn't come easy. Come to think of it ... it still hadn't been granted. Oh well, he mused silently, he must be in their good books because they let him hang around all the time. 'You mean everything Fab said about Hank was true?' he asked suddenly.

Fab and Jim turned their heads towards him slowly and said nothing. The boy imagined himself shrinking to the size of an amoeba, God knows why he felt like that. Had he said something wrong? As far as he could gather, he hadn't.

Jim suppressed the urge to laugh at this boy's discomfort and said, 'Of course. Do you think he'd lie?'

'I thought it was some kind of test,' he replied.

'A test!' Fab cried. 'What the hell for? Aren't the exams enough for you, Andrew?'

Andrew Bremenh stopped himself from answering and picked up the other half of his sandwich from his lunchbox, resting on his knees.

Taking advantage of the momentary silence, Jim exchanged a bit of sign language with Fab. Deciphering the gestures, Fab nodded his approval and Jim stood up and stepped over to the railing. Turning, he regarded each member of the League of the Gorgon Five for a few seconds, before speaking.

'All of you know Andrew Bremenh; born in West Germany, raised in Sydney, and who believes himself to be Germany's answer to H.G. Wells or Jules Verne. I want to know who among you does not believe that Andrew Bremenh is Gorgon material.'

Immediately all hands shot up in a unanimous vote. Andrew's beaming smile slowly disappeared. How could he have been so mistaken?

As he rose to leave, Jim pushed him back down onto the bench. 'Where do you think you're going?' he demanded.

'Well, it seems I'm not wanted around here, so I'm leaving,' he replied. His voice didn't hold bitterness but betrayed his disappointment.

Jim turned to Fab. 'Should we tell him?'

'I think you better,' interrupted Larry, 'he looks like he's going to cry.'

'All this was prearranged,' Fab told him, as Jim returned to his seat. 'We voted you in over a month ago.'

'Why didn't you tell me?' Andrew asked, failing to disguise the sudden excitement in his voice.

'We wanted you to sweat a little,' Tony said, 'let's just say it's part of the initiation.'

Regaining his composure, Andrew stated proudly that 'Germans don't sweat, we perspire!'

'Oh, boy!' Fab moaned under his breath and returned to his sandwich.

'Hank Andrews to the office, please,' the principal's voice boomed over the PA.

Fab and Jim exchanged glances, Andrew Bremenh now forgotten. Jim held up his right hand with his fingers crossed; Fab nodded.

'Tet, Tony,' Jim ordered, 'pick Hank's locker and bring the lunchbox to the office, and keep your fingers crossed.' He then left with Fab.

The two boys rose to obey their friend's command; Andrew stood also. This was going to be interesting, he mused. As he tried to follow them, two pairs of hands grabbed him from behind and pulled him down on the bench. Jack Talbot and Harry Callahan sat on either side of him.

'You're a Gorgon now,' Jack said, 'so you better start taking orders from Jim. He named Tet and Tony, which means that the rest of us sit here and wait.'

Reluctantly, Andrew nodded and returned to his lunch, grumbling.

AUGUST 4. 1:05 PM, WESTERN AUSTRALIA TIME

Hank left the under croft – on the far side of the main quad – where he was eating lunch with his old friends, De Boyz. It had been a long time since he sat there last, he reminded himself as he cut across the quad on his way to the office. Emilio hadn't changed at all. Still the undisputed leader of the gang and only because none of the others had enough guts to challenge him. Then there was Danny Appasee, otherwise known as Apache. Now, he was tough and Emilio's right hand. Those two were inseparable, practically brothers, since their families originated from the same part of Italy. Vic Ivanski was part Australian and part Polish. He was the one with the big mouth and a stained mirror. Hank didn't know Martin Drayner all that well, being new to the school. All he knew was that Martin was quiet but good with his fists. Ralph Sinclair was the opposite, he was good with his mouth, but no-one knew about his fists, having never been in a fight. Those were just some of De Boyz, the ones Hank regarded as his friends, anyway.

Hank's thoughts returned to the moment at hand. *What could Gardner want with him?* he wondered, passing through the second and smaller quad behind the canteen.

In front of the office was a small, tree-filled garden with a murky fishpond. Normally, he would cut through this garden to reach the office, but this time – because of the mystery behind his being called to the office – he thought it better to keep to the proper path.

As he rounded the corner, Hank recognised the deputy-principal's bald head peeping over the back of the chair as he sat at his desk, through the large windows of the office. Gardner, the principal, was leaning against a metal filing cabinet near the door. Both were looking at somebody who was still invisible to Hank but, as he neared the office, he recognised the blue uniform.

Mr. Gardner saw Hank's sudden reaction at catching sight of the policeman and as the three men shot from the office in pursuit, Hank ran for the breezeway that led to the Gorgons' Den. Hank's feet left the ground as his throat collided with Jim's outstretched arm. Like a wild animal, Hank lashed out at his attacker with all his might. The uppercut sent Jim into the door of the bookshop, Hank following in for the kill. But before he could do anything, the three men had him.

'Now,' Mr. Gardner demanded in his deep authoritative voice, 'what's going on here?'

Leaning against the door he had been thrown into, and with Fab by his side, Jim said: 'I was preventing our friend here from leaving. Senior Detective-Sergeant O'Reilly is waiting for him.'

Mr. Gardner looked surprised. First the constable and now a boy who evidently knew more than the principal of this school. 'Come with us, you two. You've got some explaining to do.'

They all headed for the office. Not one of them noticed a member of De Boyz rushing back to the under croft to report what he'd seen.

AUGUST 4. 1:10 PM, WESTERN AUSTRALIA TIME

Tony inserted the straightened paperclip he had taken from his bag into the lock. After a few wiggles, the lock sprang open and Tony said, smilingly, '*Voila!*'

Tet's hands shot in the moment the door was open and snatched the white lunchbox from its hiding place under the textbooks. A silent glance passed between the two Gorgons and after Tony had closed the locker, carefully, they turned towards the stairs. Their progress was stopped, however, when Emilio and a few other members of De Boyz blocked their way.

'Don't you know it's illegal to break into another person's locker?' Emilio asked Tet.

The young Japanese didn't answer but kept walking towards the gang leader.

Emilio's hand shot up and pushed Tet back. 'Yip, I'm talk—'

Tet tossed the lunchbox to Tony and dug his open hand deep into Emilio's abdomen while the other hand chopped into his neck. The gang leader went down. Dan Appasee, standing on Emilio's right, moved to hit the Gorgon. Catching the sudden movement in a glance, Tet retaliated with a savage groin kick. Apache fell to his knees, clutching that much-loved part of his anatomy. Tet looked determinedly at the remaining Boyz. 'Do any of you wish to die?' he asked. They made no reply but watched Apache, while he rocked and groaned, sheepishly. 'Then get out of our way!'

They moved aside making a passage for the two Gorgons. Tet signalled for Tony to precede him just in case they interfered with the one in the rear. As they reached the stairs, Tet turned and made a salute-like motion. '*Sayonara*[8],' he said nonchalantly before joining Tony downstairs.

[8]Good bye (Japanese).

Chapter Five
A Kiss to Past Dangers

AUGUST 4. 1:20 PM, WESTERN AUSTRALIA TIME

The League of the Gorgon Five watched as the patrol car, with Hank Andrews sitting in the back and a constable on his left, pulled away from the kerb and drove down the hill to turn right at the intersection.

Larry wiped the imaginary sweat from his brow and said, 'I'm glad that's over.'

'You're glad it's over?' Mike asked incredulously. 'What did you do besides sitting in the background and wanking?'

An expression of utter contempt appeared on Larry's face and before he could reply, Jim said, 'Cut it out!'

'Isn't it over?' Danny asked casually.

'Not entirely,' Jim replied. 'The police will spend the rest of today questioning Hank. He won't talk, of course, and tomorrow Fab and I can go to Police Central and question him.'

'Oh, the cops will let you?' Mike challenged.

'Yeah, they will. He won't talk to them, but he'll talk to us. When I tell Sam that, he'll let us talk to him.'

'Who's Sam?' Larry asked.

'How can you be so sure he will talk to you?' Andrew asked. He'd decided he had kept quiet long enough. 'I know Hank pretty well and when he doesn't want to talk, he won't talk. Besides, you're the one who put him there.'

'Who's Sam?' Larry asked again.

When he spoke, Jim's voice carried that familiar note of confidence. 'He'll talk to us. Get ready to deliver more pushers to the police on Monday.'

Andrew made to say something but Fab, who was closer, restrained him. 'Lunchtime's nearly over; there's no time to have an argument.'

'The term's nearly over,' Tony said, lifting himself onto the railing bordering the Den. 'We should celebrate by going to the pictures one day.'

'That's your idea of a celebration?' Fab asked. He always preferred parties, especially the ones with plenty of alcohol.

'What do you expect? A three-course dinner at the Sheraton?'

'Well, that's a start,' Andrew replied eagerly.

'Okay, it's settled,' Tony announced, with a clap of the hands and slipping from the railings. 'A three-course meal at the Sheraton ... Mr. Bremenh is paying!'

'Well, maybe it isn't such a good idea after all,' Andrew backtracked desperately.

In the remaining three minutes before the siren went, the Gorgons decided that they would celebrate the end of term by going to the cinema on the following Saturday. The siren interrupted a heated discussion on the films available. Andrew was all for seeing a re-release of *Bambi*, while Larry, Mike, and Tony chose a new kung-fu movie.

'What're you going to do, now?' Fab asked Jim as they left The Gorgons' Den.

'Go home and study for the English and history exams.'

'Or Christine Porter – whichever's more important at the time.' Fab's smile slowly disappeared when he caught sight of Jim's scowl. 'You want me to come round your place tomorrow, or meet you in town?'

'Come round, instead – that way I won't have to wait for you,' he replied with a smile. 'You better hurry before the Italian exam starts without you.'

'Oh shit!' Fab said, glancing at his watch. 'Yeah. Okay, I'll see you tomorrow. Stay hot!'

'*Tot siens*,' Jim replied, watching his friend run to S16 to get his bag. Now what the devil does 'stay hot' mean? Jim shrugged and headed for Room W where his own bag was still under the locker. Finally reaching the stairs after weaving through the Year 11 Italian students, he trotted up to the second level and again weaved through the students to get to room W.

Emilio spotted Jim at the locker and accompanied by two other members of De Boyz, approached him. 'Well, pimp, you dobbed on Hank, got him into trouble!' he goaded dangerously. He wanted Sas to try to strike at him that would justify his taking Saston apart – not that he had to justify anything he did, but just in case a teacher broke up the fight he would be able to prove that Sas had started the fight.

Jim regarded him languidly and smiled. 'Hank got himself into trouble,' he replied matter-of-factly and picked up his bag.

'Yeah – with your help. Ralph told me how you stopped him from getting away from the pigs.'

'Well, I'm happy for you,' Jim replied. 'Now, if you'll excuse me—'

Emilio stopped him from leaving and when Jim looked with distaste at the hand clutching his arm, his adversary loosened his grip and eventually let go. Why? Emilio couldn't answer that!

Jim turned to face him and hissed: 'If you ever touch me again, *kaffir*, you'll know how a beheaded chook feels!' He walked away pushing the other two out of his way.

Emilio just watched Jim head for the stairs. The Gorgon was walking slowly, casually, almost arrogantly. The bastard, Emilio told himself. Sas had made him lose face in front of his own gang members. Saston must be taught a lesson! Him and that yip, Shomira – not to mention the rest of the Gorgon-bloody-Five!

AUGUST 4. 1:28 PM, WESTERN AUSTRALIA TIME

Jim left the school grounds and was about to cross the road when a familiar voice from behind stopped him. Turning, his eyes lit up when he saw Christine approaching.

'Wagging school?' he asked as she joined him.

She smiled and nodded. 'I had social studies, English, and maths. So, I got my dad to write me a note so I could go home early. All very legal!'

'But not very ethical,' he murmured. 'Doctor or dentist appointment?'

'Dentist.'

They crossed the road in silence and after a few moments, Jim said, 'We're going to the *bioscope*⁹, next Saturday. Would you like to come – preferably without Danny?' He was referring to Christine's younger brother.

---

⁹Cinema (Afrikaans).

'Who's "we"?'

'The Gorgon Five.'

Christine looked down at the footpath. 'Oh.'

'Anything wrong?'

Why did it have to be with his gang? She asked herself. Why couldn't it be just the two of us? 'I'm supposed to help clean the house, next Saturday.'

'Oh.' He also watched his footsteps. 'Can't you make an excuse, get out of it?'

'Maybe,' she said, the disappointment evident in her words. He misunderstood the cause. 'I'm not promising anything, though.'

'That's okay.' He sounded disappointed, she thought.

After a slight pause, Christine asked, 'Why was that guy taken by the cops?'

He shot her a quick glance; his eyes betrayed the shock he felt. 'You saw?' Jim could suddenly hear his heart beating fast in his ears.

Christine nodded silently. He looked scared, suddenly, she thought. It was visible on his face. She smiled to herself as she thought that he would be terrible at poker!

Jim swallowed. 'He was selling heroin in the school,' he explained and filled her in on the happenings of the last two days.

'Now that he's been arrested, it's finished ... right?'

'No,' Jim replied, as he saw the concern on her face. 'No, it's not finished. It's just beginning. All we did was get rid of one pusher; the others will simply fill the void. So, we've got to stop the organisation.' Not waiting for a reply, he inquired about her end-of-term tests.

Christine shrugged. 'They're easy.'

'Have you learned about South Africa in Social Studies, yet?'

'No.'

'Well, when you do, I'll help you ... if you want.'

'I know! I know!' she said jokingly. 'I've heard that one before! But thanks anyway, Jim.'

They stopped in front of the Petersons' letterbox and Jim checked it. It was empty.

'Expecting a letter?' she asked, her eyes laughing.

He shook his head. 'Not particularly. But you never know.'

The two fell silent for a moment and looked at each other, searching for the truth hidden in their eyes.

Hell, but she was beautiful, he told himself. Her blue eyes fascinated him, always shining but betraying no secrets. Grosvenor had always told him that a person's eyes were your best informers. Look deep into them and you could see what that person was thinking. But with Chris, her eyes were very loyal.

Chris slipped the bag from her shoulder and moved closer to the Gorgon until their lips met. At first, from complete surprise, Jim didn't do anything. But, as the initial shock wore off, he returned the kiss.

The two teenagers reluctantly parted and, picking up her bag, Chris started up the path to her own home and when reaching the front door turned to see Jim standing where she had left him, watching her.

'Bye,' she said with a little wave and went inside.

Jim lifted his own bag from where it had dropped beside him, turned towards his own house, and fell over the letterbox! 'Bloody kaffir thing,' he swore, as he picked himself up and marched into the house. Laughter greeted him as he walked in. 'What's so funny, Julie? He asked and went into the lounge.

Julie was sitting on the settee, wiping the tears from her eyes. Giggling, she said, 'I had the same effect on Mark when I first kissed him.'

Jim's eyes widened in horror. 'You saw?'

She nodded, still giggling. 'But Mark frightened a group of ducks when he fell into one of the ponds at Hyde Park.'

Jim couldn't help but smile at the thought. The possible rumours filtering back to his friends were forgotten. 'That I would love to have seen,' he said before dropping his bag in his room.

Julie rose from the settee and followed Jim. 'What caused the kiss?'

"Nothing," Jim replied defensively.

'Girls don't kiss just for no reason,' she said. 'What did you do?'

He looked at her with his eyes wide. 'I didn't do anything.'

'Sure,' Julie replied, enjoying Jim's discomfort.

'I just invited her to the *bioscope*, that's all.'

'Oh.'

'"Oh"?'

'Does she know what you mean by "bioscope"?'

Jim remained silent.

Julie looked at him. 'You'll have to ask her again. Speak Australian, this time.'

'Yeah.'

Julie left him with that thought and went to the kitchen to start the preparations for dinner. Five minutes later, Jim appeared in the family room, dressed in a pair of black jeans and a black windcheater.

Julie noticed him from the corner of her eye and inquired about his intentions that evening. His friends normally came round on Friday nights and then the whole group would leave for town or some other destination. But this was the first time he had ever dressed like that. She felt apprehensive, then inexplicably terrified when he answered.

'I'm going somewhere with Callobar, after dinner,' he replied curtly.

Julie didn't say anything. She knew why he was going with Callobar. It was ridiculous; a young boy being exposed to such dangers as murdering criminals! She decided she would have another talk with Mark, what little that would do. But sooner or later he'd have to realise that Jim was only a boy and not one of his spies!

'What about studying for your exams?' she asked.

'I'm going to do that now until dinner time,' he replied, coming into the kitchen. Julie stood by the fridge, watching his every move. He placed slices of ham and cheese on a slice of bread. Taking a small tomato from the fridge, he proceeded to slice it. He could feel her eyes on him.

'Don't say anymore, Julie,' he said. 'Don't waste your breath. I started this and I'm going to see it through.' He covered the sandwich and sliced it. 'If you'll excuse me, I shall now retire to my bedroom and learn a century of history in one afternoon.

AUGUST 4. 1:30 PM, WESTERN AUSTRALIA TIME

Callobar found him in Records and Files at a computer console. The former Jamaican native stood in the doorway, watching him. He did not like what he had to do. Oh well, get it over with ...

Marty Torino had found the dossier he'd been searching for, through the computer's memory banks. It had been difficult trying to remember the file number or name. But finally, through trial and error, Torino had found it and the dossier now appeared on the visual display unit in digital green:

VON GAUDIN, MAXIMILLIAN EF10/1/1EGS24/2 ...

Torino quickly skimmed through the dossier: assigned to the MfS in 1956, was later transferred to the HV A. Quite impressive, Torino told himself, reading all that was on this file on the man who was once Maximillian von Gaudin!

With the number memorised, he returned to the program's index and indicated which function he wished to perform. The index faded out and von Gaudin's dossier returned. At the bottom of the digital document appeared:

IS THIS THE FILE (Y/N)

Torino pressed Y, indicating that it was, as according to the program. The dossier faded out again once more and was replaced by:

STATUS: DISPLACED, HOSPITALISED, GTG

Torino studied the display for a moment, contemplating his choices. **GTG**: Gone to Ground. No. **HOSPITALISED**: imprisoned. No. **DISPLACED**: killed without prejudice. Yes. Torino fed it into the computer. Yes, von Gaudin was dead; Torino had killed him!

Delaney had been in the Caribbean for seven months transporting kidnapped scientists and military attachés to Cuba. Torino had been sent to destroy Delaney and his operation, after the sudden disappearance of an Australian mineralogist holidaying in the Bahamas. The trail, however, had led him to Jamaica and it was there that Torino met Maria, who – he later learnt – had been hired by Delaney as a decoy. It wasn't until they were in bed that Maximillian von Gaudin appeared with the two Jamaican Indians. There was nothing he could do at the time; being naked puts anybody at a disadvantage. He made a mental note to not put that detail into his official report!

Finally dressed, he was led by the two Jamaicans to the van outside while von Gaudin remained in Maria's bungalow. Torino was thrown into the back and one of the two blacks climbed in, with a revolver always trained on him. It was then that he heard the shots! Oh well, he had thought to himself, that saves him from possible paternity responsibilities!

On the way to Santo Domingo, von Gaudin talked freely. Delaney's yacht was there waiting to take him, Torino, on his one-way trip to beyond the Iron Curtain. Upon reaching the harbour, Torino decided to take a chance at getting hold of the German's automatic pistol. The Jamaicans resisted the temptation to fire, lest they hit their employer; clearly, they hadn't been paid yet.

Onboard the yacht, Delaney ordered them to shoot. Torino jumped up and fired at the figure on the deck. Von Gaudin lay on the bitumen, an unconscious lump in a pool of blood. Glancing at the German, he remembered Maria and placed two bullets in von Gaudin's skull!

The two Jamaicans recovered their wits faster than he'd anticipated. Maybe it was the sight of their commandant being murdered in cold blood that had sobered them. Delaney had fallen; whether he was dead, Torino couldn't say. He fired at the Jamaican and one of them fell. The other fired and Torino felt the bullet hit him hard in the shoulder. He fired again and the Jamaican dived behind the van.

Torino ran to the other side of it, slid underneath, and fired upwards when the Jamaican exposed his position. A hail of bullets came from the yacht and in the distance, Torino could just hear the wailing of police sirens. He climbed in the passenger's side and lay across the seat, with the park brake poking him in the ribs, and switched on the ignition. He could hear the bullets ricochet off the bitumen and strike the van. One shattered the windscreen. Pressing the accelerator with his hand, the van inched forward despite the hand brake ...

Callobar stood beside Torino. 'Hey, Torino,' he said, grabbing a chair from the next console. 'How's the arm?'

Torino touched the shoulder gingerly. 'It hurts like hell. What you want, *kaffir*?'

Callobar frowned. Here we go, he told himself. This is called self-control. The frown vanished and he smiled. 'Don't get the wrong idea, Torino. I wouldn't stoop so low as to ask you for a favour. It's just that Jim asked me to ask.'

Torino's eyebrows shot up in surprise. 'Jim, hey? Don't you mean he ordered you? How is he, anyway?'

'He's okay," Callobar replied stiffly.

Torino laughed. 'Now there's a boy! I've heard a lot about his escapades. They're the talk of HQ. Tell him to be careful, one day he might just do a *bollemakiesie*[10] and land on his face. But anyway, what can this wounded veteran do for him, *kaffir*?'

Callobar hesitated, contemplating whether to hit this arrogant bastard. 'Jim and his mates are up against a group of mobsters,' he explained. 'Ever heard of James Slattery, Paul Edmond, or James Barton?'

Torino's eyebrows shot up again at the mention of these names. 'Slattery? Slattery of Slattery Transports?' he queried.

Callobar nodded and recounted the happenings of the last two days. 'This kid, Hank Andrews, should be in the hands of the police by now,' he informed Torino, checking his watch to make sure.

'Well, I'll be damned!' Torino said. 'Slattery's business looks legitimate. It's hard to believe he's mixed up in narcotics smuggling and possession with intent to sell.' He looked at Callobar. 'I've even bought gym equipment from his sporting outlets.'

'Well, believe it,' Callobar stated. 'We've just got to prove it and that's why Jim and I are going to look at the warehouse tonight.'

'Well, I'd like to help, *kaffir*, but I've got to be on a flight to Canberra at seven o'clock. They want me there – some technicality about my last operation. Tell Jim I'm sorry. It sounds like it would've been a *lekker*[11] lark!' With that, he rose and after patting Callobar on the back, left.

Callobar watched him strut out of the room then turned his attention to the VDU. **STATUS: DISPLACED** was all it showed. He admitted to himself that he was happy that Torino couldn't join them.

---

[10]Somersault (Afrikaans).

[11]Nice (Afrikaans).

AUGUST 4. 6:10 PM, WESTERN AUSTRALIA TIME

Jim finally emerged from his bedroom after more than five hours of studying. Julie was cooking and Mark Peterson, who had arrived an hour earlier, was reading the afternoon paper in the family room.

'How's the studying coming along?' Peterson asked, folding the paper. He was tall and well-built with a round head and rugged good looks. His blondish hair seemed to glow due to his dark tan. He was an avid surfer.

'Interesting,' Jim replied, removing a can of cat food and one of dog food from the pantry. 'Adolf Hitler was a fascinating person. He's the only fanatic who – as far as I know – had the audacity to put his ideas in writing and publish it, for all to read. Andrew must be proud of him!'

'Andrew?'

'Andrew Bremenh. A German guy at school. He's a new member of The Gorgon Five.'

'I don't think you'll find many Germans who're proud of Adolf Hitler,' Peterson said matter-of-factly. 'Austrians also, now that I think about it.'

'I know,' Jim replied. 'What amazes me is how they let him get into power. I mean, he was a man who spent time in gaol after being arrested for taking part in a riot and wrote – what could only be described as – a bible of terror. Yet, they voted him in!'

Peterson sat forward. 'If you'll remember, Germany was in economic ruin at the time. He made promises that the population believed in and dreamed about. They desperately wanted the Utopia he offered. Through the barbarism, Hitler did do a few good things for Germany. He believed every family should own a car, hence the Volkswagen. He's responsible for the autobahns and he lifted Germany out of the Great Depression and stabilised the Mark. But on the other hand, he singled out the Jews for persecution and genocide, his armies marched into the Sudetenland and Alsace-Lorraine – also, into Poland.'

Jim had been opening the two cans and disposed of the two tops. 'Hmm,' was all he said as he passed Peterson and went out the sliding door that opened onto the patio.

'Well,' Peterson muttered, unfolding the paper, 'that discussion is over.'

Julie looked at her husband. 'His mind is elsewhere,' she said with a smile.

'Yeah,' he replied, 'over next door's fence.'

'She kissed him today.'

'How do you know that?'

'I saw it happen.'

'Have you been spying on him?'

'Well,' she replied, removing plates from a cupboard, 'since you won't recruit me for ASIO, I've been doing my own spying. I may even sell my information.'

Peterson looked up from his paper. The mischievous gleam in her eye and the smile made him realise that she was joking. 'I doubt that the Communists would be interested in the report of two randy teenagers pashing on.' He went back to his paper.

Shaka was lying near the chain-link fence surrounding the swimming pool. He rose and stretched lazily, before trotting onto the patio. On Jim's orders, this was his place to wait for his food, while his master was busy in the cat shed. Some of the stray cats who had made this place their permanent home had still not gotten used to that furry monster called an Alsatian.

The Peterson four-bedroom, two-bathroom house was built of red brick, stuccoed an earthy beige, and the tiled roof was supported by a steel frame to minimise the attraction of white ants. It sat on a typical quarter-acre block, having been built in the early 1960s. Since they never had children of their own – and before the arrival of Jim in their custody – it had been decided to put in a kidney-shaped saltwater pool. This took up about half of the backyard, the rest accommodating a couple of galvanised iron sheds and a moderate vegetable garden. An impressive patio dominated the space between the pool and the back door, of the house. The cat shed, a timber-framed 'house' had been built by Peterson and Jim, and included some old furniture, with old blankets placed neatly on each one. The wooden door had a hole cut into the lower left-hand side. This gave the cats access to the interior during winter. They never spent summer nights in there, rather preferring the air-conditioned comfort of the main house. It was in here that the cats were fed. Much to Julie's chagrin, her vegetable garden served as their toilet!

Jim put the full plates on the floor among the feline crowd and took Shaka's plate to the obediently waiting dog.

Chris watched Jim, over the fence, in silence. She smiled to herself, thinking he hadn't noticed her in the shadows. But he had. 'Been there long?' he asked, not turning around. Instead, he kept watching his dog gulping down the food.

Chris's smile disappeared altogether. 'How do you do that? How'd you know I was here?'

Jim opened the gate to the pool area and approached her. There was a pile of red bricks, stacked – four high and eight across – against the Peterson side of the fence and Jim stood on them to reach Chris's height; she was standing on an old sawhorse. It was 6:25 and the sun was already down. Before coming out, Chris had turned on the patio light. Jim stopped by the hibiscus bush and folded his arms. 'I heard you breathing,' he said matter-of-factly. 'Now, why am I graced with your presence?'

'Did you mean what you said about helping me on the South Africa topic?'

He regarded her for a moment. 'No,' he said, 'I only said that because I like the sound of my voice. Of course, I meant it. Why?'

'Yesterday, we got the textbooks for the subject and were told to browse through it and even read as much as possible before Wednesday. That's when we start learning about South Africa.'

'Let me guess ... instead of reading the text, you want me to tell you all about *Die Republiek van Suid Afrika*[12], hm? Okay, where do you want me to start?'

'How about with the land?'

'Well, South Africa – the country – is small enough to go into Western Australia about one and a quarter times! It has its fair share of plains, deserts, and mountains. Also, one familiar sight throughout Africa: waterfalls. The mountain formations are practically identical throughout the continent. Yes, occasionally these mountains have peaks, but generally, they tend to be plateaux – like Table Mountain, which overlooks Table Bay in Cape Town.

'It's rich in the flora and fauna for which Africa is famous. But southern Africa, alone, is rich in diamonds. Yes, diamonds

---

[12]The Republic of South Africa (Afrikaans).

have been discovered in other parts of Africa, like North and West Africa, but south of the equator diamonds are much more abundant and of better quality. In fact, one particular beach is literally covered in uncut diamonds; you can scoop 'em up in your bare hands. Of course, you can't get within a kilometre of the *Forbidden Beach* – as it's called.'

'Why not?'

'It's heavily guarded. If diamonds were removed from that beach, it would upset the balance of the diamond trade and possibly cause that market to collapse! At least, I think that's the reason, I'm not sure.'

'The people – what're they like?'

'It depends on which people you're talking about. The English-speaking community, the Afrikaners, or the natives? Let's start with them. In South Africa, a native is usually referred to as a *kaffir*! It's not a compliment, but an insult; like calling an Aboriginal a *boong*, or a Black American a … Well, you get the idea. But they're all Bantus – that's their race. Very much like the white race is separated into different nations, so are they. In the northern Transvaal, you'll find the Tswana; Natal has the Xhosa, Zulu, and the Pondo; the Bushman is found in the Kalahari Desert, which is mainly in South-West Africa. There once was a "nation" known as the Hottentot, but the Afrikaners' ancestors made them extinct!

'The white population is divided into the English-speaking community and the Afrikaners. The English-speaking community – which are referred to as *rooineks* by the Afrikaners – consists of the English, Italians, Greeks, Germans, French, Jews, Portuguese, and even the Dutch; in fact, anybody who isn't Afrikaans-born!'

'What does *rooineks* mean?'

'It means red-necked. The Afrikaners are generally regarded, by us, as *scaapa*, hairy-backs, or rock-spiders. *Scaapa* means sheep. Afrikaner intelligence is limited, yet they rule the country! Hence the international discontent.'

'I noticed that the textbook mentioned *apartheed*. I've heard about it but still don't understand it. What does it mean?'

Jim smiled. '*Apartheid* means separate development. It gives each cultural group a chance to develop in accordance with their cultural speed. But it's also a colourful substitute for segregation, racism, and totalitarianism.

'Soweto, the native township, outside Johannesburg, is large and over-populated, with dirt roads, tin shacks, you name it – it's a real slum area. That's because the *Broederbond*[13], a secret society like the Ku Klux Klan, runs the country with a fist of iron. All the country's politicians are members of this brotherhood – and so are the church leaders!'

There was a moment's silence, and they both stared at each other, then Chris asked, 'How could you live there?'

Jim shrugged. 'That's where we happened to be living at the time and where I went to school. Our servant girl had a son, a year older than me. We were very good friends and he taught me how to make a Zulu's shield and *assegai*[14] – and how to use them properly.' He regarded a stray, which had emerged from the shed and was busy preening itself diligently. 'I'll never forget Natunga; he was one true friend,' Jim said almost to himself. Looking at the pretty blonde leaning on the fence, he asked, 'Learnt anything?'

---

[13]Fraternity (Afrikaans).

[14]Spear (Zulu).

'No!' she admitted. 'Too confusing. But I found out one thing, though.'

'What's that?'

'That I don't know you at all.'

He regarded her quizzically for a moment. 'What makes you say that?'

'The way you talked,' she replied. 'It sounded – I don't know – like, in one way you didn't like South Africa, and yet again, you missed it.'

'Because of that, you don't know me?'

'Well, you never talk about yourself.'

'I never talk about my past, Chris, because it's boring.'

'Your past is about you,' she said softly, 'I don't see where it would be boring.'

For a moment, Jim could hear his heartbeat faster in his ears. 'There are certain things about me that I can't tell you.'

'Like what?' she asked jokingly. 'Do you work for the CIA?'

What the f**k? Jim smiled at the flippant question. 'Perhaps,' he said trying to be mysterious.

'I've known you since January and all I've learnt in that time from you and Fab is that you lived in South Africa. Nothing else.'

Jim sighed. *How do you resist those beautiful blue eyes?* he asked himself. 'All right,' he said aloud, making a gesture of surrender with his hands and stepping up onto a small stack of white bricks, next to the fence.

They both leaned on the picket fence and while Jim contemplated where best to begin his narration, Chris slipped her hand into his. He looked into her eyes trying to find the reason for her sudden interest in his background and realised just how much he wanted to kiss her. But when he tried, he found he couldn't move!

Chris, knowing what he wanted to do and with a friendly smile, gently pulled his hand towards her. 'Come on,' she said.

Jim shook his head slightly. Closing his eyes, he took a deep breath. He couldn't believe it! He, James Andrew Saston, who had gone through close to two years of commando training organised by his guardian, Mark Peterson, Regional Director of the West Australian division of ASIO, couldn't bring himself to kiss a girl! It was ridiculous! He shrugged; his mind made up. 'What the hell?' he said and moved close to Chris till their lips met.

'Chris, have you fed the dog?' her mother asked from the back door.

Jim moved away so fast he fell off the bricks.

'No,' she yelled back and turned to Jim and laughed. 'You look cute. Wait a minute.' She ran into the house and a moment later came out followed by Toby, the Porters' Alsatian cross.

By now, Jim had returned to his perch on the bricks and surveyed the scene. Toby was smaller than Shaka, though he looked identical. Jim had once made the mistake of calling Chris's dog a German shepherd at which she corrected him on the fact that Toby was also part blue heeler. With childish pride, Jim had boasted that at least his dog was a pedigree!

'Now,' Chris said, getting back on the sawhorse, 'tell me "The Jamie Saston Story".'

'Jim!' he corrected her sternly. '"Jamie" is off I leave "offness" to Andrew Bremenh.'

'What's an Andrew Bremenh?'

He smiled. 'Never mind.' He regarded her for a moment, still no clue as to what she was thinking. 'I warn you, it's boring. I was born in Melbourne on the twenty-first day of January, sixteen years ago, at seven o'clock in the morning. Four hours later my mum developed internal haemorrhaging and died—'

'I'm so sorry to hear that,' Chris said sincerely.

He paused and looked at her. Was there actually moistness in her eyes? 'She wasn't a very strong woman, so my dad had said. Some months earlier – in Canberra, where my parents lived – my dad was told he and my mum were to accompany the new Australian ambassador to South Africa, as part of his staff. But when it was learnt that my mum was pregnant, it was decided that they remain in Australia till I was born. With time on her hands, my mum went to visit her parents in Melbourne.'

Chris remained silent and listened. But it was becoming difficult to hear as Jim's voice was constantly softening to a whisper as he talked. Also, she realised, he was no longer telling her the story, but thinking it all out loud.

'We lived in Pretoria,' he continued, 'and that's where I went to public school. My dad made sure I never forgot that I was an Aussie. That's why South Africa's indoctrination never worked on me. After thirteen years in that country, we finally returned to Australia. Not to Canberra – or Melbourne – but here, to Perth. Here, my dad would be far enough away from memories.'

Suddenly remembering that Chris was listening to him, he regarded her for a moment in silence while forming a suitable lie that would be accepted by her.

'My misconception of Australia was a scorched continent with tiny blots of civilisation scattered all over its face. After a few months, my dad was killed in an automobile accident—'

'Oh!' she cried. 'I'm so sorry. Now I know why you're here with the Petersons.'

'I was taken in by them,' Jim explained. 'They were friends of my parents from the Canberra days.' He hated saying that – but what could he do? – he couldn't very well tell her that his father was really an ASIO operative, that he was killed by a Soviet spy, that Mark Peterson was also connected with the same organisation and that he, himself, had been trained as an operative at the age of thirteen!

It was, he agreed, the best way of getting him out of the extreme depression that had taken hold of him after the death of his father. But that was a chapter she was not to know about. At least, not yet. 'In a nutshell, that's my biography,' he said and with a throw-away laugh, added, 'You can wake up now.'

'Very funny,' Chris reprimanded. 'How can you make fun of all that? Your life's been ... so ... tragic!'

'Don't take it so seriously, Chris. You've got to laugh away the pain – otherwise, it's going to hurt for a very long, long time. Okay, I've had it rough – but I survived whatever Fate threw at me.' Chris didn't reply. They just stared at each other. 'That's the reason I keep my past a secret,' Jim said, 'it tends to upset the people I share it with.'

'I'm not upset,' Chris said defensively, then looked at her watch. 'It's almost seven and I've got to go help Mum with tea.' She squeezed her eyes tightly shut, trying to hold back the tears that threatened to burst out.

'I better let you go, then. Besides, Julie should have dinner ready.'

Chris jumped off the sawhorse and started for the house. Halfway along, she turned and called him back to the fence.

When he reappeared, she threw her arms around his neck in a tight hug and said, 'I'm so sorry ... and I'll try to be there for you, always.' Then she kissed him.

They were still embracing and kissing when Chris's mum and Julie called them in for dinner, fifteen minutes later.

Chapter Six
Two Halves Make A Golf Ball

AUGUST 4. 7:20 PM, WESTERN AUSTRALIA TIME

When Jim returned to the family room, Callobar was sitting there chatting to Peterson. He was similarly dressed all in black. With his Luger concealed under the windcheater, no doubt, mused Jim.

'Callobar was just telling me about your planned escapade,' Peterson commented casually.

'So?' Jim replied arrogantly, annoyed with Callobar for saying anything near Julie. There had been several instances where Julie's interfering had delayed the solving of a case. Jim promised himself that that would no longer happen where he was involved!

'It seems Marty can't make it,' the West Indian announced.

'Why?' Peterson asked. 'Is he going into the field?'

'No,' answered Callobar. 'He told me he had to go to Canberra ... something wrong with a report he submitted.'

Peterson shot the West Indian a quick glance. 'I wasn't informed about that,' he stated. 'When does he leave?'

Callobar consulted his watch. 'About twenty-five minutes ago.'

'That's strange,' Peterson muttered. 'I'll need to check on that. It doesn't sound kosher!'

Jim turned to the West Indian. 'Well, what about Slattery's?' he asked *sotto voce*.

Callobar leaned forward in the armchair, resting his elbows on his knees and began clenching his hands. 'The Slattery Enterprises warehouse and transport depot is situated in Osborne Park; the offices are in a two-storey building attached to the warehouse. The warehouse is choc-a-block full of both assembled and unassembled sporting equipment of various descriptions. All came from Southeast Asia – via Geraldton.'

Jim sat on the settee, facing Callobar. 'Through Geraldton, huh?' he mused. 'It comes down by train?'

'By truck,' Callobar corrected him.

'Isn't that more expensive?'

'Yes, but also more discreet.'

'Have you eaten, Callobar?' Julie asked from over the breakfast bar. 'If so, bad luck, you're going to eat a second time.'

'No, Julie,' he replied, 'I haven't, I know better than to come Here on a full stomach. Thanks for the invitation.'

'When will dinner be ready?' Jim asked.

She stopped and looked at him. 'If you had helped, at all ... it would have been ready five minutes ago,' Julie said, petulantly. 'Since not, it's ready now. Go wash your hands!'

Heading towards the bathroom, Jim said to Callobar, who was following: 'Good! We can go straight there after dinner.'

AUGUST 4. 8:30 PM, WESTERN AUSTRALIA TIME

An hour later, Callobar's Saab entered the industrial suburb of Osborne Park from Hector Street. Slattery Enterprises occupied a large area – with a double-storey office block and an enormous warehouse. Behind the buildings were ten semi-trailers that stood like silent sentinels in their own parking bays. The Saab, like a large jungle cat, kept to the shadows – its headlights out – as it neared the property. A light was on in the office block.

A night watchman? Jim asked himself. In this day of electric eyes and electronic alarms, it was strange to find a company that still used a night watchman! Jim felt a surge of excitement at the prospect of entering the warehouse. But that watchman presented a problem. He needed to be removed!

Callobar brought the car to a rolling stop in the carpark of another company, across the road. Jim swallowed loudly. Maybe this wasn't such a good idea, after all! He recognised the first-time jitters for what they were and forced himself to overcome them.

'Well?' Callobar stated, breaking the silence that had descended since he had switched off the radio.

'"Well", what?'

'Are we going in or aren't we?' There was laughter behind his words.

'Yeah, yeah – eventually.' Jim didn't want to admit it, but he was scared. He was shaking! Two years of training to come to this moment and imitate a chihuahua during a thunderstorm!

'There's nothing to be nervous about,' the West Indian assured him. 'There's only a watchman, no elaborate electronic devices or closed-circuit television to signal the police. Besides, I don't think your friends would like it if they learnt that a Gorgon was scared.'

Jim turned and faced Callobar. 'You wouldn't dare!'

Callobar gave him a toothy grin. 'Try me.'

'You would – wouldn't you?' He thought for a moment, sizing up the ASIO agent of West Indian background. What he had said put Callobar in a very different light. Jim resolved to bury his fear and carry out the task ahead of him no matter what the consequence. 'You're right,' Jim said finally, 'I've done this many times – in theory. But this is the first time I'll be doing it for real.'

Patting the teenager on the back, Callobar said, 'Don't worry and nothing will go wrong.' He got out and circled the car. 'Coming?' There was laughter in his voice.

'Yeah,' Jim replied half-heartedly. He could hear his heart pounding in his ears again. Pull yourself together, you idiot, he scolded himself silently. Don't be so stupid, nothing will go wrong.

'Now listen,' Callobar instructed, opening the boot. 'The roller-door's on the far side. When it's closed, there's a gap between the drum and the eaves. It's too small for me which means you'll have to go up.'

'*Dankie*[15], but I have a fear of heights.'

'Well, with practice you'll lose the fear,' Callobar replied, uncaring. 'Come on, we're wasting darkness.' From the boot, he removed a double-pronged harpoon and a small harpoon-gun. Attached to the harpoon was ten – possibly eleven – metres of heavy rope. The West Indian handled this as if it were a reel of cotton.

Nervously, Jim glanced at his watch. God! Is it really this early?

The two ASIO operatives passed the office block and Jim couldn't help but admire the impressive little garden on their right. The plants it contained were mostly natives, with neat hibiscus bushes interspersed here and there. A tree Jim thought

---

[15]Thanks (Afrikaans).

he recognised caught his eye and even after passing it, he still regarded it until noticing the protea. Imagine that, he told himself, so far from home and still flourishing. He chose to take the appearance of the protea as a sign and, with renewed confidence, he turned and followed Callobar. It was fortuitous having seen that plant. After all, the protea is the national flower of South Africa. Suddenly, he felt that emptiness in the pit of his stomach. He knew that wasn't fear. He'd been plagued with that feeling for two years after leaving Africa. It was as if that dark continent was using its magic to call him back! Jim swallowed hard and pushed that hunger away from him.

They stopped before the roller door and when Callobar spoke, it was in a whisper. 'Once you get onto the drum, from his office the watchman will be able to see you if you try to descend. He has a large window facing out into the storage area. So, get onto the girders and move to a point where he won't be able to see you. You'll need this to get down.' He handed Jim a second, thinner, coil of rope. 'Of course, you'll have to dispose of the watchman before letting me in and – for God's sake – don't kill him!'

Jim was taken aback. 'Me, kill? I've never heard anything so absurd!' Subconsciously, and under the darkness, he felt under his windcheater for the modified switchblade and its reserve blades. I'll find something to help me put him to sleep.'

Callobar ignored him and pointed the gun, containing the harpoon, up through the gap to the exposed ceiling. He squeezed the trigger, slowly. The muffled detonation was barely audible as it sent the harpoon up and into the warehouse ceiling, leaving a trail of rope behind it.

Jim regarded the rope with distaste, shrugged and, throwing the second coil over his shoulder, proceeded to climb up. The harpoon's penetration of the ceiling had not been as deep as Callobar had expected and now, with Jim's weight, it was slowly moving. Ignorant of the movement, Jim kept climbing, gaining confidence with every conquered centimetre. When he was halfway up, a sudden lurch sent him swinging out and back into the roller door with a loud thud. Jim froze and as he came to rest against the door, he listened intently for the footsteps of the watchman, but all that could be heard was the loud pounding of Jim's heart between his ears.

'What happened?' Callobar asked in a whisper.

Jim looked up through the gap. Though it was dark inside, he could still make out the form of the harpoon, hanging precariously from the ceiling by one of its two prongs. 'Callobar!' Jim hissed back. 'The bloody thing is working itself loose!'

'Well, hurry up then and climb before you drop.'

Carefully, Jim eased himself up towards the drum. The harpoon held long enough for him to reach the top. Callobar caught the harpoon that Jim had dislodged once he was sitting on the drum. He watched Callobar inspect the tortured and twisted harpoon. Jim then scanned the semi-darkness of the warehouse, specifically where the watchman's office was, to the right of the door. Through the large show window, upon a badly stained desk rested an open newspaper, on which the watchman was leaning. Surveying the scene from this commanding position, Jim wasn't far from one of the girders that Callobar had briefed him on. It ran across the warehouse, parallel to ten other girders with the same triangular structure on top to support the roof. One larger girder met these perpendicularly and continued past the watchman's office. Jim peered precariously over the drum at the stacks of crates that littered the warehouse floor. The prospect of traversing the girder did not appeal to him in the slightest. One would not make a pretty sight should one slip off the girder! Oh well, he thought, swinging out onto the girder, when in doubt …

Hooking a leg on top of the steel structure, he lifted his body up and steadied himself against the triangular support before crossing, tight rope fashioned, to the larger girder. Arms outstretched and placing his feet heel to toe, Jim commenced his difficult journey. The girder inched towards him with every tender, nervous step. Upon finally reaching the large metal beam – that had, suddenly, become his god and salvation – Jim dropped and clutched onto it as if hugging Christine Porter. Regaining his nerve, Jim remembered the coil of rope on his shoulder and his Jamaican partner, outside. Rising, nervously, to his feet he repeated his tight rope performance, but with every centimetre, he was gaining confidence and his steps were further apart, and quicker. After five minutes, Jim was able to make his descent – unseen by the watchman.

Jim dropped to one knee and looped the rope around the girder, securing it with a simple knot. He dropped the remainder and it fell short of the floor. Jim glanced over the edge of his narrow platform and imagined himself falling. Instinctively, his grip tightened on the girder and much to his own amazement, found that he had to overcome his fright to loosen his grip. Finally, his will won out and he sat up. He reached into his back pocket and produced a pair of skiing gloves. With them on, he gripped the rope, swung off the girder and slid down to *terra firma*. Jim was so glad, he felt an urge to kiss the ground – but then, that would just be sick!

Oh well, first things first, and the first thing to do was incapacitate the watchman. Silently, Jim moved towards the door leading into the office block. The crates he passed, he noticed, were all stencilled: GOLF BALLS. It's wonderful to know that Perth was populated by golf fanatics. Fanatics they certainly would have to be to use up all the golf balls stored here – and here alone! God only knew how many more around the country! These would have to be opened, he decided. Inside them was the only explanation. He felt for his switchblade and when found, removed it from its pouch under the windcheater.

The door, connecting the warehouse to the office block, was open, but the other door to the watchman's office was slightly ajar. Jim pushed it open and peered in. The watchman was at his desk reading the newspaper, with the window looking out into the warehouse, directly in front of him. Formulating a plan of attack, Jim judged the distance he'd have to traverse to put the watchman out of action. Two and a half metres. Now, approach slow and careful or fast and aggressive? To move slowly was to be silent and careful, but fast was to be noisy and reckless. Normally, noisy, and reckless had fewer risks – under the supposition that one could move fast enough. He believed that this applied to him. With determination, he kicked open the door and crossed the office in two strides. As the surprised watchman turned to see the cause of the noise, a foot lashed out in a vicious sidekick that caught him in the throat. The force of the blow sent him off his chair, into the desk and onto the floor in an ungodly heap.

For a moment, Jim's eyes left the watchman and surveyed the office. The door, he noticed, had collided into a metal filing cabinet upon which stood a drip coffee set up. A pin-up board displayed the latest *Playboy* centrefold and a clipboard, hanging on a metal peg next to it. He noticed that there was an invoice attached. From the look of the office, Jim realised it wasn't only the watchman's office, but also the warehouse foreman's or dispatcher's. He moved over to the clipboard and removed the invoice. Before placing it in his pocket, he read the contents then glanced at all the crates in disbelief.

His eyes fell upon the still body of the watchman. A closer inspection showed that he was not breathing! Dropping down beside the still form, Jim felt for a pulse. There wasn't one! 'Oh gaats[16]! What've I done?' he asked himself in Afrikaans. He noticed that the watchman's neck lay at an unnatural angle. The man's neck was broken, and he was very dead! What now? What's an operative supposed to do when he accidently kills a civilian? That's one thing that Grosvenor, the man who had trained him, never explained. Without that explanation, Jim was lost. He checked the body once more – it still couldn't be real. The watchman couldn't be dead. That's impossible! A sixteen-year-old can't kill people! He rose and regarded the body. When in doubt ... ask Callobar!

Outside, Callobar paced nervously beside the roller-door. From time to time, he glanced at the steel door beside the roller door. Jim should have opened that door by now – unless something's happened! Drawing the Luger from his shoulder holster, he attached the silencer he kept in his windcheater pocket and headed for the door. From the other side came the sound of a bolt being shot back. Gun aimed, Callobar waited for whoever it may be. The door swung in slowly, the hinges creaking loudly in the stillness of the night. Callobar's free hand moved out to push it open, the gun following close behind.

---

[16]Oh gosh! Colloquially: Oh shit! (Afrikaans).

'Put that thing down, please,' Jim said from the darkness beyond the door.

Callobar gave a sigh of relief, and the Luger was lowered. 'What took you so long?'

'Your plan just had a few discrepancies,' Jim replied nervously. 'As a result, we now have one cold watchman with a disengaged neck!'

The West Indian's eyes narrowed. Suspecting the true meaning, he asked, 'What do you mean?'

Jim scratched his head innocently, searching for the right words. 'Um ... Callobar, I ... um ... I killed the watchman!'

'You what?' Callobar frowned. 'How did it happen?' he asked flatly. It wasn't really a question, but a comment demanding an explanation.

The Gorgon looked sheepishly at his feet, his hands clasped behind his back, like a penitent schoolboy. 'I kicked too hard, he fell against his desk and broke his neck. Just an unfortunate accident.' He forced a half-smile.

'What are you grinning at?' the West Indian snapped.

Jim's smile quickly vanished. 'Nothing,' he said. '... And don't go *kaffir* with me! It's not my fault I kicked too hard!'

Callobar frowned once more, and pushed past the teenager. What could he possibly say in his report? Canberra won't be too happy when they learn that a sixteen-year-old had killed a night-watchman. Kneeling beside the body, in the office, Callobar felt for a pulse. Not finding one, he moved the watchman's head. It rolled lifelessly to one side. 'His neck's broken,' he told Jim, rising. Callobar sighed, resignedly. 'It can't be helped, now. Come on, we have work to do.'

Following Callobar back into the warehouse, Jim remembered the invoice he had placed in his pocket. Fishing it out, he handed it to his partner. 'Take a look at this,' he said. 'It's an invoice for some of these crates and dated two days ago.'

Callobar unfolded it and gave the invoice the once over, then looked at Jim. 'What about it?'

'The invoice number is 59027, right?' He looked at the crates before them. 'That counts out these four crates – there's a different number stencilled on them. These ones are also out of it and these, too.' Moving around the crates, he stopped before a group near the roller door. 'Here they are. Invoice number: 59027.'

Callobar joined him. 'Well, what about it?'

'Don't you get it?' Jim asked incredulously. 'Look at the invoice. These crates are full of golf balls. If you go back and look at the ones we passed, you'll see they have the same contents! All the crates, in here, are full of golf balls! How many golf balls does one country need?'

Callobar retraced his steps and checked the crates. Jim was right, GOLF BALLS was stencilled on each crate, just under their respective invoice number. 'Jim, see if you can find something that we can use to open these crates.'

The Gorgon disappeared behind some crates, heading towards the watchman's office while Callobar returned his attention to the crates. Moving over to another collection he discovered they also carried the same cargo as all the others.

Jim returned with a crowbar and a pair of tin snips which he had found near the roller door. 'Here, I thought you might need these for the hoop-iron.'

The four metal strips surrounding the crate jumped as each was cut. Levering the crowbar, Callobar prised the top off.

Inside were cartons containing six golf balls each. Jim hurriedly removed these, piling them on the other crate. When he reached the bottom, he realised – with some disappointment – that this one did not contain what he had believed it did. He and Callobar returned the cartons to the open crate and turned their attentions to the second one, which – after a few minutes – proved to be exactly as the first. Four crates later and another pile of golf ball cartons, Jim was ready to give up.

'What the hell's going on here?'

Callobar straightened up. 'Let's try a few more. We should find something, soon. Maybe what we're looking for is towards the back.'

'Forget it,' Jim replied forlornly. 'Evidently we made a mistake.'

'Forget it? I'm sorry, but we don't forget anything. Maybe it hasn't occurred to you yet, but we got in here illegally ... that's breaking and entering. You killed the watchman and that's manslaughter! With one man dead, we are not giving up. We're staying here until we find what we're looking for.'

'What're you going to do – open every crate?'

'If we have to,' Callobar replied, emphasising the 'we'. 'One thing that Grosvenor didn't tell you is that you shouldn't get impatient. Take your time and all will come right. Look, we know that heroin is being stored in this warehouse, in these crates – somehow. We'll find the answer, just don't lose heart.' He picked up one of the cartons and inspected it. Inside were six golf balls in their individual cups, like half a dozen eggs. A little line on one attracted his attention. 'I think we've found our answer,' he announced, removing the ball. Twisting the two halves, the golf ball snapped in two revealing two small sachets containing a fine white crystalline powder. Callobar exchanged a triumphant glance with the Gorgon. 'Hurrah!'

'So that's how they do it,' Jim muttered incredulously. 'No—'

'Yes,' replied a voice, 'that's how we do it!' The warehouse lights flickered on.

From where he stood, Jim could see the men. He felt his entire body grow cold.

'Allow me to introduce myself,' the short one, in the middle of the group of six men, said with an American drawl. 'My name's Paul Edmonds – and may I ask what you are both doing in my warehouse?'

Callobar and Jim remained stock-still, neither saying a word. Instead, they kept their attention fixed on the five revolvers pointing in their direction.

Paul Edmonds was a short, stocky man attired in a grey business suit and smoking a cigarette that was fixed to a white plastic holder. His hairline had receded well away from his forehead, but what little he possessed showed it to be of an auburn colour with greying tufts at the temples. Jim estimated he was either in his late forties or early fifties. As his musings ended, Jim saw – for the first time – Edmond's small Dutchman's beard.

Jim's face broke into a smile. That beard looked as stupid on him as it did on the Afrikaners back in Africa.

Edmonds waved towards the crates. His manner was calm and confident, laced with a sense of enjoyment. He knew he held all the winning cards. Jim recognised his own attitude with despair. It had never failed him and now that attitude was aiming at him! Suddenly, Edmonds's beard wasn't as comical as he first thought.

'You're quite correct,' Edmonds said in a friendly manner, 'these crates are full of golf balls. In each ball is two sachets of that white powder we know as heroin.' He smiled beatifically. 'Please, if you are armed, drop your weapons in front of you. And may I caution you on any ridiculous actions you plan to take as my friends, here, are very trigger happy!'

Exchanging an apologetic gesture with the teenager, Callobar gingerly removed his Luger from his shoulder holster and dropped it to the ground.

'What about you, son?' Edmonds asked Jim.

The Gorgon shrugged. 'All I have is this switchblade,' he said, producing it from under the windcheater. Levelling it out and aiming it at one of Edmonds's men, Jim added: 'It's quite harmless.' He pressed the release button, the handle jerked back as the blade shot out and traversed the four metres separating them, to embed itself deep within the body of the unsuspecting mobster.

Wasting no time, and thankful for the diversion, Callobar dived for his gun and with one accurate shot brought another mobster down. The four remaining men took cover behind the nearest crates before returning fire.

'We'd better get out of here,' Jim suggested calmly when he and Callobar had taken cover behind the open crate.

'I couldn't agree with you more,' the West Indian stated. 'It's four guns to one ... and a strange pocketknife – and, somehow, I don't like those odds!'

'Nor I,' Jim admitted with a grin. 'If you'll cover me, I'll try to get the car.'

'Callobar glanced at where he knew the open door was. Between this and another cluster of crates was about three metres of open space. Crossing it would make Jim a clear target. 'I don't know,' he said. 'That's a killing ground, there. No matter how much cover I give you, it still takes one bullet ...'

Jim frowned. 'Who says I'm going that way? I'm not suicidal! I'll go straight to those crates, there, and use all these as cover. They won't see anything as long as you keep shooting at them.'

Callobar silently surveyed the scene. The crates Jim had pointed out were directly behind them and practically invisible to their enemies, due to their own crates. He nodded his approval. 'Be careful, okay?'

Two bullets bit into the crate above them. Jim waited until Callobar was able to shoot back. Keeping low, Jim moved towards the second cluster of crates and away from the mobsters. Behind him, Callobar fired two more shots, the ricochets echoed in the warehouse. Reaching these crates, he scampered behind them. His heart was in his ears again and as he crouched behind the crates trying to block out the thumping, a new sound was heard. A thin, whistling sound that stopped as the strip of hoop-iron dug into the crate above him.

The man holding it pulled it free of the crate and swung it around – above his head – as if it were a whip. Jim rolled out of the way on time and the hoop-iron hit the concrete, creating sparks. Standing now, Jim dug into the pouch for another blade, cursing himself for not reloading the switchblade earlier. His eye caught sight of another mobster sneaking up on his partner.

'Callobar! Look out!'

A shot rang out. Jim couldn't tell what had happened to the West Indian as the ominous whistling started again. This time, Jim's reflexes weren't fast enough and the metal strip cut through the sleeve of his windcheater and bit into the flesh of his arm.

'*Eina*[17]!' Involuntarily, he pushed the release, and the blade flew. Glancing back where Callobar had been, he noticed that both the ASIO operative and the mobster had disappeared. Footsteps could be heard in the warehouse. Was Callobar hurt? If so, he needed help. All thought of escape forgotten, Jim removed his blade from the dead mobster's throat and wiped the blood off on the man's shirt. 'Waste not, want not.'

Heading in the direction of the footsteps, Jim remembered the pain in his arm. It was throbbing now and for the first time, he noticed the blood, the sleeve saturated. He stopped next to a forklift to rest and caught sight of the same mobster still stalking Callobar, who was a little way ahead. Jim didn't waste time, ignoring the pain he pulled himself up onto the forklift and searched for the starter. When he turned the key, the forklift kicked into life as his foot pressed the accelerator. It was gas-powered and, therefore, quiet. Lifting the forks to chest height, Jim pushed the accelerator to the 'floor'. The sound of the fast-approaching vehicle attracted the mobster's attention, but his scream was stifled by the blood in his throat as one of the forks impaled him to one of the crates.

'Callobar!' Jim cried. 'This way!' He headed straight for the door as fast as he could, not looking back to see if Callobar was following him.

Passing the forklift, the West Indian glanced at the sight and retched. Another shot rang out and Callobar heard the bullet pass his ear. Before following Jim out the door, he returned fire and saw a mobster dive for cover.

Jim was already at the car. He jumped into the driver's seat and met Callobar in the middle of the road before speeding off.

---

[17]Ouch! (Afrikaans).

What was left of the mobsters rushed out and fired two shots at the fleeing Saab. They heard the ricochets off the bodywork and as the car disappeared around a corner, one of them brought his hand up and rubbed his large knuckle against his lower lip.

Jim turned left onto Main Street and kept the car at a reasonable speed, always checking the rear-view mirror for any signs of pursuit.

Callobar looked at Jim and suddenly realised who was driving. 'What are you doing?'

'I'm not too sure, but I think it's called driving!'

'You know what I mean,' Callobar retorted, 'you don't have a licence. Pull over!'

'Oh, for f**k's sake!' Jim cried. 'I killed three men tonight and you're worried about a bloody driver's licence! You need to reassess your priorities, my friend!' Despite the protest, Jim pulled over into the carpark of a Catholic church and climbed out of the vehicle.

The two swapped seats and, as he climbed into the passenger's seat, his arm hit against the door and Jim winced as the pain erupted from the deep cut caused by the hoop iron.

Callobar looked at him. 'What's wrong?'

'Don't worry about it,' Jim replied, 'get moving.'

Jim was cradling his left arm and Callobar shot out a strong hand and dragged the teenager's arm towards him. Jim screamed with the pain and the West Indian saw the savage cut through the separated part of Jim's windcheater. 'Oh, shit!' he swore. 'We need to get this tended to before Julie murders me!'

The Saab exited the carpark, cutting off an old grey ute whose driver never really noticed them. Callobar sped up to avoid a collision and glanced at Jim. 'We'll go back to my place, and we can clean up that injury.' They drove in silence for a while, then Callobar asked: 'Where did you get that knife?'

Jim looked at Callobar. 'Really?' he replied. 'I impaled a man to a wooden crate with a forklift and you ask about a little knife?' Shit! This arm was really starting to hurt. He tightened his grip on it, the pressure minimising the pain. 'I bought it,' he finally said.

'Not doing what that thing did,' Callobar shot back.

Jim smiled weakly. 'Well, maybe I did modify it a little.'

'How do I even put that into my report?' Callobar asked, turning right at the traffic lights on Wanneroo Road. 'A night watchman with a broken neck, a mobster killed by a switchblade that spits out its blades, and another pinned by a forklift. What do I tell Peterson, Jim?'

When no response came from his passenger, Callobar shot Jim a worried look. The teenager was sitting still, the seat belt preventing him from falling forward. He realised that Jim had merely passed out.

Chapter Seven
Non-Police Brutality

AUGUST 5. 8:00 AM, WESTERN AUSTRALIA TIME

'So that's how they do it!' Fab said incredulously, eyeing the two halves of the golf ball which lay on the pink map of Australia on Jim's student desk.

Jim slid open one side of the pine wardrobe and removed a tracksuit top. He was dressed completely in blue, except for the tan desert boots.

Fab's green tracksuit top clashed with the brown slacks and blue shirt that he wore. 'We are taking it with us?' he asked.

Jim checked the mirror to see if his hair was presentable and decided that it needed combing. 'Yeah,' he replied, constructing a reasonably straight part on his left side. Putting the two halves together and placing the golf ball in the safety of the tracksuit's pocket, he motioned to Fab to precede him out of the room. 'Hold on,' he said to Fab and walked to the kitchen where Julie was busy checking her shopping list. Mark was still in bed, Jim noted by the quiet in the house. 'We're going now,' he commented.

She looked up from the notepad she held in her hand. 'Okay,' she said with a smile.

'Bye,' Fab called from the entry hall, before closing the door behind him.

'Mark was still asleep, Fab. You shouldn't have yelled,' Jim said, as they walked up the road to the bus stop. 'If you keep doing that, he'll kill you one day.'

Fab remained silent for a moment. Then asked how Jim had gotten hold of that golf ball.

Jim explained the events of the previous night, omitting the carnage that they had left behind and of the stitched-up wound on his arm.

When Jim had awakened from his blackout, Callobar had given him a cup of black coffee with nothing else but two tots of brandy added. It had helped with the throbbing pain of the freshly stitched cut on his arm. Even now, it was still throbbing.

'What's going to happen now is that those thugs are going to carry out a massive clean-up of that warehouse and try their best to quieten Callobar and me.'

'You mean they're going to try to kill you?'

'Perhaps,' Jim admitted. 'So, that'll be the last time we're to be seen on the streets, okay? At school we're all right – they wouldn't dare try anything there.'

'You sure?' Fab asked anxiously.

'Of course, I'm sure,' Jim replied confidently. 'It's too risky on their part; they'll expose themselves and become more visible to the police. Besides, it's not the 1920s and we're not in Chicago!'

Fab wasn't convinced. 'Yeah,' Fab said, 'but we're dealing with members of organised crime, and they do tend to be dangerous!'

Jim stopped and faced Fab. 'Look,' he said angrily, 'if you're too scared to participate why don't you go straight home and play with your little Matchbox cars? I'll go question Hank by myself.'

'Don't be stupid!' Fab snapped back, 'I'll come with you. And I'm not scared – just worried … and nervous.'

Because the bus was cruising down the small slope towards the bus stop, the boys broke into a run and dashed across the road in time to let the bus driver realise their intention and apply the brakes. Only a few stops were made as the bus wound its way towards the Perth CBD and finally turned into the bus lane that skirted just behind the Perth Entertainment Centre, to come to a halt at the Bus Terminal on Wellington Street. The driver killed the engine and the passengers disembarked.

The traffic, building up on Horseshoe Bridge, got a chance to move off as Fab and Jim joined the rest of the pedestrians at the corner waiting for the walk signal. It blinked on and the two Gorgons, followed by some others, marched diagonally across the intersection, and down William Street towards Myers. Turning left into Murray Street, they continued past the various department stores and then crossed over at the second set of lights. The usual crowd jostled past them at the Plaza Arcade, but after various detours around and dodging gossiping groups, they reached Hay Street Mall.

Police Central faces the WACA Grounds in the suburb of East Perth, some two kilometres from the city centre. The two buildings were connected by a dual-level corridor, one storey above the ground. Fab hesitated as they approached the four steps to the door of the police station.

Jim turned to face his friend. 'Aren't you coming?'

The young man, of Italian origin, looked at the plants growing on either side of the steps. 'You know,' he told Jim, 'I've gone past this place hundreds of times, but this is the first time I'll ever have gone inside.'

'Yeah, yeah,' Jim said. '"One small step for man ..."' He opened the door, muttering on about a first time for everything.

Inside, a uniform-clad officer was conversing with a man, dressed in an impressive grey suit, standing on opposite sides of the counter. The officer glanced at the two boys, excused himself, and asked them, 'What can I do for you lads?'

Fab and Jim exchanged looks and Jim replied, 'Yes.' Casting an uncomfortable eye in the direction of the man in the suit, he said, 'I'd like to see Senior Detective-Sergeant O'Reilly, please.'

At the mention of the name, the man in the suit stepped forward. 'You want to see Sam O'Reilly?' he inquired.

Jim looked him up and down with an air of disdain and directed his answer back to the constable. 'Yes. It concerns a boy who was picked up at Tan—' He looked hard at the man who now stood by his side with a broad grin on his face.

As if sensing the doubt in Jim's mind, the man said in a reassuring manner, 'Don't worry, I'm not a reporter, I'm a cop!'

Confirmation of this fact from the constable only made Jim even more uncomfortable. 'About a boy who was picked up at Tannen Heights Senior High School yesterday afternoon, for the possession and selling of drugs.' As he uttered the statement, he could feel his confidence returning.

'What information have you boys got?' the man asked.

'I'd rather discuss that with Sam – er, um – Mr. O'Reilly,' Jim answered.

'... And your names are ...?'

Jim felt really in control now. 'My name's Saston, Jim Saston. My silent friend beside me is Fab Arterro.'

'Well, Saston Jim Saston, what do you want with Detective O'Reilly?' the man demanded sarcastically.

On hearing Jim's name, the constable squinted. Saston? Sounds familiar ... 'Hey, Bill, I know that name!'

'From where, Doug? It doesn't ...' He turned back to Jim. 'Hey, it's you!' he uttered with a laugh, extending a finger, and pointing to Jim in astonishment. 'You're that one! Sam – um – O'Reilly's told me about you – you're the kid who competes with him!'

'What?' cried Doug, clearly puzzled as he stared from Bill to Jim and back again. 'How can this kid be a competitor? Why he doesn't even ...' Doug's words trailed off as he noticed Jim's face change.

'I'll explain later, Doug,' Bill promised, 'First I'll take these two to Sam.' He led the way to the elevator and pressed for the second floor, then ushered them down the corridor and stopped before a door marked 'Senior Detective-Sergeant Samuel O'Reilly'. Bill rapped his knuckles on it then opened it before the knock was answered. Bill stated, 'Sam, there are two young men here to see you.'

Bill motioned for the two Gorgons to enter, and following behind them, closed the door.

Senior Detective-Sergeant Sam O'Reilly looked up from a report and removed his wire-rimmed glasses. His greeting smile slowly disappeared as his eyes focused on Jim's face. 'Oh, God!' he muttered. Now this glorious day was officially destroyed by this interfering teenage bastard! Many-a-time he had been tempted to demand that Mark Peterson get a cage in which to put James, but that action would anger the Child Welfare Department! God curse government institutions! 'Hello, James,' he said finally, ice coating his words. He looked at the other lad, wondering who he was.

'Fabrizio Arterro,' Jim commented. He didn't like being referred to as 'James', and O'Reilly was well aware of that.

O'Reilly nodded towards him. 'Sit down,' he said, shortly. 'Now, what do you want, James?'

Jim removed the golf ball from his pocket. Placing it on top of the desk in front of the detective, he replied, 'Take a look at this.'

O'Reilly looked down at the white object on his red blotter. At last, he said, 'I can't be sure, but it looks just like a golf ball.'

Jim ignored the sarcasm and picked up the ball. 'That's what it looks and feels like, but—' his fingers pulled the two halves apart '—when you do this, you find that some things just don't seem to be exactly what they look like.' He dropped the small bags of heroin out onto the blotter.

The two detectives exchanged astonished glances. Bill picked up one of the bags, produced a pocketknife, and made a tiny incision in the plastic. He raised his powder-encrusted finger to his mouth and, when the taste registered, nodded to O'Reilly.

'Where'd you get this?' O'Reilly wanted to know, pointing to the ball.

Jim smiled knowingly. 'Callobar and I got it – and you know from where … and how.'

O'Reilly caught Bill's questioning glance. 'Callobar's a … a Jamaican immigrant,' he said. 'Lawyer by profession, amateur detective by hobby.' He caught Jim's eye and received an approving nod from him. O'Reilly didn't like lying but at times it was necessary. In this case, it saved a lot of questions about the intelligence organisation that two people in this office knew little about. He lifted a pen from the blotter and began rotating it between his thumbs and the first two fingers of each hand. Realising he was fidgeting, he put it down on the blotter, calmly. 'Okay,' he said at long last, 'are there any more of these?'

Jim nodded. 'They're all in crates – and every crate is full of golf balls. I suggest you get your hands on that stuff before they move it all.'

'What's the hurry?' Bill asked.

'Let's just say that their lease is about to expire,' Jim replied calmly.

'Great!' O'Reilly cried out and shifted nervously in his chair. He could feel Bill's puzzled eyes on him again. *Damn him!* O'Reilly thought, damn James and ASIO – and most of all, Slattery! It was no joke having a sixteen-year-old boy strut in here with the evidence that a fully trained undercover officer failed to obtain. Especially when the report of the post-mortem carried out on the charred remains of that officer lay on the desk in front of him. It was no joke, at all. This report proved that the men behind the drug pipeline were willing to commit murder to protect their investment. But then, why shouldn't they? The Slattery organisation was only an offshoot of the Las Vegas-based Valentine Mob – and Rick Valentine was no stranger to murder, so O'Reilly had been told.

He remembered back to when he had briefed Graeme Chesston on the job he had volunteered to do. That had been the first time he had met the man who was playfully called 'The Cat'. A cat has nine lives – as the saying goes – and, ironically, this case had been Chesston's tenth; The Cat had used up all of his lives! Now, where Chesston had failed, James had succeeded and left God knows how many dead!

O'Reilly sighed. 'Bill,' he said, 'get a team out to Slattery's warehouse and stop any loading of crates.' By now, Slattery's people would've cleaned up all signs of any night-time activity. But in case they hadn't, Bill Hammer would return with a lot of questions, so he began preparing himself for the explanation. He had done that in the past, explaining ASIO's participation in some of their cases. Every time ASIO was involved, they led to a bloodbath behind. Now, from what James had cryptically said, he had graduated into that league, and that meant that sometime during the case the situation would arise where he would have to tell Hammer the truth about James Saston and Callobar. He watched as Hammer left.

Clasping his hands together, O'Reilly sat forward, resting his forearms on the edge of the desk. 'Now, James, I've got something to tell you.' He picked up a sheet of paper. 'This is a report on a body that was discovered in a burnt-out car north of Eneabba. Denture checks have identified the body as that of an undercover police officer who had been investigating this drug case. The back of his head was caved in due to a blow – a bloody hard blow! The body was missing two hands and two feet, what does that prove?' He waited for an answer, but none came from the two Gorgons. 'It proves that his cover was blown and that they had tortured him! In a fit of pity, I guess, his torturers did the right thing by him and bashed him one, killing him! The body – or what was left of it – was placed in an old Ford, dumped, and set alight. Evidently, the body would be completely incinerated, but some well-timed rain put an end to that.'

Jim swallowed loudly. If Sam was trying to scare him, he was doing a great job! He glanced at Fab, sitting a little way behind, who had turned a deathly white. 'How long's he been dead?' he asked in a shaky voice.

'Two days – but he'd been reported as missing for a few weeks. Now you get an idea what type of men we – the police – are dealing with.'

So that was it. A secret weapon, Sam? It didn't work. Jim nodded in agreement and the detective smiled. 'Yeah, Sam, I see – but it doesn't change my mind. I told you on the phone why I'm here.'

'Yeah,' O'Reilly replied with a sigh. 'I thought you were coming in on Monday.' Oh well, he told himself, at least I tried. 'Hank Andrews is in the interview room, next door. He was brought here at five-thirty this morning, from the detention centre. If we keep inconveniencing him, sooner or later he'll tire of it and talk. You can go in and talk to him – but it won't help, he simply won't say anything.'

Jim rose and grinned. 'Want a bet?' he said and walked out of the office, Fab following.

Once in the corridor, Fab seemed to have found his voice and stopped his friend from opening the door to the interview room, in which Hank sat and waited. 'Maybe we're getting too involved in this thing,' he said nervously. 'That poor cop. What a thing to do to a person – death must've been a blessing!'

Jim's grip tightened on the door handle as he closed his eyes and tried to erase the subject from his mind. 'Fab, if you don't mind, let's not talk about it.' He took a deep breath and walked into the room.

Hank sat at the head of the table, his back to Fab and the door; Jim paced round the room. 'Okay, I'll try again,' he told the seated boy, 'and again, and again … until my patience runs out.' He placed his hands on the table and brought his face close to Hank's. His sore arm throbbed painfully but chose to ignore it. The wound had behaved itself all morning and remained numb, so why was it playing up now? 'You know, Hank, the human jaw contains some thirty-odd teeth. If you're lucky and start talking, you'll probably be able to keep two or three of yours. If not, when I've finished with you, you're going to need false ones!'

'Are you trying to scare me, kid?' Hank threw back defiantly. 'If so, it's not bloody working ... and besides, that's assault!'

'You're right,' Jim agreed placidly. 'But you're overlooking one very important fact – I'm not supposed to be here, nor's Fab. The police will deny any allegations you make about us coming here and bashing the living f**k out of you – so you're pretty well on your own!'

Hank remained silent. Jim looked past him at Fab, who shrugged nonchalantly. In one quick move, Jim grabbed Hank's long greasy hair and smashed his face down on the table. As blood trickled from his nose and forehead, he whipped around his fist knocking the side of Jim's injured arm, then made a break for it dashing towards the door, screaming 'Help!' at the top of his lungs.

Fab's arm was leaning against the door stopping any further escape for Hank. As he glanced at Jim, whose face was closed with pain, Fab brought his knee up to connect with Hank's midsection. Jim grabbed at Hank's arm as he got back to his feet and sent him into the table – hank's groin painfully taking the blow of the table's sharp corner. With tears streaming down his cheeks, Hank collapsed into a chair feebly trying to kick back at Jim or Fab. 'Bastards!' he muttered under his breath.

'Did you say something, Andrews?' Jim asked pleasantly, casually pulling Hank's head backward.

'Yeah,' Hank said, lunging towards Jim, his arm lashing out as he moved. The hand – now clenched into a fist – hit Jim in the ribs and the Gorgon was thrown by the surprisingly strong blow.

Fab's own clenched fist came down on Hank's forehead, sending him to the floor.

With the speed of a stallion, Jim was back on his feet diving towards Hank, pain banished away beyond the memory until it was time to feel it again. Without thinking, Jim pummelled Hank's back, aiming each blow along the boy's spine. He had the intention of smashing Hank's vertebrae, rendering him a paraplegic or, if he was lucky, a quadriplegic! Fab had to use all his might to pull Jim off his victim.

Holding Jim in a bear hug, he yelled to Hank, 'See? He's a madman and if I let him go now, he'll kill you!' Fab's words were emphasised as Jim frantically pushed against Fab's strength and weight. Though it seemed like the usual put-on – the good cop/ bad cop routine – Fab knew it wasn't a put-on. He knew that if he let go of his friend now, Jim would certainly kill Hank Andrews!

'Kill! Ha!' scorned Hank as he got to his feet, stretching his aching back. He felt his self-confidence returning.

After an hour and a half, they still hadn't gotten Hank to talk. He was proud of himself. Yet Hank had to admit it, the cramps he had been feeling for the last eight hours were getting worse. More so now that that bastard, Saston, had hit him continuously in the back.

'Okay,' Fab said and loosened his grip on Jim, as if in answer to Hank's leer, and watched as the massacre began. He knew better than to prevent him from what he intended to do. No point in getting bashed up as well.

Jim's mind was a blank, except for the primeval desire to inflict as much pain as humanly possible on the person of Hank Andrews! This thought brought an evil glint to his eyes. His method of fighting was of a trained and drilled operative, skill was his weapon, knowing where to direct his blows to maximise pain. By contrast, Hank's dodging and weaving was just a scared, cowardly flight of movement.

Hank adopted the classic boxing stance, fists clenched, waiting for Jim's attack. Jim's attack, unfortunately for Hank was not classic or fair. The Gorgon twisted to his left and brought his right leg up and smashed his foot into Hank's solar plexus, sending him into the wall. The pain in his back shot up along his backbone and he slid down into a squatting position. Jim continued the twist and his left foot connected with Hank's chin, sending his head smashing back into the wall. Jim heard Hank's teeth click violently and he smiled. Without stopping, Jim swapped feet again and his right foot buried deep into Hank's groin!

Hank groaned and his hands dropped to his prized possession. 'Stop!' he wheezed. 'Please, stop. I give in, just, stop!'

'Can't hear you!' stated Jim.

'Jim!' Fab said, pulling Hank up and pleased to hear a small whimpering sound from the bleeding lips of the beaten drug pusher. 'He's had enough, for f**k's sake!'

'Strange,' Jim commented. 'Nowhere near death yet cowering already. Ever think about those other lives you helped destroy – huh, Hank, huh? I know of Rick Devlin, Tracy Palmer, Lenny Dorrington, Peter Farmer, Marie Machik, Linda Small … The list is endless, Andrews. All died of ODs!'

'Don't forget Geraldine Palmerston and Jack Davies,' Fab added. 'Both died because the rubbish they were taking was laced with strychnine.'

'How many more of them have to die before it affects your conscience?' Jim wanted to know. 'You know, it doesn't matter how many more kids die from taking the heroin that you sell, you'll only be charged with pushing it not with what it actually is – murder!'

'It's not murder!' Hank glared at Jim defiantly, the venom dancing in his eyes. 'If they died it's only because they don't know how to use it.'

'But you know how to use it, don't you? Of course, you do, because you're also hooked on it – aren't you? Aren't you?'

Hank broke eye contact and stared at the floor or tabletop. Fab wasn't too sure.

'Who knows?' Jim carried on, 'maybe you used more than your share and started taking it out of your customers' packets, hm? That means you'd have to redistribute the stuff. Wouldn't you? You'd substitute the missing portion with something else. What did you use? Actual sugar, flour, or … strychnine? Where'd you get the strychnine, Andrews? What kind of sick person would give you strychnine?' Jim trailed around to the other side of the table, theorising. 'With the strychnine in your possession, you added it to the heroin and sold it, knowing full well it would kill them! You sold it to two kids – a Year 9 and a Year 10! They died from administering that poison! That, Andrews, is premeditated murder! And you know something? Western Australia never did away with the death penalty, so that means that you're going to be put away in Longmore for two years and the day you turn eighteen, they're going to take you away for your appointment with the long drop. Happy birthday, Hank Andrews! You want to know why? Because you're the only drug pusher caught at Tannen Heights Senior High School and, naturally, the blame of the strychnine poisoning's going to fall on you! Irrespective of the fact that you might be innocent of the whole thing! But someone's neck needs to stretch for it!'

'No, I won't!' Hank said quickly in a shaky voice, hardly believing what he said himself. 'They don't kill people, anymore!'

'How do you know?' Fab asked.

''Cos they don't!" Hank cried.

'Why not?'

''Cos that's murder!'

'So, you're allowed to commit murder, but the state isn't?' Fab replied sarcastically.

'Listen, like I said – that's their fault. They get hooked, they die, not me – that's not my fault!' Hank yelled. 'They can die, it's their life, not mine! Theirs!'

Now Fab wanted to hit him. 'What right have you got to control it, Andrews?' Fab asked, clenching his fists. 'What makes you so big and important … Henry?'

'Don't call me that!' Hank screamed.

'I can call you what the f**k I want … Henry!' Fab retorted.

It was about time Fab joined in, Jim told himself. 'Amazing how people talk, isn't it?' he asked casually, removing something from his pocket.

'What do you mean?' Fab queried.

With a wicked smile, Jim replied, 'Well, when they want something badly enough …' he paused for a moment and regarded Hank '… like this!'

'Where'd ya get that?' Hank cried excitedly, though remaining seated.

Fab looked from the small clear package, containing a white powder and needle that rested in the Gorgon's hand, back to Jim. What was he playing at and where the hell did he get that?

Subconsciously, he passed his hand across his brow to remove the thin layer of sweat that had gathered there.

Hank, suspiciously, regarded Fab with interest. He obviously didn't know anything about this, so it must be sugar.

Jim noticed with satisfaction that Hank's eyes were betraying their owner's hunger. A few more steps ... 'Well?' Jim said. 'Well, you going to talk?'

'Why? Why should I?' Hank asked insolently.

'Because you're a dope addict,' Jim replied.

'No, I'm not,' Hank returned quickly in defence. Too quickly, perhaps?

'Oh well, then that means that you are not suffering from withdrawal symptoms, and which means that you won't need this then, will you?' returned Jim, moving over to the door. 'I'll just return this to the evidence locker.'

'Hey, hold it!' yelled Hank. 'Maybe ...'

Jim stopped and turned. 'Maybe, what?' He asked, his hand resting on the door handle.

'Maybe we can make a deal! Yeah? Okay?' Hank licked his lips.

Jim squinted and eyed Hank suspiciously. But he already knew the sort of deal Hank wanted to strike. 'What sort of deal?'

'You give me that,' Hank suggested greedily, pointing to the white-filled package and the hypodermic in Jim's hand, 'and I'll give you all the names you want!'

'How can we even believe what you say?' Fab asked phlegmatically, hardly believing the drama that was playing out before his eyes.

'Well if he doesn't tell us the truth,' Jim replied matter-of-factly, 'we'll simply come back and throw him out the window. They do that in South Africa, from the roof of John Vorster Square!'

Hank went pale but nodded towards Jim's hand.

Jim pulled back his hand. 'No,' Jim said with an evil smile, 'You talk first.'

Hank leaned forward eagerly, his words barely audible in his rush to get the heroin. 'There's three more ... Bill, Graeme, and Cyndy,' he murmured, suddenly rushing towards Jim.

Fab looked at his friend, nodded, and pushed him down back onto the chair.

'Surnames!' Jim stated, beginning to turn the handle.

'No! Don't go!' grovelled Hank, his hands outstretched in desperation. 'Bill Flynn. Graeme Madden, and Cyndy ... Cynthia Johnson!'

Jim shot an astonished eye at Fab and then returned his attention to Hank. 'Cynthia Johnson? Year 10, short, red-head, cute face?"

Hank nodded. His eyes were glued to what Jim held.

'One of Chris's friends?' Fab queried.

Jim nodded absently, thinking over what he'd just learnt. Is Cynthia's little venture known to Chris's group, and if so, who in the group buys? That was what he was now worried about. He thought better not to contemplate it and pushed the subject from his mind. 'What about the supplier?' he asked automatically.

'Dunno,' shrugged Hank. 'Please?' he whispered, his eyes never leaving their target in Jim's hand.

'Where does he get it from?'

Hank shrugged dumbly. 'I dunno!'

'Why is it, Andrews, I get the feeling your lying?' He watched the hope dissolve from the other's face.

Then Hank did something that neither of the Gorgons were prepared for: He began to cry!

At that point, Fab decided that that was all he could take and left the interview room.

Finally bringing the tears under control, Hank cast a pathetically pleading look at his antagonist. 'Look, I told ya everythin' I know,' he blubbered. 'I'm not holdin' nothin' back!'

Jim stared at Hank for a long time, never saying a word. 'Okay,' he said finally and threw the hypo and the pack to the back of the room.

Hank sped towards it like nothing less than lightning. Kneeling on the ground, he ripped open the package and then just stared at the contents in disbelief. 'Ya f**ken bastard!' he shouted. 'That's icing sugar! Not heroin!'

Jim gave a thin and evil smile. Before he left the room, he turned where Hank had collapsed into a sobbing heap. 'You know something, Andrews, you're a pathetic pile of rubbish.' With that, he closed the door. He noticed his hand was shaking and forced it to stop.

Fab was looking out the window at the traffic on the causeway. He couldn't have been looking at anything as his tumultuous thoughts blinded him. He sensed Jim approaching and turned to face his friend. 'What did you give him that dope for?' he demanded.

'Didn't you hear him? That wasn't dope. It was icing sugar.'

'Icing sugar?' Fab repeated. 'That's bloody disgusting! Why would you do something so cruel?'

'Oh, come on, Fab, think about it. He pushes dope, he takes dope a bit – he hasn't been near the stuff for about forty-eight hours. He'll be desperate – willing to talk. I get a small package that looks like heroin – and a needle – used for one of my injections, and flash it around a bit. His desperation blurs his reason and heightens his hunger for that shit! Then he surrenders his will to my suggestions.'

'And it all was nothing but sugar?' Fab spat out.

Jim raised an eyebrow innocently. 'It was sugar … sweet sugar!'

'You tortured him, Jim!' Fab accused. 'How the hell could you do such a thing? Especially here, in a police station! We have laws … we live according to rules. You broke those rules, those laws … and that's okay with you?'

Jim remained silent as he stared at the causeway. Living by the rules, the laws, only helped to assuage the conscience. Those who live solely by the rules leave them open to lethal attack and Jim determined a long time ago that that was never going to be him. Better to be pessimistic and trust no-one, than be the betrayed optimist! 'Yes,' Jim said, turning to Fab. 'My conduct does not weigh upon my conscience and never will!'

Fab frowned. 'What? How can you even think like that? What the hell happened to you?'

Jim's face reddened. 'My father was killed. He didn't die of natural causes but was gunned down - like a dog - in the streets! So, excuse me if I don't reflect your values. There was a job to be done and I did it!' He started to walk to O'Reilly's office. 'You coming?'

'I'll be there in a few minutes,' Fab muttered. He started thinking that being in the Gorgons and, even thinking of Jim as a friend, was not healthy.

133

Chapter Eight
Mr. Simos Reports

AUGUST 5. 9:02 AM, WESTERN AUSTRALIA TIME

Callobar awoke just after nine and spent half an hour in the shower to remove the final traces of sleep from his body. With a towel wrapped around his waist, he lumbered into the kitchen and plugged in the kettle. Where the shower had failed, coffee would triumph.

From a pile of dirty dishes, Callobar removed a dirty mug. A quick rinse and it was clean. The last clean bowl in the house was removed from the cupboard and placed on the breakfast bar. One day, he told himself, he'd have to do the dishes ... or buy a set of paper plates and cups. As the kitchen resounded with the whistling of the kettle, Callobar poured the steaming liquid into the mug. With the mug of coffee and a bowl full of cornflakes he moved to the family room, switched on the television, and watched the Saturday morning cartoons.

When his grandfather's clock announced the tenth hour, he decided it was time to dress and go and meet Jim at the Petersons' house. Regretfully, he switched off the television and added the bowl and mug to the tower of dishes in the sink.

With one glance out the window, he decided it would be too warm to wear black. So, putting on a pair of cream slacks and a light blue sports shirt, he remembered that his keys were on the dining-room table with the stuff he had used to clean and bandage Jim's wound, which the boy had received from the strip of hoop-iron at the Slattery warehouse the night before. He returned the first-aid kit to the cupboard in the laundry, where he also kept a small assortment of weapons. With the keys in his pocket and one last look at the grandfather's clock, he headed for the front door.

Something small, lying on the doormat, attracted Callobar's attention. He frowned as he removed a set of blue rosary beads. Smiling to himself, he returned them to their container. Some devout Catholic feels generous today, he mused and slipped his key into the car and unlocked the door. He reached over and popped the beads into the glove box.

The white light erupting from the front of the car was the last thing Callobar knew; the sudden heat was the last thing he felt.

AUGUST 5. 11:05 AM, WESTERN AUSTRALIA TIME

Sam O'Reilly returned the phone to its cradle, sighed, and buried his face in his hands. The dissected golf ball still lay on the desk before him. Maybe the news of the experience of the late – and unlucky – Graeme Chesston may not have deterred James Saston, but the latest news he had would, that he was sure of. O'Reilly didn't like being the bearer of bad news, no policeman does, but it was an unfortunate part of the job to inform the next of kin, a loving husband or wife – or some meddlesome amateur, who didn't fully realise the danger he was inviting, of a death.

Hammer sat quietly in the chair that Jim had occupied almost two hours before. Since his return from the warehouse, he had been entertained by O'Reilly's version of the boy's biography – or at least – what little his superior knew of it. Hammer couldn't help wondering how Jim had managed to accept the death of his father so easily. The only parent the kid ever knew, one minute alive and well, next – according to the case described by O'Reilly – a bullet-riddled corpse in a twisted auto-wreck. Hell, some people's lives were rough! But this kid must have had nerves of steel to go through the ordeal of identifying his father's body and accepting the fact that he was now totally alone. Another kid, of the same age, would probably have cracked up and joined a group of layabouts, who would help carry his grudge against society – vandalising and looting property, fighting, terrorising housewives, and harassing pensioners. Kids who, by the age of sixteen, would have spent anything from six to twelve months at Longmore Detention Centre. No! Hammer decided. There's something wrong with that story! Between his father's death and now, something had occurred that had occupied both Jim's mind and time – and playing amateur detective was just the fallout of it!

'What's up?' Hammer asked. 'What was the phone call about?'

O'Reilly sighed. 'I'll tell you in a few minutes,' he replied. 'First, I want to know what happened at the warehouse.'

It was Hammer's turn to sigh, and he leaned forward. 'We managed to stop one semi, as it left the warehouse. It was carrying the last of the crates, the warehouse was empty! They must have spent all night clearing the place out.'

'Don't you believe it, boyo,' O'Reilly stated. 'They took time out to plant a car bomb!'

'A car bomb?'

136

O'Reilly nodded, silently.

'Where? How do you know?'

'That lawyer, I told you about, the one that helps James. He's dead! A bomb in his car.'

'A car bomb in Perth? What's this city coming to?' He made a low whistling sound. 'That means that they're going to try to kill our young friend, next door.'

'That's right,' O'Reilly agreed. 'Knowing James, he isn't going to like what I'm about to suggest. Bill, arrange for Joe to take James and his friend home.'

After one knock, Jim entered the office. 'Hank's ready to … to talk to you, now,' he said, stopping in the doorway, the grin of victory dropping from his face. He sensed the change in the atmosphere, had felt the tension's thickness.

Hammer rose and said to no-one in particular: 'I'll see to it.'

O'Reilly looked up, distracted from his train of thought. 'What? Oh, yeah. Take care of it, Bill.' He glanced past Jim and through the open door saw Fab standing in the corridor. The teenager didn't seem to want to come in, so O'Reilly gestured to Jim to close the door and sit down.

Jim lowered himself into the chair, and asked, 'What's wrong?'

O'Reilly sighed. 'I told you earlier that we're dealing with a dangerous gang of men,' he replied. 'A few minutes ago, I received a telephone call that proved, not only are they well informed but also that they don't hesitate to strike back! The call was to inform me that a car in Joondanna exploded on ignition, killing the driver … Callobar!'

Jim's mouth fell open as the colour drained from his face, he felt his stomach drop. After a few speechless moments, he asked, in a trembling voice: 'How'd they find out so fast?'

The detective shrugged.

Jim slowly shook his head as this new development set in his memory like cement. 'No,' he muttered to himself. 'Now Mark's going to take me off this assignment!' He regretted the words as they spilled from his mouth. A friend of his was dead and all he could think of was being taken off this stupid case!

O'Reilly found it hard to contain his own feelings at James's statement, but with strict self-control and the thought of having this nuisance finally out of his hair, he forced a smile. 'Really?'

'You don't have to sound so happy about it!' Jim snapped back.

'I don't mean to, James. But you've got to agree it is the safest thing to do.'

Reluctantly, Jim did agree for the sake of the guys at school – and Chris. He'd never forgive himself if anything happened to any of them. It was bad enough that Callobar was now dead because of it all.

O'Reilly lifted a pen absently. 'What did you find out from your "friend"?'

'Not much,' Jim replied, grateful for a change of subject. 'Hank doesn't know anything about the warehouse operation – that's for sure! But he did manage to give us the names of three other pushers in the school. Can you have them picked up on Monday? Chances are they'll only lead us back to the newsagent, Craig St. James. By the way, have you guys picked him up yet?'

'No,' O'Reilly said, 'we're watching him instead. Sooner or later, he's bound to get another little shipment which he must pass onto his distributors. We have his phone tapped and all I can tell you is he has a contact in Highgate, 'cos he's received about three calls in two days. The other guy's voice is familiar, I've heard it somewhere before, but I can't place it. The tape is being compared to the voice patterns of known criminals, with no luck, so far.' He regarded Jim intently. 'I've arranged for you and the other boy to be taken home, in view of what's happened.'

'Thanks,' Jim replied, rising from his seat. 'I'd better go and face the music.'

'Well, before you do, can I have those names?'

Jim hesitated at first, his mind racing. Finally, he decided it would be safer for Chris if all three were named ... and picked up. He grabbed a pen and a piece of paper and scrawled down the names.

O'Reilly regarded the names on the memo pad. 'Bill Flynn, Graeme Madden, and Cynthia Johnson,' he read aloud.

'Well, I'll be off.' With one hand on the door handle, Jim turned to face the detective. 'When your blokes are finished, can I listen to that tape?'

O'Reilly raised an eyebrow. 'I thought you were out of it?'

'After this, Mark won't let me continue with active work. But I'd still like to hear that tape.'

The detective gave a sigh. 'I'll see what I can do, James.'

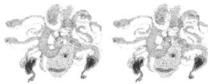

AUGUST 5. 2:15 PM, WESTERN AUSTRALIA TIME

Peppermint Grove is one of the influential areas in the city of Perth, some of its occupants being the owners of large and successful businesses in and around the city. Others were partners – if not sole owners – of the mining and drilling companies operating at Kalgoorlie or up in the north-west.

Paul Edmonds's two-storey Tudor-style house was on The Esplanade, overlooking Freshwater Bay. It was from here that he conducted most of his business and rarely ever visited the warehouse in Osborne Park. When he felt the urge to escape the noises of the city, he would retreat to his stud-farm south of Jandakot.

A dark brown Volvo, with blue personal plates, pulled up behind Edmonds's black Mercedes-Benz. The driver, a short, stocky man with dark skin and Slavic features, climbed out and, after straightening his navy-blue tie and expensive tailored suit, walked briskly to the front door. Thirty seconds elapsed before the usual large-knuckled gorilla answered his three loud raps – his trademark to his friends and business associates – on the carved maple door.

'Good afternoon, Mr. Barton,' he greeted the man cheerfully. 'How are you today?'

'Not complaining, Mr. Simos. Mr. Edmonds's on the patio. Just walk right through.'

'Thank you,' he replied, and marched through the lounge and adjoining games-room, onto the patio. Edmonds was reclining on a simple deckchair, wearing only a pair of shorts, giving his hairless chest and legs a chance to receive the sun's rays and tan the white skin, despite the winter season.

Simos glanced at the three girls by the kidney-shaped pool: a brunette, a blonde, and a red-head ... all wore skimpy bikinis. The redhead was preparing to dive off the board. The blonde and brunette, he judged, were at least sixteen years old. The red-head, possibly in her mid-twenties! Simos turned his attention away from them in the heated pool, and focused on his client.

Edmonds reached for his glass of Scotch and soda on the glass-topped table on his right and noticed Simos admiring the three beauties. Feeling a twinge of jealousy, he immediately attracted the Greek's attention with a sudden bark of his name, which succeeded in startling the girls and thus causing the red-head to perform an embarrassing bellyflop.

Simos pulled up a patio chair and placed his briefcase on his knees. *How could those girls go swimming this time of year?* he asked himself. It wasn't cold, but it was chilly. Chilly enough to give one a bout of the flu!

'Well, how did we go on our gamble?' Edmonds demanded, sitting forward. 'Did we make a killing?'

'Half a killing, Mr. Edmonds, I'm afraid,' Simos apologised nervously.

The smile vanished from the American's face, his drink returning to the table. He was annoyed and was going to make sure that this greasy wog knew it. 'Which half?' Edmonds snarled.

'The Negro.'

'The boy got away?'

'Not away,' Simos corrected him quickly, 'he simply wasn't there at the time.'

'What did the Christian have to say?'

'I must confess that I haven't been in contact with the Christian, as yet. You must admit, Mr. Edmonds, that this morning's job was really 'a stab in the dark', to coin a phrase. Taking into consideration the time given to prepare the hit.'

'Will you shut up? Don't give me your stupid blabber, just go and tell the Christian that that kid has to be hit – and hit now!'

During Edmonds's rant, no-one but Barton had heard the faint knock on the door, and when Barton returned it was in the company of two other men.

'What is it, Barton?'

Before Barton could answer, one of the other men answered, 'Mr. Edmonds, I am Senior-Detective Sergeant O'Reilly,' he said, showing his ID, 'and this is Detective Hammer. We'd like to ask you a few questions concerning some crates which, until this morning, had been kept in the Slattery Enterprises warehouse.'

Edmonds cast a malevolent eye at the Greek. That wog would pay for this!

Without invitation, O'Reilly lowered himself into a patio chair, opposite Edmonds.

AUGUST 5. 7:30 PM, WESTERN AUSTRALIA TIME

It wasn't until the cats were about to eat that Jim noticed that the amount of food dished out into the four plates was uneven. He quickly snatched them up and redistributed the food fairly. Throwing the can in the dustbin, he glanced momentarily at the seven cats eating in the privacy of their own shed and then at the German shepherd on the patio. It was the first time that he had fed these animals ninety minutes late. But it couldn't be helped; since Fab's departure early that afternoon, Jim had stayed in his room staring at the opposite wall as he lay on his bed, thinking. Thinking about what? Strange, now that he tried to remember what had occupied his mind for the past seven hours, he couldn't. All he could recall was Julie looking in and asking if he was alright.

Before he rushed out to feed the yard's furry population, Peterson had stopped him and a suggested word in private and the two retreated to the privacy of Peterson's study.

'I know what you're going to say, Mark,' Jim pre-empted. 'Callobar's murder has raised the stakes and I've brought the attention of these mobsters onto The Gorgons and Chris, next door.'

Seated behind his desk with his fingers laced together as if in prayer, Peterson sat and listened. 'That's very mature of you, Jim. I must admit that I'm somewhat surprised by the attitude. Honestly, I expected more of a battle from you. At least you're looking at the bigger picture and realise that your actions may place civilians in danger. I'm just disappointed that it took Callobar, losing his life, to make you see it all.'

Jim harrumphed and leaned on the desk which separated them. 'The reality is I can't spread myself far enough to keep everyone safe, Mark,' he began, 'that's why I'm dropping the caper. Callobar was a trained operative ... he knew the score. Once the other drug pushers in the school are picked up ... we're finished with the whole thing.'

Peterson gave a slight nod. 'Okay,' he said, unclenching his fingers. 'I'll inform Sam and your principal.'

Jim straightened. 'You do that. I have cats to feed ... and Shaka.' With that, he turned and left the study.

Peterson watched him go. Julie came in, looked behind her, and closed the door. 'Did you talk to him?' she asked, the stress evident in the slight tremor in her voice.

Peterson nodded, still looking at the closed door.

'Well?' Julie wanted to know, 'how'd he take it?'

'He said he's out of it all, because of Callobar's death.'

Julie lowered herself into the seat, sudden relief in her demeanour. 'Oh, thank God,' she said.

Peterson grunted in assent, which was laced with doubt.

Julie regarded her husband. 'You don't believe him?'

'Not for one second,' Peterson replied.

'Why not?'

'Because his eyes betray his anger,' Peterson admitted. 'Blend that with the kind of training he's had, and you just know he's going after those mobsters.'

'What will you do?' Julie asked, fear in her voice.

Peterson looked at his wife. 'He'll be safe,' he assured her. 'Jim'll be under constant observation. I'll organise a small task force to back him up.'

'Make sure nothing happens to him, Mark. Promise me that no danger will come near him.'

Peterson smiled. 'He'll be safe. I promise.'

Jim sat on a patio chair looking at Shaka, yet, not seeing him as he tried to recall the thoughts of that afternoon. The crates, the boxes, the golf balls, the six men ... four dead; he'd killed three. He, Jim Saston, had killed three men - four, counting the night watchman! These flashes lasted only a few seconds and were replaced by a Saab - Callobar's Saab. He could see the tall Black man in his mind's eye climb into the car, the hand turning the key and the flame shooting out from under the hood, engulfing the car and its driver ...

Jim squeezed his eyes shut. Trying to drive the image away. 'No!' he shouted, shaking his head to force the picture out of his mind.

Behind him, standing on the sawhorse, on her side of the fence, was Chris Porter. She watched and listened quietly and had decided to go and leave him to his demons. Though she didn't really know Jim, she knew his - or any other guy's - pride would be shattered if he knew that she had witnessed his moment of weakness.

Jim's voice stopped her from leaving the fence. Wiping tears off his cheeks, he approached the fence conscious of the puffiness of his eyes. 'Callobar's dead,' he told her on reaching the fence. 'Those bastards put a bomb in his car!'

Chris didn't respond. Instead, she watched a tortoise-shell cat as it left the cat-shed, licking its mouth and heading straight for Shaka. She knew who Callobar was, having met him a few times previously. Her eyes returned to Jim, and she asked uncomfortably, 'That bomb … was it also meant for you?'

Jim nodded reluctantly, even after he'd done so he still couldn't be sure he'd done the right thing. 'It was meant for both of us because we discovered how they got the sugar from Geraldton to Perth and throughout the rest of the country. I guess they wanted to shut us up.'

Chris grabbed his hand. 'Why don't you stop all this before you get hurt?'

Jim gave a very thin smile. She cared, she really cared! 'I've been ordered to stop – by Mark – and I will … soon,' he assured her. 'Fab and I talked to Hank this morning. He named three other pushers operating in the school.'

'There are more?'

Jim nodded. Now, he decided, comes the hard part – telling her that one of her friends was a pusher. 'How well do you know your friends, Chris?'

Confused by the question, Chris hesitated before responding. 'Okay, I guess. Why?'

When Jim replied, his voice was low, and Chris had to move closer to hear. 'What would you say if I was to tell you that one of your friends was a pusher?'

She moved away, raising her voice as she replied, 'I'd say you're bloody stupid!'

Jim's eyes widened in surprise at the language. He had expected a reply of sorts, but not one so volatile. 'Keep your voice down," he said firmly. "I'm not stupid and one of your friends is a pusher: Cynthia Johnson!'

'Cyndy!' she cried. A strained smile transformed her pretty face. 'Now I know you're joking, Jamie!'

He glared at her. 'Jim - not Jamie! As I said, Hank named the three other pushers and one of them is Cynthia Johnson!'

Chris shook her head, vehemently. 'I don't believe you; I reckon you're lying! I reckon Hank's lying! How can you believe him? He'd say anything to be free. You say I don't know my friends? I talk to her! I know how she feels about drugs!' she stated venomously.

'I said she sells the stuff, not take it! Listen, Chris, whether she sells the stuff or not, it doesn't matter to me! Cynthia Johnson has been named as a pusher and I've passed her name to the police. If she's innocent then they'll let her go, no harm done!'

'No harm done? What about her bloody reputation at school? What about her family? What about her feelings?' Chris yelled back. 'No harm done, indeed!'

Jim's face went blank. That had been the one thing he hadn't thought about. It hadn't occurred to him that Hank may have been lying! He shrugged absently and said, 'I don't know. But I know that she isn't innocent and on Monday you'll find that out for yourself when the police come to pick them up!'

'Why wait till Monday, why not this bloody weekend?'

Why all the 'bloodys'? he asked himself. 'They'll all be at school on that day, and it saves the police the trouble of running around trying to find them. Besides, I want to be there when they are picked up, it'll be the last active part I'm taking in this affair.'

'Last active part – is that all you care about? Just your good time!' yelled Chris and then immediately felt guilty when the hurt showed through Jim's face. She averted her eyes. 'I'm sorry,' she said. 'I didn't mean it like that. It's just that she's my friend! I am sorry … about you having a good time.'

'I know she's your friend – but I can't help that. But I still hate starting something I can't finish.'

'But I don't want to see you – or anyone else – get hurt.'

Jim smiled. 'You won't – now.' He drew closer and kissed her lightly on the lips.

Her arms went around him with difficulty because of the fence, and drew him even closer. It stopped as suddenly as it had started.

'I've got to go in now,' she muttered, and jumped from the sawhorse.

'Bye,' he said softly to no-one in particular, before going in.

Chapter Nine
The Body In The Bushes

AUGUST 6. 9:35 AM, WESTERN AUSTRALIA TIME

Jim rose late the next morning, showered, and dressed in the space of an hour and a half. He had brunch on the patio, watching three cats stalking a turtledove who had come to feed on the back lawn. The bird was stupid, he told himself and sent Shaka out to scare it away. The cats sadly watched it fly off to perch on the highest branch of the almond tree, at the back of the yard.

Few clouds were visible today, he noticed. Though the sun was out, it was still chilly. That's August for you, he thought, one step to spring but not far enough away from winter. Callobar liked spring, Jim remembered. Every spring, if he wasn't on assignment, he'd go camping down south to fish. That won't happen anymore, he reflected grimly.

'Jim, are you alright?'

He regarded Julie for a moment before answering. 'Yeah, I'm okay.'

Not really content with his reply, Julie suggested upon him taking Shaka for a walk.

'That's actually a good idea. I'll see if Chris wants to come with me.' He disappeared inside and soon returned with a leather leash. 'Shaka!' he called, and the dog sauntered over to sit obediently at his master's feet as Jim attached the leash.

Danny, Chris's brother, answered the door. He regarded Jim lazily and said, 'Hi. She's not up yet.'

'What? At this hour? What a lazy bug!'

'She gets up after twelve on Sundays.' Danny's eyes were glued to the activity on the television screen.

Jim chuckled. 'Where's her bedroom, I'll get her out of bed.' Before entering the house, he ordered Shaka not to wander off. The dog lay down to wait, the end of the leash in his mouth.

Danny led the way to his sister's bedroom in silence.

'Where are your parents?' Jim asked, noticing the emptiness of the house.

'They went to visit some friends.'

The bedroom was definitely a girl's room: pink walls and fluffy toys were adorning the top of the wardrobe, shelves, and the headboard, which doubled as a small bookshelf. Hanging from a hook in the ceiling near her bed, was a macramé hanging pot with light Chinese mobiles and more fluffy toys attached. Suspended from the central light was a witch on a broomstick.

He looked at the sleeping girl on the bed with one bare arm around a large grey toy cow! Once more, he surveyed the room and realized that the fluffy toys were all animals. Like Circe, he mused silently, referring to the sorceress of Greek mythology who had the habit of turning men into animals ... usually pigs! Careful not to awaken her, he moved closer and kissed her gently on the lips. Her arm tightened around the cow, a wistful smile appearing on her pretty face.

'Good morning,' he said with a grin.

Chris's eyes were immediately open. 'What're you doing in here?' It was more an accusation than a question.

'The book told me to brave all challenges and awake the Sleeping Beauty.'

'Get out!' Chris screamed while clutching the sheet to her body, desperately trying to cover herself. 'Out! Out! Out!'

'Yes, Memsahib,' Jim replied, bowing slightly with his palms together.

'Out – now!' she demanded.

Jim moved briskly out of the room back to the lounge where he joined Danny and stared at the television set.

'Don't worry, she's always like that,' Danny drawled in between spooning cornflakes into his mouth. His eyes never left the WAFL game on the television.

'I never worry,' Jim replied with a finality that surprised even him.

'She just likes yelling at everybody,' he continued, ignoring Jim's comment.

Jim stood, feeling in the way. He could hear the shower going and suddenly stop.

'Oh, sit down, Jamie – um – Jim. Sorry, but Danny's so rude,' gestured Christine apologetically.

She looked fresh from her shower and was dressed a little more appropriately: a pair of light blue jeans and a white blouse outlining her figure perfectly, Jim told himself. Casual, but perfect!

'Sorry about before,' she apologized when they were out walking Shaka. 'I thought you were Danny.'

'Danny gives you a kiss to wake you up?'

Chris looked at him, then down at Shaka. 'Tell your boy that he's a bloody idiot,' she said sweetly. To Jim, she said, 'No. He does not ... unless he's suffering from a death wish!' Her eyes were cold.

'That's alright, then,' Jim replied with a grin.

'No, it wasn't – and will you stop acting so ... so ... formal!' With that she ran up and down the road, moving mainly in circles around him.

'You're crazy,' he called to her, 'you know that?'

'And inexhaustible?' she asked, shaking her head slightly. Her smile disappeared then, and a sense of sadness seemed to envelope her.

The suddenness of it surprised Jim. Why he didn't know, but the fact was it did. 'Chris,' he whispered gently, holding her hand, 'want to tell me?'

She tried to move her hand away, but Jim was insistent and grasped it tightly.

'You're blaming me, aren't you,' he asked, 'for what is going to happen?'

'She doesn't push,' Chris insisted. 'Her sister died! She doesn't push!'

'I hate to say it, but, yes,' Jim said, 'she does.'

'No!' Chris yelled, turning to face him, her eyes ablaze. 'She doesn't! You're just a liar. You like getting people into trouble, I can see that now.' With that comment, she had run a few metres ahead and into the school grounds. She stopped at the drinking taps next to the pool on the oval.

Better to wait till she calmed down, then walk her home, Jim told himself, in total silence if need be. Oh, well, the romance was lovely while it lasted. Knowing that Chris wouldn't accept the fact that her friend might be a pusher, he decided to leave the subject

151

alone until after she was picked up. Maybe that would prove to her that he wasn't lying.

Chris's scream rang loud and clear, the terror evident in her voice. It sent Jim and Shaka down the oval at a pace at which Jim didn't realise he could move. When he got to Chris, he looked around for the cause of her distress. Seeing nothing, he was puzzled by her tears. Even Shaka seemed unsure and began smelling around the area.

'Chris,' Jim's voice stated urgently, trying to comfort her, 'I'm here. It's alright.' Forgetting all his stuffiness and formality, he held her shaking body to his. He hugged her confidently and this seemed to settle her, Jim could feel the racking sobs diminish. When she had finally calmed down, he kissed her lightly on the forehead. 'What was it?' he asked.

'That!' she said, pointing to the undergrowth growing to one side of the taps and around the side of the changerooms to merge with an untrimmed bush. Jim's eyes moved frantically over the area that she had pointed out but couldn't see anything.

'Whatever it was, it's gone now,' he said, trying to comfort her.

'It can't move!' she cried at him. Why couldn't he understand? Her tears flowed again as she buried her face into his shoulder.

'Why can't it?' asked Jim, completely bamboozled and still unable to see anything that could cause distress in the undergrowth.

Her answer was so soft, he had to place his ear close to hear her. ''Cos he's dead!'

The statement hit him like a sledgehammer. 'Who?' he questioned urgently. He held her at arm's length.

'Him!' she said, pointing at the bushes again.

This time he saw it – the finger that was bent at an unnatural angle. The leaves had been bent back to reveal to Chris something she had never expected. Shaka was looking at him expectantly, wondering why his master had taken so long to understand. Chris's body was again racked with dry sobs as Jim's mind worked, desperately trying to figure out what to do.

'Chris,' he said, surprised by the steadiness of his voice. 'I want you to go to my place and get Julie to call the police.'

'No,' she said quickly, perhaps too quickly, the fear plainly showing in her eyes.

'Chris, you have to,' Jim insisted. 'I can't go. I have to stay here to watch over the evidence.' He looked into her eyes. 'I'll be alright.' He noticed her eyes flare when he said, 'the evidence' rather than 'the body', knowing it sounded hard and cruel – but that was how he felt at this moment. Finding dead bodies in bushes was not his idea of a fun time. Hades was being kept busy this weekend!

'Okay,' she replied in a tiny, weak voice.

It was only when she had left that Jim began to worry about her. 'Shaka,' Jim commanded, in Afrikaans, 'go after Chris. Look after her!'

The German shepherd hesitated. He looked in the direction the girl had taken, then looked back at Jim. With a whimper, Shaka moved off at a run to join Christine. He had smelt Jim's fear, even though he understood the command.

Chris was happier when the German shepherd had fallen in step with her. Her own paranoia had made her believe that someone was following her and felt better with Shaka next to her. The two kept a steady pace until turning into the street on which they lived. Then Chris broke into a run, the dog pacing beside her. They turned into the Peterson's front yard and Chris pressed the doorbell before hammering the front door. Excited, Shaka began barking.

'Have you forgotten your ...' Julie began as she swung open the door. 'Christine.'

Chris rushed forward and fell into Julie's arms, crying uncontrollably.

'Christine,' Julie said, holding the girl tight in her arms, 'what's wrong?' Then she realised that Shaka was there barking excitedly. Terror, not fear, tightened her stomach. 'Christine,' she forced herself to say, 'what's happened? Where's Jim?'

'Jim's waiting back there,' Chris said automatically. 'He's dead!'

Julie's stomach dropped. 'Jim's .... Dead?'

Chris pulled away from Julie and looked her right in the eyes. 'No. The boy at the school. He's dead. Jim told me to get help.'

'Wait, Christine,' Julie said, taking charge. 'Tell me all of it ... more slowly.'

Slowly the story came out. How Chris had followed the mouse into the bushes and had moved the leaves back to see where it had gone. The finger had not been in her sight as her hand bumped into the head of the boy. She's actually touched it! Chris shuddered at the thought. Then she saw the finger, and there was blood all over the leaves.

'Okay, Christine,' Julie assured her, 'but where is Jim?'

'With the boy ... um, the dead .... dead ... dead ... body, the boy's dead body,' Chris replied with finality.

That figures. 'Okay,' Julie said. 'Get in the car. We're going to get him.'

'Who, Jim or the dead boy? The dead body! We can't!' Chris said, desperately.

'Why not?'

'Jim said you had to ring the police!'

Julie stopped and regarded the girl and realised the girl was right. She turned back into the house. Julie went straight to the phone and dialled O'Reilly's direct line. When O'Reilly answered the phone, Julie said, 'Sam. It's me, Julie. Jim said I should ring you right away.' Had she heard correctly? Did Sam just sigh deeply?

'What does he want?' O'Reilly asked. He sounded tired.

'Jim and his girlfriend just discovered a dead body at the high school!'

'Put Jim on, Julie,' he said.

'Well, I can't,' she replied. 'He stayed there to make sure no-one tampered with the body.'

Of course, he did! 'Okay,' O'Reilly said. 'We'll get a unit out there as soon as possible. Tell James to keep his hands off everything. He won't listen, of course, but at least you'll have tried.' He hung up and Julie stared at the receiver in her hand.

She hung the receiver back in its cradle and was about to rush off when she had another idea. Julie removed the receiver and dialled Mark's number. When her husband answered, she told him all she knew, and he promised to rush home. Julie replaced the receiver and herded Chris and Shaka into her car.

Chris was silent as she thought about what she was experiencing. She knew what had happened. Somebody had killed him and dragged his body into the bushes to hide the evidence. The evidence? She shuddered. What a horrible word. But anyway, they didn't count on Christine Porter's curiosity!

With switchblade in hand, Jim explored the area for clues. It's ironic that Paul should be found dead in the same place where Hank and he had had the blue, which Jim had witnessed. That had been Wednesday, it was now Sunday morning and rigor mortis had set in, in more than just Paul's body! The boy's body was set in that position for all eternity, at least, until the funeral director found a way to fit the body into a coffin! Callous, I know, he told himself. But one simply couldn't feel any sympathy for Paul – after all, he was an addict! Having missed out on his week's quota, Paul must have been desperate for some sugar. God knows where he got it from, but he definitely put too much in the syringe. Jim had seen the rust-coloured stain that was congealed blood on Paul's arm and the bruise that marked the tiny wound. Entering the science block from the alley, Jim surveyed the area taking it all in with one glance.

Nothing. Nothing of interest, no clues – nothing. He resigned himself to the fact that there was nothing around to disprove the fact that Paul had come to the school to commit suicide! He wished he knew more about suicides, he admitted to himself. Where do suicides go when they want to end it all? American businessmen, during the Great Depression, would jump out of their office windows ... Like that would have been a quick death! Spies had the last lower molar, on either side, drilled out and a cyanide capsule placed in there for them to break the cap – that sealed it in – and break the capsule to kill them quickly, so they wouldn't be able to be questioned! The favourite exercise for America's criminals was to trick the police to shoot them dead. 'Death by cop', it was called. There was always the overdose of chemist-bought drugs, but those people always did that in their own homes. The same with slashing of wrists, also done at home.

Illicit drug overdoses were always accidental ... or the product was tainted and, therefore, lethal! Could that be the case here? Besides, who would have supplied him? Chances are one of the three that Hank had named. Something told Jim that he had dismissed the scene too quickly. Paul's presence here just did not gel. Did he always come here to shoot up? No, of course not. Teenagers, meeting each other clandestinely at the school grounds. It was here that girls and guys met without their parents knowing. Maybe addicts also met each other here to shoot up in company! *Was that even possible?* He asked himself. If that was the case, then there would be evidence of a second person!

Keeping his distance and crouching down, he examined the scene with a renewed sense of determination. He noted the lie of Paul's body, beneath the bushes and the surrounding scrub. With this second examination, Jim started to think that Paul couldn't have been alone. He hadn't crawled into those bushes, he'd been dragged. Jim could now see the drag marks and the pushed-up sand, where the other person had pushed Paul far into the recess of the bushes and scrub. The effort had required the other person to exert pressure to conceal his body. Did this mean that the other person wasn't strong enough? Jim, now intrigued, it did seem that Paul Matthews was in the company of someone else! This meant that there would be two sets of footprints plus Chris's own.

'Jim!' Chris called out. She heard the running footsteps from where she stood – near the Olympic-size pool – and crouched holding Shaka close, hoping that it was Jim approaching.

'What's wrong?' Jim asked breathlessly, regarding the spot where Paul's finger was sticking out of the bushes. Now that he knew what to look for, that finger couldn't be missed!

Chris pointed to him accusingly. 'What is that?'

Jim realised that he was holding the switchblade and that she had never seen it, till now. 'What?' he replied, concealing it behind him.

Chris didn't pursue the matter; she didn't have to, what she felt was amplified by the look in her eyes. If looks could kill, Jim mused, he was dead, buried, and decomposing! 'Where were you?' she demanded.

'I was in the science block, looking at the scene from that perspective.'

She turned and looked out across the oval. Only when he heard a sob, did Jim return the switchblade to its hiding place and approach Chris. He turned her around to face him and hugged her.

'What's wrong, Chris?'

'I'm sorry for crying,' she replied between the sniffles, 'I don't mean to.'

Jim gave her a gentle squeeze. 'Hey, you've got nothing to apologise for.' He brought his face close to hers.

Chris pulled away from him. 'Jim, please, don't. Not in front of him.'

'Who?' Jim looked around. They were the only two people there. *Where was Julie?* He wondered. Surely, she wouldn't have let Chris come back here alone, only in the protection of a dog.

'Paul.'

'Chris, he's dead! He isn't going to see anything we do. He's probably halfway to Heaven by now. Hell, more likely!'

'How can you say something like that?'

Jim let go of her. 'Oh, come on! Chris, the guy was a drug addict – he's not worth the sympathy!'

'How do you know?' she retorted. 'Have you talked to him? I mean, really talked to him – found out what he wanted out of life? No. Of course, you didn't. The great Gorgon Five wouldn't be interested in that! All they're after is to see how many feathers they can stick in their caps, or how many lives they can f**k up!'

'Is that what you think of me?' he asked, his anger beginning to rise.

'Yes!' she answered, crossing her arms determinedly.

Don't. Don't do it! Say nothing! A small voice told Jim. 'I think you'd better start coming back to Earth, my dear. This is not the Land of Oz or Wonderland, it's the twentieth-century Australia where drugs are a very real problem. There—' pointing to Paul's body '—is one very real example. And Hank Andrews is another. Paul was going to die, anyway. Without heroin he couldn't function, it had taken too much out of him. They're the ones who killed him – Hank Andrews and his crowd – not me! But that doesn't matter to you … I'm the poor bastard that's trying to prevent another person from taking an OD – and if getting your friend is going to do that, then, by God, I'm going to do it!' Good one! His inner voice said. This is why we can't have nice things!

Chris had stopped listening and was struggling to get out of his hold, to get away from his voice which now held so much venom. She broke free and ran.

Jim swore under his breath and glared at the body in the bushes. You idiot, Saston, he berated himself. What did you do that for? Now, where's she gone? He glanced up the road; no sign of her. He wanted to go after her but knew that that was impossible, someone had to stay with the body until the police arrived. 'Shaka,' he called, looking around for his dog.

The German shepherd trotted over obediently from another clump of bushes, where he'd been sleeping.

'Go with Christine, Shaka,' Jim ordered in Afrikaans. 'Look after her.' He didn't have to repeat the command. Shaka took off after the irate girl, picking her scent up straight away.

Jim felt better. At least Chris would be all right now that Shaka was with her. After all, he had trained the dog himself, to obey him whether he spoke to Shaka in English or Afrikaans. At Jim's command, Shaka would bite, maim, or even kill an antagonist. Jim knew that his dog would do exactly as he had been ordered; he would protect Chris Porter in whichever way he saw fit.

His eyes focused on Julie's approaching form. *Where had she been?* No matter ... at least she hadn't seen the switchblade. She would have done her nut if she had seen it.

'Christine just ran past me, crying,' she said. 'So did Shaka, for that matter. What happened?'

'We had an argument,' Jim stated. 'She couldn't handle it and ran away.'

Julie noted the bitterness in his voice, so there was no need for her to say anything. 'I rang Sam,' she said, '... and Mark. They all should be here soon.'

Jim turned away. 'Oh great,' he said. 'This day's getting better and better!'

'I thought you might need Mark's support,' Julie stated. 'You know that Sam doesn't like you very much.'

Jim faced her. 'He doesn't like me because he hates the idea that I can do what is necessary to solve a case. He has to obey stupid rules and ridiculous codes of conduct.' He watched flashing lights quickly approaching. 'It's the lecture from Mark I don't need. All I've done is secure a crime scene!'

'Don't be ridiculous!' Julie snapped at him. 'He knows full well that you didn't do anything active, here. You did everything right.' She thought about the sobbing girl. 'Well, there's a bridge you have to fix and eat lots of crow.'

'What?'

'Girls don't run away crying,' Julie said, 'as a general rule. Which means you said something stupid! That means you will have to apologise to her.'

Jim bit his lip and said nothing. Instead, he focused on the group of uniformed and plain-clothed police coming to join them.

'Where is it?' O'Reilly asked upon reaching Jim and Julie.

The Gorgon pointed towards the bushes, near the drinking trough. 'The body's there.'

Bill Hammer went to join the forensics men at the body site, while his superior remained with Jim and the lady.

'Do you know who it is?' O'Reilly asked.

Jim nodded. 'His name's Paul Matthews. He's a Year 10 at this school and one of Hank's customers.'

O'Reilly was jotting it down in a small leather-bound notebook. 'Did you find the body?'

'No, a friend of mine did.'

O'Reilly looked up and around. 'Where's your friend?'

'She couldn't handle the stress of all this and left.'

'She?' An eyebrow shot up.

'Yeah,' Jim replied, the anger rising, 'is that okay with you?'

'Jim!'

Jim looked sideways at Julie and lowered his eyes, contemplating the ground.

'Her name and address.'

'Her name's Christine Porter and she lives next door to us.'

'Now,' O'Reilly said, still writing in his notebook, 'why did she really leave?'

'We had a bit of a fight, and she went home.'

'She found the body,' O'Reilly stated, 'she wasn't supposed to leave here till we arrived and question her.'

'Then maybe we should be taught that in school!'

'Jim!' This time it was Peterson who had snapped out his name.

O'Reilly turned and shook hands with Peterson. 'What are you doing here?'

'I'm here to support Jim,' Peterson said.

'He doesn't need support. He needs to be controlled!'

'Sam!' Julie snapped. 'That's a horrible thing to say.'

O'Reilly stared at both of the adults and brought his eyes to Jim's. 'I'm sorry, James.'

Jim smiled. 'That's okay, Sam. Look, she was upset. How would you feel if you were a fifteen-year-old girl who had just come across the first dead body she'd ever seen? Not every girl is Modesty Blaise, you know.'

O'Reilly sighed. 'Well, we've still got to talk to her. We need a statement from her – after all, she's the one who discovered the body ... right?'

'Yeah, she did,' Jim answered.

Just then, a dishevelled-looking man accosted them. He was puffing a lot, as if he had tried to run from the Catholic school, up the road. Jim introduced him as Mr. Fuller, the school caretaker.

'What's going on here?' he demanded of O'Reilly.

'Er – nothing to be alarmed about,' the senior detective replied. 'This young man has discovered a dead body, over there, by the taps.'

'A what?'

'A dead body: corpse, cadaver, shell devoid of life.'

'I know what it is, officer, there's no need for brevity. But what I'd like to know is, what was this boy doing on the school grounds?'

'I was walking my dog on the oval,' Jim said sounding very innocent. O'Reilly's eyes narrowed as he watched Jim's face. 'He got away and made a beeline for here ...'

'Where's your dog now?' Fuller asked, looking around for the supposed canine.

'I ... er ... I was here with my girlfriend. My dog was very distraught, so she took him home.'

'Right,' Fuller replied, producing a notebook, 'what's her name?'

'She doesn't go to this school,' Jim explained, 'she's a student of St. Jacob's, up the road.'

Fuller sighed and O'Reilly commiserated with him. 'Well, what's your name?'

O'Reilly caught the twinkle in Jim's eye, as they exchanged looks. 'Paul,' Jim replied obediently, 'Paul Matthews.'

Fuller scribbled the name down. 'Right. Mr. Gardner will want to talk with you tomorrow.' With a self-satisfied smirk, the caretaker turned to go but was stopped by Peterson's grip on his arm.

'Why will Gardner want to talk to him?' Peterson asked.

'This kid was trespassing,' Fuller replied. 'Mr. Gardner will be informed.'

'He was trespassing?'

'Yeah,' Fuller said, squaring up to Peterson, 'he was trespassing.'

'Where are the signs?' Peterson asked, looking around.

'What signs?'

'The "no trespassing" signs.'

'This is government land,' Fuller began, 'that's why he's trespassing.'

'If that's true,' Peterson said, going in for the kill, 'why aren't the school precincts fenced off? There are no signs visible, which means you haven't been earning your wages. I am an officer of the Federal Government and if Gardner wants to talk to my ward, then he'll be talking to me also!'

Fuller stepped back.

'Don't do just part of your job ... do all of it! I'll be telling Gardner that.'

'Fine,' Fuller said, producing the notebook and tearing off the page with the name Paul Matthews scribbled on it. He crumpled it up and dropped it on the ground and stormed off in the direction of his cottage, at the end of the school precinct.

Peterson returned to the small group just as Hammer approached with a notebook in hand. 'We have a slight case of murder – or a second death if this is part of the drug case.'

'I think it is,' Jim put in quickly. 'He was an addict. How do you know it could be murder?'

Hammer exchanged looks with O'Reilly who sighed. 'Because if it was just a routine OD, then there would be a syringe lying around. Did you find one?' Jim shook his head silently. 'Also, you'll find that the index finger, on his right hand, is broken. It doesn't matter how violent the spasms he went through; they shouldn't cause him to break bones. Besides, his hands are covered in dirt and blood, and he's lost a fingernail, which indicates that he was dragged along the bitumen post-mortem.'

Jim scowled and O'Reilly grinned. Finally, after all these months of being proven wrong by this boy, he was wrong for once. Wrong? Well, you could say that. O'Reilly felt a twinge of jealousy. Why did it have to be Hammer who caught James out?

An ambulance appeared next to the police cars and the two paramedics approached them with a gurney.

O'Reilly pointed to the bushes, where two other policemen stood. The team of forensic experts had already left. 'The body's there.'

'Well, if you gentlemen no longer need Jim,' Peterson began, 'I'll take him home.'

'All right, Mark,' O'Reilly said. 'We'll be over that way later to talk to your neighbour's daughter.'

'Can I come with you when you do?' Jim asked.

'Why?' Hammer asked with a smile. 'Are you her lawyer now?'

AUGUST 6. 5:05 PM, WESTERN AUSTRALIA TIME

Julie handed the cup of tea to the detective. 'Thanks,' O'Reilly said and took two biscuits from the tray on the coffee table.

Jim closed the sliding door and turned to face the two detectives and Peterson. 'She still isn't home,' he told them. 'It's been four hours since she left the school grounds.'

'We can't wait around for her to return,' O'Reilly said. 'When she decides to come home, give me a call.' He drained the cup in one gulp. It was only when he began to gasp that he realised that the liquid he had passed down his throat was only just under boiling point.

Jim chuckled. 'We should've warned you about Julie's tea, it's always scalding.'

'"Scalding" isn't the right word for it,' he whispered, tears streaming down his cheeks. 'Just call me when she gets home.'

He turned to Hammer, who was sipping at his cup gingerly; even his pinkie was sticking out! 'Drink that and let's go.'

Hammer looked despairingly at Jim and Peterson.

'You can leave it,' Peterson said with a smile. 'Julie will understand.'

'Thanks,' Hammer said with a sigh of relief and placed the cup on the table.

Jim showed them to the door and, as Hammer moved towards the car, he stopped O'Reilly. 'Sam, can you wait a day before talking to Chris?'

O'Reilly regarded Jim suspiciously and considered the request. 'I guess so,' he said. 'Why?'

'Look, after what's happened today, and her not returning home, means that she's upset. Let her get a good night's sleep and when those three pushers are picked up, take her also. Arrest her, that way she won't get a reputation as a dobber when she returns to school. Let's face it, the police aren't too popular among my generation.'

Reluctantly, O'Reilly nodded his agreement. He could see Jim's motives behind his asking and hoped the Commissioner would also understand. 'All right, James, as long as you promise she'll be at the school tomorrow.'

'She will be,' he assured the detective. 'I know her better than she thinks I do.'

Jim waited until the car had disappeared down the street before returning to the backyard. 'Chris where are you?' he asked the window of her bedroom. For the first time in a long while, Jim Saston prayed.

Chapter Ten
The Battle of Tannen Heights High

AUGUST 7. 8:30 AM, WESTERN AUSTRALIA TIME

From the Gorgons' Den, Jim could see up and down Jewel Street while he waited for Fab to arrive. Occasionally, he'd wander into the school to look, in vain, for Chris.

Shaka saw his master first and ran to where Jim stood. On reaching him, the dog placed his huge paws on Jim's chest and began lapping at his face.

'Shaka, down!' Jim ordered. The Alsatian obeyed immediately and sat down at the boy's feet, brushing the ground with his tail. 'I'm glad to see you, too. Where's Chris?'

The German shepherd turned his head and regarded the two approaching girls.

When they reached Jim, Chris said, 'I'm here, okay? Now, get your stupid hound away! I kept on telling him to go home, but he wouldn't listen. I thought you said he was trained and always obeyed?'

'He does obey,' Jim replied matter-of-factly. 'But he'll only obey me.'

'Well,' Chris said coldly, 'you owe Cathy two cans of dog food. Inflation!' With that, the two girls walked off. Before disappearing around the corner, Cathy glanced back at him and giggled.

Jim could feel himself going red. 'You know, Shaka, if I didn't have any manners, I'd order you to go and bite her one on the arse.' He crouched down beside his dog and petted him. 'You can't stay here, boy, so you better go home. Julie's there, she'll let you in and if you don't tell her you've eaten, she'll probably give you something. Go on.'

The dog took off at a run, nearly bowling a Year 9 girl over. She screamed as she moved away from the definitely mad animal.

'Isn't that wonderful … a dog and his idiot of a master.'

The smile vanished from Jim's face, as he turned. 'That's not funny, Fab,' he said. 'I have something to tell you …'

As the two Gorgons marched into the school, Jim filled his friend in on the happenings of the day before. The discovery of Paul Matthews's body, his argument with Chris, and her disappearance until this morning.

'Where has she been?'

Jim shrugged. 'A friend's place.'

Fab shook his head in disbelief. 'It's hard to believe that four days ago we were forcing him to tell us all about Hank Andrews. Now he's dead.'

'What's more,' Jim added, *sotto voce*[18], 'he was murdered.'

'Murdered?' Then Fab remembered where he was and lowered his voice. 'I thought you said it was an overdose?'

'It was,' Jim replied. 'But he didn't administer the sugar himself. Somebody else did … somebody who wanted to see him dead. That's what the Gorgon Five are going to try and find out.'

---

[18]Whisper (Italian).

'What about the drugs?'

'It's in the hands of the police, after today.'

'You're giving it up? Just like that? I can't believe it. That's the first time I ever heard you say you're giving up without finishing. What does Callobar have to say about all this?'

Jim sighed regretfully at the mention of the West Indian's name. Why did Fab have to say that? Jim could have done all right without the memories. But he remained silent and was relieved when Danny Fletcher joined them, at the lockers.

AUGUST 7. 12:20 PM, WESTERN AUSTRALIA TIME

The police cars pulled up outside the high school and two detectives and constables marched down the five steps to the office door.

Seven members of The League of the Gorgon Five were absent from the Den and the three remaining members watched the four policemen till they vanished through the office doors. 'Here we go again,' Larry muttered to no-one in particular.

On the other side of the school, in the main quad, a group of six Year 10 boys sat in a circle on the grass while they ate, joked, and swore. Occasionally, a boy from another group would meander over and would exchange a few words with them.

Sitting not too far from these six, near the stairs and the breezeway, were Fab and Mike Daniels. At various times, one – or the other – would glance over at the group and keep an eye on its members. Holding his bag tightly, as if it contained the Crown Jewels of England, sat Bill Flynn.

Outside Room Q, a general science classroom, sat three Year 12 boys. One was the school's head boy; the other had won an award for a chemistry essay he had composed for a national science competition; the last one was a drug pusher.

Andrew Bremenh and Tet Shomira sat nearby eating their lunch quietly – waiting!

Danny Fletcher and Jim were outside room T, the senior school biology classroom, also waiting, but not to help Andrew and Tet escort Graeme Madden to the office. Jim knew there would be trouble when it came to taking Chris and Cynthia to the office. If it was the last thing she did, Cathy would make her opinion heard. Somehow, Jim thought, Tony would have his hands full.

Sitting on the stairs outside S16, a social studies classroom was Tony Waters. He glanced between the treads at the group of giggling girls – Chris's group, aptly named by the Gorgons as the Nutcracker Suite! – and regretted having boasted that he worked better alone. Now he wished he had insisted on help; those girls were capable of anything, even now they could be planning on how to upset the Gorgons' plan. He wondered what they were saying ...

A group of girls was gathered outside S18, another social studies classroom, laughing and chatting – disjointedly – as usual.

'"Mary had a little lamb, her dad shot it dead" – um – hey, Jo, what's the rest? Huh?' Cathy asked, signing Ordina's autograph book while she waited for the conclusion of the limerick.

'What's the rest of what?' Jo wanted to know.

'Like the one about Ordina sitting on the garden fence ...,' laughed Kelly.

'Ah you,' laughed Ordina. 'You rottena to me – you wrote thata one.'

'What was Mary's dad sitting on the fence for?' questioned Joyce, clearly puzzled.

'Laughing at Gordon,' answered Cathy.

'What are you talking about, Cath? I don't follow you,' Chris said.

'Gordon who-a?' Ordina asked.

'Chris's Gordon!' replied Cathy.

'Chris's new boyfriend? You didn't tell us – you naughty, naughty—' stated Joyce, wagging a reprimanding finger at her friend.

'He's not a boyfriend!' Chris said shyly. 'And he's a Gorgon – not Gordon.'

'Yeah, that's right, Gorbon … no wrong – um – Gorvin. Something like Marvin, but with an "O" and a "G" – Gorvin,' apologised Cathy.

'Gorvin what – who?' questioned Kelly, completely lost.

'"Gorvin what' is right," agreed Marlene, just coming into the conversation, 'and they're watching us now!'

'Gorgon Five,' whispered Chris more to herself than anyone else – but, by then, the subject was completely different.

'Heya, Marlene, hearda about a Paul?' commiserated Ordina. 'Really funny thata. Never thoughta he'da do it.'

'Knock off the Ding accent, Ordy, you don't have it and you know it!' Ordina hunched over and looked shattered.

'Hey – what right you got to push Ordina around?' Cynthia protested. 'If she-a wanta to have a Dinga accent, she's alloweda to have a Dinga accent. Right, Ordina?'

'Righta!' Ordina agreed.

'What are you so stroppy about, Mars?' Cathy asked. 'Oh, sorry, I forgot …'

'That's right!' agreed Sue, sarcastically adding, 'He dropped Celia to go out with you – and now you're all stroppy 'cos his comment was he'd rather die than go out with you. And you missed out, didn't you?'

'Stop being so bitchy!' pleaded Chris in a tired voice. Now she was glad that she hadn't told Cathy everything. Cathy did have a big mouth, even though she was a good friend.

'We know that Paul's dead – okay, Marlene? Just don't give us any of that shi—you know what. We all feel the bloody same way – okay? And that's not going to change anything now! What was that poem you wanted to complete, Cath? Something about "Mary had a little lamb"? – yeah …'

Cathy regarded Chris and smiled. She may be a bit weird, but she did know how to put a person in their place and dissolve a heated situation. 'Yeah. I still can't remember the end of that. Does anybody else know it?'

'Something about … "it got filled with maggots, and …"?' Jo said.

'… "Each of your chicks ate some of it",' yelled Rod.

'Oh, PO[19], Rod, now you made me feel sick,' Kelly giggled.

'Uh – uh – uh – I'm dying …!' yelled Cathy, falling dramatically to the ground.

'I'll give you mouth-to-mouth,' Brett eagerly offered, rushing over from where his group was sitting.

'No way – yuck!' screamed Cathy. 'Call the ambulance, the doctor … I think I might have rabies, cholera, VD!'

The two groups dissolved into laughter.

The music, supplied by a conservative radio station, filtering through the school's PA, stopped to be replaced by Mr. Gardner's

---

[19]Abbreviation for 'piss off' (Strine).

uneasy voice. He barked off three names and demanded those three people to report to the office. The subdued music resumed.

Bill Flynn's mouth fell open as he heard his name called. Looking around, he spotted and recognised the two Gorgons approaching him from the stairs, near the breezeway and undercroft. Forgetting the value of his bag's contents he charged through the middle of the circle towards the canteen.

Fab and Mike exchanged quick glances and sprinted after him. Most students sat on benches at the perimeter of the quad and Bill's flight was made unhindered, but the two Gorgons were fit – and fast runners. In a flying tackle, Mike brought Bill down.

Sitting on their side of the under croft, away from where Fab and Mike had been sitting, were the twenty-three members of De Boyz. Ralph Sinclair manoeuvred his sandwich to his mouth, carefully making sure that it did not collide with his large, hooked nose. Taking two large bites from it, he re-entered the discussion concerning the virtue of a particular Diploma girl that they all knew. Ralph knew Bill Flynn, who lived only a few houses down from him and had a sexy sister of nineteen who was known to be very easy – though untried by himself. To his surprise, he watched as the short, chubby Year 10 darted away from his mates with two of those Gorgon bastards after him. 'Hey!' he spluttered, bits of wet bread shooting from his mouth. 'They're at it again – look!'

Emilio Meshattro looked up to see Mike tackling Bill and, eventually, Fab and Mike dragging him off towards the office. 'They're at it again, all right. Sas won't learn, will he? Well, it's about we taught the League of the f**ken Gorgon Five a bloody lesson!' A murmur of agreement floated around the gang as they all gathered in close to listen to Emilio's plan.

Graeme Madden wasn't at all pleased to hear his name called, and – much to Andrew and Tet's surprise – foresaw the futility of trying to escape justice and marched down to the office. Unknown to the people in the Deputy-Principal's office, was the fact that Graeme Madden was the favourite nephew of an influential magistrate.

As the two Gorgons followed him down, they met up with Bill, Fab, and Mike. Tet glanced at Bill and then, at Fab. 'Now the hardest part is up to the others,' he said.

Tony put his lunch away and placed his bag near the wall where he would retrieve it later, if he was still alive, and walked casually towards the girls. Before he knew what was happening, Danny and Jim joined him.

'Hey, look! Goon Squad has come to town!' yelled Cathy, standing up to greet the approaching Gorgons.

'I don't know what you've done, chickadee, but if you're up against them, Gardie, and the cops, I reckon they have to get a search warrant to get you,' Marlene said to Cyndy, with a gleam in her eye.

Chris was the only one in the group who noticed and understood the remark. Evidently, Marlene Manson knew more about Cyndy than anyone else.

'Let's charge!' Cathy cried.

Jim nudged Tony forward. 'You said you could handle this alone, let's see you do it.'

Reluctantly, Tony approached the group of girls. 'Come on, Chris and Cyndy Johnson – might as well get it over and done with,' he said simply, looking uncomfortably at the other girls. Was it his imagination, or were they all coming towards him?

God, Jim said to himself, just like a Zulu impi! He watched, with a growing spark of excitement, as the girls, in one fluid movement, completely surrounded Tony.

Some of the girls kept back, keeping a wary eye on the other two Gorgons.

'I suppose we'd better help him,' Danny stated.

Jim smiled. 'I think you're right – they may kill him, otherwise.'

Tony surveyed the circle of people around him, with a growing dismal feeling. 'Oh, shit!'

Unfortunately, he didn't see Sue help a girl up onto her back. With a flying leap, Ordina was on Tony's back, scratching and biting like a wildcat. Tony shrieked in pain, frantically trying to tear the girl – or whatever it was – off his back. While his attention was wholly focused on Ordina, Jo thought it was time for her to make her move.

Tony's mind was a million miles away when Jo's shod foot smashed between his legs. Pain blotted out everything as he fell heavily to the ground, Ordina scrambled from his back.

'Can I kick him again?' Jo cried. 'Please, can I kick him again? Please, pretty please?'

'I think he's had enough,' laughed Rod. 'He might want kids one day.'

Brett leaped forward and slammed his fist into Tony's face. As blood poured down, he punched him once more in the eye.

Jim and Danny exchanged glances and stepped forward.

'That one's for hurting my Ordina!' cried Brett.

'Your Ordina?' yelled Ordina. 'Since when?'

'Aah ... nothing! Don't worry about it,' shrugged Brett, stepping back sheepishly.

'Hey, hold it, mate,' stated Ordina, grabbing Brett by his shirt, 'you owe me a kiss!' Oblivious to the action going on around them, they kissed.

Danny rushed forward to help his incapacitated friend. Seeing a foot, he laughed to himself and hopped over it. The pain of another leg connecting sharply with his kneecap was enough to catch him off guard.

A chair, held by Kelly, helped to pin him against the lockers of S18. Oh, well, I begin by fighting girls, next I'll take on the world, Danny thought to himself. His retaliation was a swift kick aimed at Rod, who was helping the girls. Laughing, Rod saw the kick and avoided the collision. The next thing Danny knew was that he was on the ground and that Ordina and Kelly were both kicking him in his stomach.

As the wind was forced from his lungs, the dry retching began. Hell, fighting with girls wasn't worth it – there were much easier ways to die!

Jim, who had stood back and watched the embarrassing defeat of his fellow Gorgons, realised that barging into the middle of the melee was definitely not a wise move. The next best thing to do was to find Cynthia's dope to show the girls – maybe then they would come to their senses and act more lady-like. But, somehow, Jim doubted it. He glanced over to where the bags had been left, he guessed at which one was Cynthia's and reached for it. With the bag nearly in reach, Jim's progress was halted by Joyce's foot pinning his hand to the ground. Jim swore at the pain and struggled to free his hand. He grabbed the girl's offending foot and twisted it sharply.

Joyce yelped in pain.

Realising that Joyce was in trouble, Cathy grabbed Margaret and both girls ran to help their friend. As Margaret kicked Jim in the kidneys, Cathy took a good aim and, with precision, kicked Jim in the groin.

Chris started forward, then forced herself to check the urge to go to Jim's aid and just watched as her friends took care of her next-door neighbour.

Jim fell heavily to the ground, trying not to balance any of his body weight on his kidneys or groin, as both were throbbing immensely.

'Having trouble, Master Saston?' came Hammer's laughing voice from the back of the crowd that had gathered to see the fun.

'Oh, God,' Jim murmured before picking himself up.

The crowd of Year 10s and other cheering students. Moved away from the scene.

Hammer moved towards the girls' bags and grabbed the one labelled 'Cyndy Johnson'. Tipping it upside-down, he emptied the bag of its contents.

Cathy cringed as the makeup set in Cyndy's schoolbag opened and perfume sprayed everywhere.

Stepping out of the perfume's reach, Hammer produced his pocket-knife and stabbed the bag and sliced it open.

'Hey!' yelled Cathy, 'I'm going to report you to the Royal Society for the Prevention of Cruelty to Bags!'

'Shut up!' Hammer barked.

With a very hurt expression, Cathy moved back into the crowd.

All watched as the contents fell from the gash in the bag and clattered to the floor. Various shades of lipstick, eyeliner pencil, two compacts, two different coloured nail varnish, and lots of small cotton cylindrical objects all crashed to the ground. Nothing suspicious seemed to be among the debris. The boys in the crowd laughed as they recognised the cylindrical objects.

There was a cry of embarrassment and Cynthia Johnson buried her sobbing face on Chris's shoulder. She hugged her friend and exchanged glances with Jim, who looked stunned.

Hammer looked at Jim, realising that he had overstepped his brief. He picked up the bag and searched through it, desperately. Hammer glared at Jim once more as he lowered the bag.

'Try this one,' Jim said, rising. His hand was still on the bag he had originally picked as Cynthia's. The weight of the bag alone proved it wasn't just typical Year 10 exercise books and files.

'You better be right, mate,' Hammer muttered. He put his hand into the open bag and removed another makeup bag. This one he opened properly and looked at its contents carefully. Hammer's cry of triumph proved that something incriminating had been found. 'Whose bag is this?' he demanded, looking up at the small crowd.

'That,' Cathy began slowly, unbelievingly, 'that's Marlene's.'

Jim looked at Chris and Cynthia apologetically. That bastard Hank Andrews had lied! God, he was a fool! Chris had stated that Cynthia wasn't involved, and he refused to believe her. What a fool he was! Jim scanned the crowd and noticed that Marlene was not there. Where the hell had she gone? 'Where's Marlene?' he asked.

'She's run off when you picked up her bag,' another Year 10 girl said. She was not a member of The Nutcracker Suite.

Hammer turned to the deputy-principal, who had accompanied him. 'Seal the school. We need to get her.'

'We can't seal the school,' the deputy-principal replied. 'Do you see any gates and fences?'

Hammer sighed. 'Okay,' he said. 'We'll just have to put out an all-points bulletin on her. We'll get her. Eventually.'

Jim looked at Chris and moved his head slightly, indicating the direction of the office.

Before she could move, Hammer asked, 'Whichever one of you is called Christine Porter, we'd like you to come with us also.'

'Why?' demanded Cathy defiantly.

Hammer looked at her. What a loud-mouthed little bitch. 'Accessory after the fact!'

What? Chris cried within, looking at Jim for an answer. Why?

Jim sensed what Chris was thinking and shook his head slightly, to indicate that all would be fine.

'What fact?' Cathy persisted.

Hammer round upon her. 'The one you'll be booked for if you don't keep your nose out of what doesn't concern you!'

'It's okay, Cath,' Chris said, 'I'll be back soon.'

Cathy nodded, pretending that she didn't see any tears, and turned to go.

'Before we re-join the others at the Den,' Jim said quietly to the other six, as they left Chris and the two pushers in the hands of the police, 'I suggest we go get our bags, they may not be safe where they are, scattered around the school – besides, it's untidy.'

All but Mike had an exam after lunch, and they decided to accompany him to his next class, which happened to be at the science block. Discussing the possible events of the next five days, the Gorgons didn't notice that the four entrances to the

Science Block had been staked out by De Boyz. Tet was the first one to notice them; he tapped Jim on the shoulder and indicated the threat, over his own.

Jim glanced around and felt his stomach tighten. The other five, as they noticed their antagonists drawing closer, stopped talking and eyed them warily.

'What's all this?' Fab demanded, stepping forward.

But much to his surprise, it was Jim who answered. 'It's commonly referred to as a "death circle". But what puzzles me is – is it the area within or the perimeter of the circle, which the gods have condemned to death?' He smiled with that air of confidence that Fab had learned to recognise as instant success.

Fab discovered that he actually felt pity for De Boyz, as they didn't know what they had initiated.

The circle became noticeably smaller as Jim talked. While De Boyz formed a proper circle, the Gorgons turned to face their opponents. Andrew stood in the middle trying his very best to act inconspicuous.

Jim singled out one of the rival gang's three possible leaders. 'Very impressive, Emilio, but we don't need an honour guard; we're modest heroes.'

Emilio stopped and rested his fists on his hips. 'Ha!' he bellowed. 'Heroes? Is that what ya call yourselves? I – we – don't call you that. You guys think you're all great 'cos ya dobbed in six people to the pigs, well you're now goin' to get what ya deserve!'

Andrew gulped loudly.

Jim shook his head slowly. 'You know, Emilio, in South Africa there are many natives. The Zulu happens to be one of the greater nations and they have a saying which happily fits this situation: *Wena funa eiffa, mena bulala wena!*'

Emilio Meshattro frowned momentarily distracted, then glanced at his friends for silent reassurance. 'What does that even mean?' he asked cautiously. Somehow, maybe due to Jim's over-calmness, Emilio knew that his gang's actions were futile.

Jim took a deep breath, letting the silence and tension eat into his opponent's nerves. He saw Emilio's tough mask drop for only a second and made his decision. '"If you want to die",' Jim translated steadily, '"then I will kill you"!' The second part he translated slowly, menacingly.

It had the desired effect on Emilio and, before Jim had finished the phrase, Jim twisted to the right as he lifted his leg in a side kick. The ball of his foot, reinforced by the sole of his shoe, hit Emilio directly in the throat – hard enough to remove him from the fight; soft enough not to kill.

Dan Appasee watched in horror as Emilio collapsed and lay prostrate upon the grass. He didn't have time to retaliate as Jim jabbed him in the midsection and with a quick chop – to the back of the neck – put him out of the fight also.

Tet had proven his skill as a karate student, having disposed of Charlie Harren with a savage groin kick, and giving another a deep stomach jab which forced his partly digested lunch out of his mouth. A quick twist from Tet, and Charlie ended up face down in his own vomit.

Vic Ivanski, Joe Gordonson, and Ralph Sinclair had Tony pinned to the ground while a fourth member was busy kicking him. Summoning all of his strength, Tony threw his captors from him and grabbed the kicker's foot, sending his own into the other's crotch. The boy uttered an agonised howl, but that didn't satisfy Tony who twisted the foot until something in it snapped.

Mike took care of Joe Gordonson, sending him head-first into the brick wall of SR3. But a sneak attack from another member sent Mike to the ground.

Andrew, still trying to make himself invisible, had been pushed back towards SR2 and as Ralph moved in to take care of him, he suddenly lashed out with a side kick that caught the unsuspecting gang-member in the solar plexus.

While engaged in his own private battle, Danny Fletcher felt Ralph fall into him. Thinking that he was being attacked from behind, he hit Ralph hard in the kidneys. Andrew watched him fall and brushed himself off before relieving another boy of consciousness.

Yet, another member of De Boyz, Philip, had acquired a remnant of a rusted bike rack and entered the brawl, flailing it like a club. Fab was in a lot of trouble trying to prevent getting hurt by two other guys, Damien, and Joe. When they caught sight of their club-bearing friend, they beckoned him over.

Spying the slight movement of Damien's head, Fab glanced quickly over his shoulder and came face-to-face with Philip. Even though there wasn't much Fab could do with arms pinned tightly to his sides, an idea still managed to crawl into his mind. Now, all he had to do was wait until Philip got closer. With the faintest smile appearing on his face and adopting Jim's reckless optimism, Fab suddenly heaved his body up – using Joe's own body as his fulcrum – and rapidly kicked out at his approaching enemy's hands. As his feet connected with the piece of metal, it shot back and cut, deep, into Philip's forehead. Screaming,

Philip collapsed. His huge body crashed hard onto the grass. The shock of witnessing what had happened to his mate made Joe, subconsciously, back away from Fab and loosen his grip. Fab leapt away before Joe could recover from his shock and grabbed the boy's head, brought it down sharply on to his knee, and tossed the limp figure into Damien.

Damien's reactions were fast but uneasy. He ungraciously cast Joe – with a shattered nose – aside onto the bitumen and jumped forward. As he lashed out viciously, Fab blocked the blow with his forearm and grabbed his opponent, bringing him into an awaiting, raised knee as he twisted around and sent his foot into the other's midsection. The last thing that Damien remembered was that he was on a merry-go-round – or was he?

From under his shirt, Martin Drayner produced a small fishing knife and lunged at Jim. Because of the cut he had received three nights before – which Jim could feel bleeding again – and the beating he'd got from the girls, Jim decided that he had taken enough punishment today. Now it was time to dish out his own indiscriminate brand of punishment. The kind that those Afrikaans bastards had felt by his hands, in the Zulu fashion of no mercy!

Instead of kicking away the knife as he had been trained to do, he lost his temper and grabbed Martin's hand, pulling the surprised boy towards him. Martin gazed; eyes widened with terror as Jim turned the knife on its owner. 'You're carrying a knife, *kaffir*!' Jim said. 'Now, let's see if you've got the balls to put it into yourself!' He pushed on Martin's hand, bringing the knife's point close to Martin's chest. Like a wild animal, Martin fought to get this madman off him. *This isn't what's supposed to happen*, he kept telling himself. Jim backhanded him across the face and brought the knife down, once more. As Martin tried to deflect the weapon from its intended target, the action caused the knife to slip closer to his chest, the point going through the fabric of his t-shirt and slicing across the skin, leaving a line of blood welling up. The shock made Martin let go of the weapon and Jim hit him repeatedly until he was pulled away by Fab and Tet.

Vic Ivanski and the other five, still standing, did not hang around; instead, they abandoned their friends and bolted towards the breezeway of the main school building.

Straightening up, Jim asked, 'Anybody hurt?' He felt shaken by the realisation that he was prepared to kill Martin Drayner! His kidneys hurt by the surge of adrenalin that his loss of control had caused. He stood uneasily, absorbing the pain, vowing that such a moment must never re-occur!

'Nothing that won't heal,' Fab replied between pants and gasps; he was out of condition. So much for the high school physical education program! Fab's arms ached, his legs ached, and, most of all, his stomach ached; he'd taken enough punches to last him a lifetime.

Jim surveyed the field of battle: Emilio was still unconscious from Jim's kick to the throat; the bloodied piece of metal lay where it had fallen, but Philip was nowhere to be seen; two other members of De Boyz were rising from where the evidence of their lunch lay in a mixed puddle, and another sat alone clutching his leg, his foot hanging, almost lifeless. He was crying. Nine others were scattered about, but Jim just ignored them.

'Enjoy your time in high school,' Mark's advice swam in Jim's head. 'It's the greatest time of your life!'

Jim frowned. 'Let's get out of here,' he said with disgust, as he stepped over Emilio's body.

AUGUST 7. 12:45 PM, WESTERN AUSTRALIA TIME

'I want the League of the Gorgon Five in my office. Now!' the principal, Mr. Gardner, barked over the PA.

From the two exam rooms, as well as SR2 and Room W, emerged the ten members of the League of the Gorgon Five. Silently, they gathered at the office.

The receptionist touched a button on the switchboard. 'The Gorgon Five are here, sir,' she said softly.

'Get them in here!' he snapped.

Jim led the way in and stood defiantly before the red-faced administrator.

'I have just been on the phone to some parents who were informed that their sons are all in hospital! Now ... I don't care if you boys want to play detectives and clean up society of its drug offenders – but I will not condone gang warfare in my school!'

'Now just wait a *blêrrie*[20] minute!' Jim snapped back at the principal, oblivious to the fact that he was now talking with an Afrikaans accent. 'Just calm down and stop screaming like a *kaffir*!'

Fab rolled his eyes up to the ceiling. 'Oh, God,' he muttered under his breath.

Mr. Gardner's face turned a deep crimson. With his eyes bulging, he resembled something out of a science-fiction movie. 'How dare—'

'I dare quite a bit!' Jim cut in. 'It's not our fault that De Boyz came to us looking for a fight. I'm not so weak to turn the other cheek, so, we fought back. We are the victims here! No wonder people in this country don't want to get involved, they're too afraid of repercussions. They wanted to fight because we helped the police to rid your school of drug pushers!'

The principal glared at Jim for a few moments. 'That may be so,' Mr. Gardner replied calmly, 'but that doesn't change the fact that one boy is in a coma, with a nasty bruise across his throat – he is lucky to be alive, according to the ambulance attendants! Six others require stitches; one has a ghastly cut down his face and says that one of you attacked him with a weapon—'

'That's a lie!' Fab cried.

Mr. Gardner ignored the outburst and continued. 'Another one has a cut across his chest, made by a knife. Which one of you carries a knife?'

'None of us do,' Jim lied. Better they don't learn about the switchblade, its new 'function' may be a bit too difficult to explain. 'Our hands are the only – and best – weapons we have, and they're not even concealed.'

'Be that as it may, the fact still remains that a fight took place on the school grounds and that some of the participants were seriously injured. That is serious enough to call in the police and, I'm sorry, but my report to the Regional Office will have to suggest your subsequent expulsion from this school.'

Larry swallowed loudly. What would he tell his parents? What would they all tell their parents? Jim was the only one who didn't seem worried. Instead, he smiled knowingly, as if amused by a secret known only to him. Larry eyed him suspiciously.

'Could I possibly use your phone, sir?' Jim asked.

Mr. Gardner regarded Jim in surprise for a moment. He'd known this boy since Jim had started high school and had always been interested in his progress. The principal had been the first person to inform Jim of his father's death two and a half years ago, and had been surprised at the way he had taken the news. Instead of breaking down and weeping, Jim had avoided his eyes as the meaning became clear: that he was alone … completely alone. The boy had a lot of pride, maybe too much, he'd thought that day. Mr. Gardner thought that now, as Jim and his friends stood before him. 'Yes,' he acquiesced, slightly perplexed. 'All right.'

Jim quickly dialled a number not found in the white or yellow pages, and which was known to only a few people in Western Australia. Once finished, he waited. 'Hello?' Jim said, after what seemed an eternity; the Afrikaans accent was gone. The Gorgons all exchanged puzzled glances, they were all curious at Jim's calmness, if not his actions. Who could he be phoning? They all wondered. 'Connie? It's me, Jim. Is Mark in? … Good. Can I talk to him? … Hello, Mark, it's Jim, I seem to have a bit of a problem. The principal will explain.' He handed the receiver over to Mr. Gardner and herded his group out the door, but he remained in the office. 'They'll wait out there.'

The Gorgon Five stepped out of the office and talked amongst themselves.

'It's not our fault we won,' Fab stated.

'It doesn't matter who won,' Tony replied. 'The bad publicity that will result from this is what we're all going to be punished for.'

'I think it's going to be worse than that,' muttered Larry, 'especially with Jim talking to Gardie.'

'What could they be talking about?' Mike wanted to know.

'Maybe he's got a few million bucks stashed away and he's buying off the old man.'

Mike regarded Larry for a moment. 'Mitchell, if you had a mind, you'd be dangerous!'

'Having to look at your ugly face all the time, it's a wonder I haven't turned to stone. You make Medusa look—'

'Will the pair of you just shut up?' Fab said sternly. 'Knowing Jim, we won't get into trouble.'

'What could he possibly say to the old man?' Andrew asked.

'That's the one thing about Jim,' Tony put in, 'you never know how he does it, but he can perform a miracle most of the time.'

As if on cue, the principal's door opened, and he and Jim emerged from the office. The Gorgons gathered around them, each wondering what their fate might be.

'Boys,' Mr. Gardner said, a wide grin appearing on his scarlet face. 'Thanks to your friend here, and another person whom I talked to, I must tell you that what I said earlier, in my office - about your possible expulsion ... Well, it was a bit hasty. Now that the situation has been fully explained to me and a few questions answered, I'm glad to tell you boys that I have no intention of having all of you expelled ... or suspended.'

'Saved,' Larry said. The Gorgons glared at him.

'But I'm sure you're aware that I can't just let this fight go unpunished. Jim and I discussed it and have decided that, as a suitable punishment for fighting, all of you should do a week of scab duty next term.'

The Gorgons glared at Jim.

'Maybe being expelled isn't so bad,' Larry suggested.
The Gorgons glared at him.

AUGUST 7. 11:20 PM, WESTERN AUSTRALIA TIME

The fire was burning nicely, and the Phillips television set was displaying the opening sequence to *Star Trek*. Craig St. James entered the lounge, carrying a cup of black tea and a small plate with five Milk Arrowroot biscuits, and sat in the armchair, which was positioned directly in front of the set. He took a tentative sip of the steaming liquid as he listened to William Shatner recite the well-known blurb which ended with the antiquated futuristic theme.

A knock at his door disturbing his peace and quiet, not to mention his night-time routine, made him wince and he rose to answer it. He regretted having to move away from the fire. There was another knock. Why didn't the bloody idiot use the doorbell? It had cost him enough to have it installed.

'Okay, okay,' he grumbled. 'Do you even know what time it is?' He unlocked the door and opened it to reveal a familiar face staring back at him. 'Oh, it's you. What do you want?'

'We need to talk, and I have a message to deliver,' the visitor stated.

St. James sniggered. 'Reduced to a messenger, hey? Did you f**k up?'

The visitor crossed the threshold and St. James closed the door and ushered him into the lounge.

'It's cold out there,' the visitor said.

St. James sighed. Play the good host, then he'll leave that much sooner. 'You want a cuppa?'

'Please.' He sat on the settee without removing the raincoat he wore. 'Coffee.'

St. James rolled his eyes, but left the lounge, mourning the fact that he was missing his show. 'What do we need to chat about?' he asked as he removed a cup from the cupboard. He grabbed a teaspoon and dipped it into his tin of Nescafe and removed a heaped spoon of the granules. This bastard's not going to sleep for a month! 'Sugar?'

'Please,' came the answer from the lounge. The visitor opened his raincoat and reached for the Smith & Wesson, resting in the shoulder holster, and removed it. He checked the action and, from a pocket, removed a thick cylinder which he screwed onto the pistol. Once done, he slipped the gun into the folds of his raincoat. The kettle began to whistle, and the visitor picked up that day's copy of *The West Australian* from the coffee table. He opened it at a random page and began to read whichever article his eyes had zeroed in on.

St. James returned to the lounge, carrying the steaming cup of coffee. He placed it in front of the visitor.

The man lowered the paper and regarded the cup. 'Milk?'

'Damn, I forgot to ask.' Swearing beneath his breath, St. James returned to the kitchen.

The visitor dropped the paper and gripping the gun, followed his host into the kitchen. 'You know that a few more of your distributors have been picked up by the cops?'

'Yeah,' St. James replied. 'But what can you do?'

'Edmonds is worried that they'll talk to the police and point at you.'

St. James grabbed the glass bottle of milk and straightened from the fridge. 'So?' he replied, surprised to see his visitor in the kitchen. 'He knows I wouldn't talk. I've dealt with the cops before. They're toothless tigers that have been neutered by society.'

'Yeah, well, this time's different. Your operation, feeding the high school, has been washed up by an annoying kid and his gang. That's got Edmonds pissed.'

'Why?' St. James wanted to know. 'I'll play dumb like I usually do. Nothing's different.'

'Word on the street is that the cops have federal help this time.'

St. James tightened his grip on the glass bottle. 'Federal?'

'Yeah, federal. Chances are the cops won't be questioning you, this time. You think you can play dumb with federal agents questioning you?'

St. James puffed out his chest, trying to make himself seem braver than he was. The truth was that the mention of federal agents had rattled him. 'It'll be a piece of piss.'

The visitor shook his head, slightly. 'Edmonds thinks you don't have the balls to hold out against them.'

'Then, what does he suggest?'

'This.' The visitor whipped out his Smith & Wesson and placed a bullet between St. James's eyes.

The bottle of milk fell from the dead fingers and shattered on the linoleum floor. A bullet hole was visible on the far wall and blood, brain, and skull fragments had sprayed out and covered the sink and the once-clean dishes.

The visitor calmly unscrewed the sound suppressor and blew the heat away, ignoring that the heat of the metal could be felt through the leather gloves he wore. The suppressor went into a pocket, the Smith & Wesson was popped back into the shoulder holster. Just as calmly, he removed his gloves and put them in his blazer pocket. As he did that, a set of rosary beads fell onto the floor. The visitor sighed and put the gloves back on before picking up the rosary beads, which he placed on the kitchen table, then stepped around the dead body and hefted it up by the armpits and dragged it out of the kitchen.

Chapter Eleven
Flunked?

AUGUST 8. 8:50 AM, WESTERN AUSTRALIA TIME

The day had started, as usual. The black clouds wetting everything in sight as the school buzzed excitedly about the events of the previous day. Christine Porter was back at school, but Bill Flynn and Graeme Madden were permanently absent. With Cathy and Cynthia, Chris strolled around the school, desperately searching for Jim. She had to see him, tell him something she knew, something she had to pass on to the police. But wherever she looked, Jim was not to be found. Tony and Tet were at the Gorgons' Den, talking; Fab was at his locker, studying; Larry, Mike, Jack, and Harry were at the canteen; while Andrew, the newest member, was with a group of boys she didn't know. Danny Fletcher wasn't here yet, she told herself, maybe Jim was with him. But her hopes were dashed when, while passing H18, she glanced up at Fab and spied Danny beside him, also studying.

The siren went and Chris realised that Jim wasn't coming to school today; he probably didn't have an exam. Suddenly, she wished she hadn't come to school either. Heading to her class, she decided that halfway through the day she would go home.

Cathy and Cynthia walked some distance behind Chris, chatting about Marlene's sudden disappearance yesterday.

'It seems that Chris knew all about it, before it happened,' Cathy stated.

'What?' Cynthia responded. 'But how?'

Cathy shrugged. 'Don't know, but she's awfully upset today, poor chick ... I'd never have guessed that Marlene was a dope pusher, especially since her ex was involved. Oh well, shows how little you know about people.'

'Will the League of the Gorgon Five please come to the office?' demanded the voice of the deputy-principal over the PA.

'Ha! Looks like they're in trouble again,' Cathy quipped, more to herself than anyone else.

AUGUST 8. 8:55 AM, WESTERN AUSTRALIA TIME

Fab and Danny exchanged looks.

'What about our exam?' Fab complained and with a lot of swearing, he returned his pencil case to his bag and left it at S16. He followed Danny to the admin office.

They all congregated there and waited for one of the staff to notice them.

'Here we go again,' sighed Larry. 'What now – and where the hell is Saston?'

In Jim's absence, Fab assumed control. 'Larry, shut up!' he said sternly and turned to where the deputy-principal was talking to two men. Fab recognised Bill Hammer, but the other detective was unknown to him. 'Now what do they want?' he mumbled to himself.

'What?' Danny asked, who also recognised Hammer as one of the arresting officers from the day before.

The Gorgons gathered closer together. Maybe Jim's influence didn't work this time and the police were here to take them away. What happened? Did one of De Boyz die – or something worse?

Larry was the first one to find his voice. 'They've come to arrest us. Let's get out of here; I'm too young to go to Fremantle Gaol.'

'If we get arrested,' Mike told Larry, 'It'll be worth it – because I'm going to kill you if you don't shut the hell up!'

Hammer came forward and greeted Fab. 'So, this is the rest of your gang? You've got quite an army here. My name's Bill Hammer and my partner here is Detective Rod Turney, and we would like to talk to each of you, concerning your interrogation of Paul Matthews. Let's start with you' – he consulted his notebook – 'Fabrizio.'

He led Fab into the registrar's office and shut the door behind him. Fifteen minutes later, Fab emerged, the displeasure evident on his face, and Tony was called in.

'What happened?' Mike asked.

'They just asked me about what we got out of Paul that day. They most probably think we know something about his death.'

'What about Jim?' Andrew asked.

'He's at Police Central,' Fab began, 'listening to tapes.'

'What?'

Fab shrugged. 'That's what I was told.'

'We're being grilled here and he's listening to music?' Larry complained.

They all looked at him. 'What?' he asked.

'Not music, you idiot,' Fab said. 'He's listening to interview tapes! God, you're dense.'

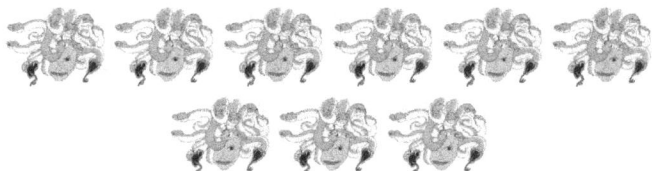

AUGUST 8. 9:05 AM, WESTERN AUSTRALIA TIME

O'Reilly switched off the tape recorder. 'Well, what do you think?'

Jim pointed at the recorder. 'There's something about that voice – not St. James, but the other one ...'

The detective narrowed his eyes as he regarded the teenager. 'What?'

'There's something ... familiar ... about that voice – but I can't place where.'

'Maybe St. James can ... I've had him sent for.'

'Can you play the tape again?'

O'Reilly rewound it and pressed play. The tape ran for half an hour before the two seated in the office were disturbed by the ringing of the phone.

Swearing under his breath, O'Reilly picked up the receiver while Jim turned off the tape. 'O'Reilly.'

Jim glanced around the office, trying to place the voice of the unknown man.

'What!'

Jim's eyes returned to O'Reilly at the sudden outburst.

'When did this happen?'

Jim's heart missed a beat. *Now what?* he asked himself. Had something happened at the school? Was Chris all right? 'What happened?' he asked as the detective replaced the receiver.

O'Reilly didn't answer but just looked blankly at the teenager on the other side of the desk as he pondered the ramifications of what he had just learned.

'Sam, what's wrong?' he asked anxiously, rising from his seat, and fearing the worst.

'That pusher – St. James – he's dead!'

'What? How? When?'

'His body was just found in the main bedroom of his house.' He gestured for Jim to sit. 'He was nailed to the wall ... in the crucifix position!' Sam crossed himself.

Jim grimaced. 'Oh my God!'

'The officers who went to pick him up found a set of rosary beads at the foot of the bed.' Sam sighed. 'It looks like "The Christian" has been at it again.'

Jim frowned. 'The Christian?'

'A hired killer who works mainly for Edmonds. Every killing on this case – except that of this boy, Matthews – has had a set of rosary beads close by.'

'Callobar's?' Jim asked, tentatively.

Their eyes met and O'Reilly nodded. 'We found the remains of a set of rosary beads in what was left of the glove box.'

'The rosary beads are his calling card?' Jim surmised.

'Yes. That's why he's called "The Christian". Chesston told us about him in the last report we ever received from him.'

'Have you been able to identify him?'

The detective shook his head. 'No-one on our files, or that of Interpol or the FBI, are known as The Christian. So, we still don't know who he is – or what he looks like.'

Jim's eyes returned to the tape recorder. 'St. James has a late-night visitor, and they banter about a message that needs delivering,' Jim begins. 'I'm certain that I have heard that visitor's voice somewhere.'

'Well, we can assume the visitor's voice is that of The Christian,' O'Reilly replied.

'There's something familiar about it,' Jim persisted. 'That American accent is so over-exaggerated that it has to be fake.'

'How can you be sure?' Sam wanted to know. 'How many Americans have you talked to?'

'Well,' Jim said, 'there's Wally, Wally's two sisters. Also, his mum and dad. So, that makes five. How many have you spoken to?'

Sam refused to answer and just looked at him. 'Have you heard this voice before?'

Jim remained silent as he pondered the question. He wanted to say no, but he also wanted to answer yes. 'It's not the voice itself; it's certain inflections within the speech pattern that seems familiar,' Jim said. He looked at Sam inquiringly. 'Does that make sense?'

'I must be getting tired,' Sam replied, 'because it does seem to make sense and that worries me.'

'Let's hear the tape again,' Jim suggested. 'Maybe I'll be able to figure out what's troubling me about that voice.'

O'Reilly shook his head. 'What's the point? We've listened to it five times and haven't gotten anywhere. You think you can identify the voice, but you can't.'

Jim sat forward. 'It's not so much the voice that I'm trying to identify. It's difficult to explain ... It's all about the annunciation—'

'Annunciation?' O'Reilly uttered. 'This has nothing to do with religion.'

'What?' Jim replied. 'Okay, so I don't know the exact word. Let's try "inflection", then. The way we speak is unique to each of us.' O'Reilly frowned. 'We both speak English, but certain words in our speech patterns will be pronounced in a different manner. Stress may be put on different parts of a word that we both use. This is because of our different accents, cultural ties, even race, and nationality. "The Christian" is not an American, despite the fact that he is using that accent. The soundings are all wrong.'

'You finished?'

Jim looked at O'Reilly. 'Yeah.'

'All you needed to say was "I want to listen to the tape again instead of waffling on".'

AUGUST 8. 10:00 AM, WESTERN AUSTRALIA TIME

The door opened and the last Gorgon to be questioned left the office to re-join his friends. Hammer, coat off and tie loosened, approached them.

'Well, boys,' he said, 'thanks for the help – but none of it was of any use to us. Are you sure there isn't anything else that happened before, during, or after speaking to Paul Matthews?'

Larry made a slight gesture which the detective spotted immediately. 'I don't know if this is important or not, but just after we questioned Paul, I started going around with a girl. She kept asking me about why we had to talk to Paul and why he and Hank had had a fight at school, one day. Unfortunately, ...' His voice trailed off, just as it dawned on his fellow Gorgons that Larry had betrayed them, sold their secrets, to a non-member, and what was worse – a girl! 'Guys,' Larry pleaded as he turned to face them. 'Hold it a sec – hey, it isn't my fault I talk in my sleep, is it?'

'You're going to have to answer to Jim for that,' Fab said flatly.

'You guys can figure all that out afterwards,' Hammer said, then turned to Larry. 'What did you tell this girl?'

Larry shrugged. 'About how Paul took heroin, and how he dobbed on Hank. There could've been more – I don't know, exactly.'

'Well, we'll call this girl up and question her. What's her name?'

Larry blushed and avoided the eyes of the other Gorgons. 'It won't help, because it's Marlene Manson,' he admitted sheepishly.

Fab couldn't help but burst out laughing. 'Marlene Manson? Oh, you couldn't have chosen better, you idiot.'

'Marlene Manson?' Hammer repeated. 'The same Marlene Manson that went missing yesterday after being outed as one of the pushers in the school?'

Larry nodded but remained silent.

'Why the hell couldn't you have told us this yesterday?' Hammer yelled.

'I didn't know she was a bloody pusher!' Larry yelled back. 'That miniscule detail never came up.'

The Gorgons began laughing.

'That's probably the only thing that didn't come up!' Mike uttered.

'Shut the f**k up!' Larry yelled.

'That's enough!' the deputy-principal said. 'Now, if you're no longer needed...' He regarded Hammer, who nodded '... then get out.' The Gorgons looked from Hammer to the deputy-principal. 'Get out!'

'That doesn't help my exams any,' Fab muttered, as he filed out of the anteroom with the other Gorgons.

'What do we do?' Danny asked.

'F**ked if I know!' Fab retorted. 'Let's find Dalby. Maybe we can take an alternative exam.' They moved off from the rest and headed for the mathematics faculty office.

The mathematics faculty office was located upstairs, tucked in between Room Q and the girls' toilets, overlooking the small quadrangle behind the canteen. Fab knocked on the door tentatively, and when one of the teachers looked up from their backlog of marking, asked to speak to Mr. Dalby.

'One minute,' Dalby's voice called out. 'Let me just finish this poor excuse of homework.' After a few minutes, Robert Dalby approached the faculty doorway. 'What's up?' he asked. He never bothered with long strings of rhetorical banter and always kept his explanations short and sweet. Some students found his approach refreshingly simple, while others found him aloof and cold.

Fab liked him. 'We had to miss our maths exam.'

'Why?'

'Well,' Danny started saying, uncertain whether or not Mr. Dalby would commiserate with them. 'We were called to the office and have been questioned by the police.'

'Then you failed!' Dalby stated flatly and turned to go.

'What?' Fab cried. 'No way. We were summoned to the office and, as students, we are expected to obey. It's not our fault that we missed out on the exam.'

Dalby turned and regarded the two Gorgons. 'Yes it is,' he said flatly. 'You chose to be distracted by extracurricular activities, not authorised by the Secondary Education Authority, and you, now, want me to invent marks for both of you.'

'No,' Danny stated. 'We want a chance to do the exam!'

'Really?' Dalby looked from Danny to Fab. 'I suppose that you will promise not to talk to any of the students, in your class, about the exam. Hmmm? Forgive me for not being that naïve. I will ponder upon the matter, and you will be advised soon. Good day.' He abruptly turned away from the two students and went back to his desk.

The female teacher who shared the desk with Dalby, looked at the doorway and looked at the two stunned students who, eventually, moved away. 'You're an arsehole, Rob!' Felicity Baker said, smiling. 'Why didn't you just tell them that you already have another exam paper for them to do?'

Dalby grinned at her. 'They're young,' he said. 'They need to learn all about suffering. Besides, those two happen to be the top students in that class. Without their grades, the bell curve will be extremely shallow ... and we can't have that!'

'No, we can't,' Felicity agreed and returned to her own marking.

'This is f**ked!' Fab vented as he and Danny moved away from the faculty office. 'I'm going to get a fail just because Jim wants to play detective?'

'Well, I'm getting a fail also,' Danny muttered. 'I don't think that Jim should cop all of the blame—'

'F**k off! Of course, he does,' Fab snapped. 'Why did he have to start all of this shit, right now? Hey? Why not next term ... early? Oh no! That wouldn't work for Jim Saston! He needs to be the hero right now because his dad was killed!'

Danny stopped and looked at Fab. 'Just listen to yourself, Fab, what the hell is bothering you, besides the stupid exam, and stupid Mr. D,' he said in a lower voice. 'It may be bad luck, for us, but everything will work out. It has to.'

Fab gave a derisive laugh. 'You keep believing that, Danny. I saw the true Jim Saston when we were questioning Hank, at the cop shop. It wasn't pretty. He tortured Hank! Made him believe that he was getting some heroin. He laughed that he fell for a sugar substitute. Jim doesn't give a damn about Hank and those other pushers, at all. Hell, he probably doesn't even give a f**k about us! We're only here to back him up! Well, you know what? I've f**ken had it with him and his stupid civic crusade!'

'Come on ...' Danny said. 'You don't really mean that. It's just your frustration and anger talking.'

Fab regarded Danny. 'No,' he said. 'I'm being very level-headed. You should have seen him. Heard him also. You know he blames society for the death of his father. He admitted that he didn't share our values and was unapologetic about his conduct. I swear you need to watch him and the way he acts. He'll sacrifice us if the situation warrants it!'

'I don't believe that,' Danny stated.

'Well, be warned.'

'He'll be back tomorrow,' Danny said. 'We can talk it out then.'

They reached the lockers and Fab fumbled for his keys, eventually finding them. 'I'm starting to believe that he has no respect for the law and, maybe, even democracy as well.' He inserted the keys into the lock and opened his locker, then just looked dumbly at the contents. *Why had he even opened this?* he asked himself. He didn't even have his bag! It was still outside the examination room. Fab swore and closed the locker.

Danny just watched him bemusedly but said nothing.

'I'm out of sorts,' Fab said.

'And it's Jim's fault, I suppose?' Danny asked.

'Yes, it is, for God's f**ken sake!' He slammed his locker door shut with such ferocity that the small, open padlock fell off. 'F**k!' Fab swore, bending down and retrieving it from under the bench. He held the padlock up triumphantly. 'You watch,' he said, placing the padlock on the locker and pushing the bolt home. 'Everything's going to go south, soon, and Jim won't know what to do. We'll pay for that ... dearly!' He left Danny with that thought and headed for the exam room to retrieve his bag.

Danny shook his head and let out a deep sigh. He sat down and wondered what Fab's tirade meant for their group. It sounded like Fab wanted to leave the group. If he did that, nothing would ever be the same again. Things had changed dramatically when Wally's family had returned to Pittsburgh. *Yeah, we kept in touch with him by mail and occasional phone call, without their parents knowing, but his everyday presence was sorely missed.* 'Shit!' he said and went to get his bag from outside the exam room.

AUGUST 8. 10:36 AM, WESTERN AUSTRALIA TIME

O'Reilly pressed the stop button on the tape recorder. 'Well?'

Jim looked at him expectantly. 'Well, what?'

The police detective released a pent-up sigh. 'Have you figured out what was bothering you about The Christian's voice?'

Jim returned the steady gaze. 'No.'

'Then we have gotten nowhere,' O'Reilly said

'What do you mean? You have the tape. It incriminates Edmonds ...'

'Can't be used,' O'Reilly returned.

'Why?' Jim demanded obstinately. 'You have St. James and The Christian mentioning Edmonds's name. Besides that, you can hear the sounds of The Christian killing St. James. What more do you need?'

O'Reilly looked away. 'We need a warrant,' he said. 'Without one, this tape is inadmissible as evidence.'

'What?' Jim exclaimed. 'That's absolutely stupid! You have the evidence right there and you can't use it? No wonder criminals exist! That's the fundamental flaw in democracy! Wait,' he looked at O'Reilly. 'How did you get this tape, if you didn't have a warrant?'

O'Reilly looked at the teenager. 'Mark had them placed in the St. James house,' he admitted. 'As a favour.'

Jim gave a laugh. 'What?' He stopped as pictures flashed in his mind's eye. Jim rose from his seat and moved over to the window that overlooked the causeway, the Swan River, and Victoria Park. He reviewed the mind pictures as quickly as they flashed on his mind. Some images he missed, they were moving in and out of his consciousness so fast. He was able to identify which hardware would have been used and where the operative would have placed them throughout St. James's house. Like a flash of bright light that made Jim involuntarily squint, the process and identification of what he had been unable to identify about The Christian's voice revealed itself. My God! Jim admitted to himself. So, he's The Christian! Surely, that's not possible!

O'Reilly watched Jim and saw the change come over his face. 'What's wrong?'

Jim looked at the detective. He opened his mouth to reply, but something stopped him. What if he was wrong? He'd look foolish and cause irreparable damage to someone's professional reputation! No, he told himself, better keep the revelation to himself ... for the moment. 'Nothing,' he replied, 'I'm just getting a headache. I need to go home.'

O'Reilly nodded and reached for the phone. 'I'll get a patrolman to drive you home,' he said.

'I can drive him,' Hammer said, entering the office. 'I go off duty in half an hour.'

'How did it all go?' O'Reilly queried.

'Fine, I suppose,' Hammer replied, sitting in the seat vacated by Jim. He turned to face Jim. 'Your mates don't know much about what they're involved in. Are you purposefully keeping them in the dark?'

Jim turned and smiled. He made a slight gesture. 'Well, you know how it is ... it's a matter of need to know. There are some things that they don't need to know.'

Hammer chuckled. 'You sound like some sort of a spy,' he said.

O'Reilly and Jim exchanged knowing glances.

Jim laughed and moved to stand by the desk. 'Good one,' he said. 'You're the ones playing spies by planting bugs in a suspect's house. I didn't know that you cops were allowed to do that.'

'Believe me,' Hammer assured Jim, 'I was against that part of the case. We've ended up with stuff that we're not allowed to use in court. So, it was a wasted exercise. Just like questioning your mates.'

'I could have told you that they wouldn't be able to help you guys.'

Hammer chuckled. 'Yeah. That guy, Fab, just kept harping on that he was missing his exam—'

'What?' Jim said, straightening. 'You interfered with his exam timetable? He'll be furious!' Jim turned to O'Reilly. 'I need to go home now and ring Fab.' He looked back at Hammer. 'You never get between Fab and his exams, assignments, or homework! He's going to blame me for this!'

Hammer's eyes narrowed, mockingly. 'Yeah, I think he is.'

'Great!' Jim said. 'You can take me home, right now. See you, Sam!' He led the way to the door, then turned to face O'Reilly. 'I'll get back to you ... when I figure out what's bugging me about that voice.' Jim left the room.

Hammer and O'Reilly exchanged looks and, as he headed for the door, Hammer said, 'Bye.'

Chapter Twelve
Two Minus One
Leaves None

AUGUST 9. 9:50 AM, WESTERN AUSTRALIA TIME

A new day and the police were back! Hammer beckoned Barry Enton into the principal's office and watched as Peter Balfour left, before closing the door. Barry was the last of three boys in Tannen Heights High fitting the description given late last night by an anonymous tip! Another two had been named by a few teachers, including Mr. Gardner and the deputy-principal, following the police debrief to the teaching staff in the staff room earlier that morning.

The search for Marlene Manson had taken a different course. Since vanishing from the school, she hadn't been home and no-one who had been questioned knew where she had sought shelter and succour. Then the anonymous call had mentioned the existence of a boyfriend and gave a relatively vague description. Despite the fact that logic dictated that most anonymous calls, made to the police, were misleading jokes, false reports, hoaxes … they still had to be investigated. Hammer couldn't help feeling that he was chasing his tail.

Because the Gorgons had named this one, Hammer had decided to leave Barry for last, maybe hoping that this boy would bring the morning's proceedings to a climactic end. But if this Barry was not Marlene Manson's *spunk*[21] then he would have to proceed on to the Catholic school, Saint Jacob's Co-Educational College, up the road. And what if the guy wasn't there? Hammer shrugged, pushing the thought from his mind and moved away from the closed door. 'Okay,' he said to the seated boy. 'Barry Enton, isn't it?'

The teenager nodded nervously. He'd never been involved in a police investigation before. What would his parents say? They're going to go mental when they find out. He wondered if he should tell them anything. What if he kept quiet and someone else told them? Should he take that gamble? Barry was unsure what he ought to do.

'All right, Barry,' Hammer said in a friendly manner, as he sat opposite. 'We'd like to ask you a few questions.' He indicated towards Turney, who was leaning against the plate-glass window. 'Your parents have been informed that we are questioning you, concerning the arrests that occurred two days ago.'

'Why me?' He gulped visibly, his Adam's apple bobbing up and down.

Hammer smiled at the teenager's discomfort. 'You're in Year 11?' he asked, referring to an open file, 'so I suppose you know the Gorgon Five?'

'Yes, sir, I do.'

'What do you think of them?'

Barry shrugged. 'They're okay, I guess.'

Hammer looked up from the file. 'You guess? Don't you know?'

---

[21]Boyfriend, fantasy love. Actually, it means semen (Western Australian Strine).

'Well, I don't know them that well. I know Jim, Fab, and Tony ... that's about it.'

'How long have you been a student here?'

Barry gave the detective a quizzical look, trying to understand what this was all about. 'Since Year 8, sir.'

Hammer's eyes dropped back to the open file. 'Do you know a girl called Marlene Manson?'

The teenager kept quiet for a few moments trying to remember the person. 'I've heard about her, but never met her.'

'She's in Year 10.'

Barry nodded. 'I know.'

Hammer looked up. 'I thought you said you never met her?'

'I haven't, just heard the rumours about her.'

'What have you heard?'

Barry shrugged. 'That she was a bit loose – er – and that she was going out with Hank Andrews.'

The two detectives exchanged surprised glances. 'Are you sure about that?'

Barry started to relax, having noticed the surprise of the pigs; he sat back in the chair. 'Yeah,' he replied. 'They were going around together for about two years.'

'Was this common knowledge?'

'I don't know,' Barry replied. 'I don't think everybody knows. This is high school. Everybody starts a new relationship every week ... some even score, in that short time. Marlene's got a slutty reputation, so Hank was sitting pretty for two years!'

'How come you're the only one to have said this?' Hammer wanted to know.

'I don't know,' Barry replied, his confidence growing. 'Maybe you haven't asked the right questions.'

Hammer blinked and failed to see Turney's smile. 'Why didn't the Gorgons tell us this?' Hammer asked no-one in particular.

'Because no-one tells the Gorgons anything,' Barry offered. 'They're tolerated, but not trusted. The gossip never gets to them ... or to anyone who seems to be on friendly terms with them.'

'So, they're not your friends?'

Barry shook his head. 'No. They're acquaintances. Nothing more. After Year 12, I won't have to see them ever again.'

Hammer stared at the teenager, saying nothing.

'Can I go now?'

Hammer exhaled noisily. 'Yeah, get out.'

Barry rose and left the office.

Turney sat in the empty chair. 'Well, he's a nice human being.'

'Yeah,' Hammer replied absently. Interviewing Barry Enton had certainly been climactic. But they still hadn't found Marlene Manson! If the teenager was telling the truth, then they had a good idea as to where she was being sheltered: the Andrews house! He'd organise for a couple of female constables to go there and ferret her out. Unfortunately, Sam O'Reilly had stated that the students at the Catholic school needed to be questioned. Oh, well, Hammer told himself, time to give the brothers and nuns at Saint Jacob's heart attacks!

At Saint Jacob's, the teachers were very helpful once they had gotten over their initial shock. One of their students involved in drugs? Ridiculous! The students come from the best Catholic families in the area. Besides, selling that poison was a sin! Despite this pious fact, the teachers managed to give the two detectives up to ten students' names. Nine were found quite easily and questioned with no results. The tenth, and last teenager, Tony D'Bombardino, was nowhere to be found.

Following an extensive search that proved futile, the two detectives were about to throw in the towel when the principal, Brother Samuel Webb, stopped them.

'There is one place that we haven't searched,' he offered.

'Where?' asked the two detectives.

'The church.'

'What?' Hammer asked.

'The church,' Webb repeated. 'He may be in there.'

'Why would he be there?' Hammer asked. 'He should be in class, like everyone else. Don't you guys practise discipline here?'

Webb blinked. 'He happens to be quite pious. There's a good chance that he may enter a seminary in two years. So, of course, we give him a certain leeway when it comes to the school rules.'

Turney regarded the brother in disbelief. 'You're joking!'

'No. Why should I be joking?'

'Where's the church?' Hammer demanded.

'This way. Follow me,' Webb ordered.

The church was on the far side of the school, looking out onto the next street. It was a product of the form of modern architecture and at first glance did not seem much like what it professed to be. The detectives had expected to be led to a normal Gothic edifice, mirroring the Norman style. Instead, this church was mostly glass with a single sloping roof from the back to the front. At first glance, it looked like a gigantic wedge of cheese. The sight of the structure made Hammer realise that he was hungry!

The three men approached the building in silence and, just as silently, entered. Silhouetted against the coloured light, streaming through the stained-glass window, was the figure of a man, kneeling, as if in prayer.

'Anthony D'Bombardino?' Turney called. He listened in awe as his voice returned to him in a continuous echo.

'Shhh!' came a remonstration from the kneeling figure. 'You are in the House of the Lord.'

'Are you Anthony?' Hammer asked in a whisper despite his atheistic views.

Webb sat in a pew and watched the discomfort of the detectives with slight amusement.

'Yes, my brother,' the teenager acknowledged as he rose to face the detectives. 'How can I help you?' He stood with the light from the burning candles, on the altar, forming a halo around his head.

'Ah, um, ah,' Hammer started looking at his partner, uncertain how to pose the question.

'Do you know a girl by the name of Marlene Manson?' Turney asked.

'I know of no such person,' the teenager admitted.

'What about Hank Andrews?' Hammer had found his voice.

'I don't know anyone by that name.'

'Okay,' Turney replied. 'That's all we needed to hear.' He grabbed Hammer's arm and dragged him out of the church, Webb following them out the door.

'God go with you, my brothers,' Tony said.

'That kid's too pious to be a crook,' Turney stated.

'He probably doesn't even know what heroin is!' Hammer said.

Webb led them through the school and to their waiting car. Disgruntled, the two detectives returned to Police Central and reported their findings to Senior Detective-Sergeant Sam O'Reilly.

O'Reilly and Jim were still listening to and analysing the tape for what seemed the millionth time, when Hammer entered the office. Jim turned and regarded the detective as the recorder was switched off.

With a sigh, Hammer dropped into a chair next to Jim. 'We didn't get anywhere.'

'Nothing at all?' O'Reilly queried in surprise.

Hammer shook his head. 'Nothing to go on. But if you like a bit of gossip – here's something.' He turned to Jim. 'You guys aren't in the know.'

Jim's eyes narrowed. 'What does that mean?'

Hammer sat back, making himself more comfortable. 'According to our sources, the Gorgons are merely tolerated ... not trusted and not really liked.'

'Hell, I already know that,' Jim replied.

'Watch your mouth!' O'Reilly admonished.

'Sorry,' Jim apologised, 'but nothing new has been stated. I know that the Gorgon Five are not really liked by the students at the high school, but who cares? Certainly, the actions of the last few days have shown that druggies won't be tolerated. It's one of the reasons that I wanted you guys to pick up the pushers at the school.'

'That kind of advertising can also make you guys a target,' Hammer stated.

Jim gave a derisive laugh. 'From the members of my cohort? You've questioned some of them. They're morons! The girls are only interested in fashion and make-up; the boys are so sex-starved that they can't even figure out how to flirt and seduce a girl.'

'Speaking from experience, are you?'

Jim turned to O'Reilly. 'What? Well, no, actually there's more to life than just sex—'

'Such as?'

Good question. Jim looked at Hammer. 'Living life; taking part in the hunt.'

'Some would say that sex is part of living life,' Hammer offered.

'Sex is a distraction to fill in idle time,' Jim said pompously, his mind racing through numerous arguments to outwit these two flatfoots. 'That's one of the reasons that incidents of syphilis and gonorrhoea are on the rise in this country.' *Thank you, Health Ed.,* he silently thought.

The two detectives exchanged looks. 'Well, someone's had his idle time thoroughly filled,' Hammer stated.

'What does that mean?' Jim asked.

'Hank Andrews and Marlene Manson seem to have been an item ... for two years!'

'What? That's not possible. I would have heard about that.'

Hammer sat forward and looked Jim in the eyes. 'No, you wouldn't. You Gorgons are only tolerated to the point that schoolyard gossip is never discussed within earshot of any one of you guys. It seems you Gorgons are kept out of the loop.' He turned to O'Reilly. 'Marlene may be hiding out under the protection of Hank's mother. I've sent a couple of constables to search for and detain her.'

'We're out of the loop?' Jim mumbled.

'Yeah,' Hammer said. 'Doesn't look like you're not making a lot of new friends at that school. You could always transfer to the Catholic school, up the road. It seems they have Australia's first Catholic saint already in residence.'

'What are you talking about?' O'Reilly asked.

'Turney and I met him,' Hammer informed them. 'It was weird just talking to him.'

'Maybe he's on drugs,' Jim offered jokingly.

'He's on something,' Hammer replied, 'but it ain't drugs!' He looked at the tape recorder on the desk. 'What'd you find out from the tape?'

Jim sighed. 'Nothing. Absolutely nothing. Only a lot of talk.'

'But James reckons there's something familiar about one of the voices,' O'Reilly explained, switching the recorder on. 'Let's see what you think.'

They listened quietly as the late Craig St. James started the conversation, which would last for the next fifteen minutes.

AUGUST 9. 6:00 PM, WESTERN AUSTRALIA TIME

As always, Chris waited at the fence for Jim. But as six o'clock came and went, Jim did not show up. She looked around nervously and noticed that Shaka was gnawing on a large bone, near the cat shed. *Where was Jim?* she asked herself. She had to see him. It was important! After experiencing Cyclone Tracy, the tempest responsible for the destruction of part of the city of Darwin, not many things could scare Chris Porter! But she wasn't ashamed to admit to herself that she was scared now – bloody scared! For some reason – mysteriously unknown to her – only Jim would make her feel safe. Where was he? Is he going to let the cats starve? 'Jim!' she called. 'Jim!' She waited, but he did not come out. A sly smile appeared on her pretty face as an idea formed. The idea was mischievous, low, cruel, in bad taste and, therefore, should work. Cupping her hands to her mouth, she called:

'Jamie ... Jamie Saston!'

Almost immediately, the Petersons' sliding door opened, and Jim stomped out. 'Are you mad?' he said as he approached her. 'How dare you call me that?'

'It got you out here, didn't it?' she replied sweetly. 'And how are you going to apologise if you're not out here talking to me?'

'What! I apologise? What the hell for?'

'For the way you carried on about Paul the other day,' she replied.

'Oh, that. If I remember rightly, you're the one who carried on.'

'What do you mean, me? You're the one who didn't care; you're the one who went on and on and on ... Jamie!'

Jim winced at the mention of that variation of his name and noticed the sweet smile on Chris's face. Then he noticed that while her mouth was smiling, her eyes were not; they betrayed her worry. 'That's not my name so if you don't mind, refrain from calling me that.'

'"Refrain"? What does that mean, Jamie? Huh, Jamie! Come on, tell me, big boy. Come on, Jamie.'

Jim remained quiet as he glared at the girl. For a slight moment, he wondered how difficult it would be to change his name. 'If you're going to act so childishly, I'm going back inside, and you can stay here and talk to yourself.'

'If that's the way you want it, then go and let me die,' she said soberly. The mischievous smile was gone, replaced by a thin line for a mouth with lips taut from fear. Her eyes started to water despite her attempts to prevent it. Chris began to shake from the effort.

Jim couldn't help frowning. 'What are you talking about?'

'Nothing!'

He shrugged. You've got to be cruel to be kind. 'If that's the way you want it,' he replied and turned to leave.

'Hey, where're you going?' Chris called. 'Aren't you going to apologise first?'

'Not if you're going to carry on like this.'

'I'm not carrying on,' she said quietly.

Jim took a step towards the fence; towards her ... concerned about the way that she was acting. He stopped himself. No. She wants you to weaken, Saston, so don't. 'Then, what do you call it?' His voice was hard as stone.

Chris remained silent as she counted the horses in her mind's eye.

The stone began crumbling. She certainly knew how to make someone feel evil, he told himself. Relentingly, he stepped up onto the neat stack of bricks, next to the fence. 'I'm sorry,' he said before he could stop himself. 'What's wrong, Chris? What's troubling you?'

'I'm scared,' she whispered.

'Scared? But you told me that after Cyclone Tracy, nothing could possibly scare you ... ever! What are you scared of?'

'I heard something yesterday.'

'What was that?'

'It's about Paul Matthews.'

Jim sighed. 'What about him?' he asked, failing to disguise the annoyance that this re-occurring ghost caused.

'No,' she replied. 'You don't want to know.'

'Yes, I do.'

'Why?'

God, she is exasperating! 'Because if something is scaring you, then I want to help. After all, I'm not a Gorgon for nothing. What do you know about Paul?'

Chris hesitated.

'Come on,' he urged gently.

'Because you're a Gorgon ... is that the only reason why you want to help me?'

'Of course, not – you know that. At least, you should know that. I thought it was obvious why I was always out here talking to you. Especially in the rain, at times. I wouldn't do that for any other girl.'

Chris lowered her eyes and contemplated the picket fence for a moment. To Jim, she looked fragile, at that moment. Like an object that could break at the slightest vibration. Awkwardly, because of the fence, he wrapped his arms around her.

'Aren't you going to tell me?'

Chris's eyes rose and locked onto Jim's. 'I know who murdered him.'

Jim was thunderstruck. He let go of her, taking a step back, forgetting that he had been standing on a narrow stack of bricks. His arms swung in a circular motion as he lost his balance and fell backwards into the pool. His head broke the surface, and he squirted out saltwater and swam towards the shallow end and climbed out. Jim squelched back to where she was and noticed that she was laughing so hard that tears were streaming down her face. 'I need to get changed,' he said and that made her laugh even harder. 'Come on over and we'll talk.'

'All right,' she said between her bouts of laughter. 'We can only talk, okay ... nothing else.' Chris exploded into more laughter.

'Well yeah, we're only going to talk since I've had a f**king cold shower!' he muttered under his breath. 'How funny my misfortunes are!' Jim walked away and back to the house, his shoes squelching loudly as he went. 'Very funny, indeed!' Jim stopped and turned back to look at the place where Chris had stood. What had she meant by that comment? What did that mean? Was there a possibility ...? He slid back the sliding door and stepped in.

'What the hell happened to you?' Peterson demanded, looking up from his copy of *The West Australian*.

'I might get laid,' Jim replied, not thinking.

'What?' both Petersons asked at the same time.

'I ... er ... fell in the pool,' he replied. 'Christine's coming over.'

'You need to get out of those wet clothes before you freeze to death,' Julie insisted. 'Go, I'll get you some dry clothes. Thank heaven I did the washing today.'

'Why is Chris coming over?' Peterson wanted to know.

Jim stopped in the archway that opened onto the hallway leading to the bedrooms. 'She said she knows who the murderer is.'

'Which murderer?'

'Paul Matthews's murderer,' Jim called from his bedroom.

'Does she now?' Julie said, entering Jim's room with a pile of folded clothes. She placed them on his bed and picked up the soaked jumper, shirt, t-shirt, and socks he had taken off. She looked at Jim. 'Come on, the jeans and your underpants,' she stated.

Jim looked at her defiantly. 'Not while you're in the room.'

Julie laughed. 'I do your laundry and, before your dad and you left for South Africa, I changed a nappy or two. Believe me, you don't have anything that I haven't already seen.'

Jim's eyes widened in surprise. 'I don't care what you've seen in the past, you're not seeing anything now.'

'Neither will Christine,' Julie said. 'You'll receive her in the lounge.' She turned her back on him and walked out.

Jim went to the bathroom and grabbed his towel, bringing it back to his bedroom. He quickly dried himself and dressed in a freshly folded t-shirt, underpants, jeans, socks, windcheater, all black. As the doorbell rang, he had returned to the bathroom and combed his hair. Jim spotted Peterson's aftershave and splashed some onto his hand and rubbed it on his face, almost screaming from the stinging sensation. He grabbed his towel and rubbed his face until the stinging ceased. He could hear Julie's voice welcoming Chris into the house.

Chris and Julie were in the kitchen, talking, as he entered the family room. As he passed, Peterson began sniffing the air and gave a wry smile as he eyed Jim.

'Hi,' he greeted her, feeling awkward.

Julie lifted her nose and sniffed, regarding Jim. 'Has that dog brought something dead into the house?'

Chris laughed as she got a whiff of the aftershave.

'You can have privacy in the lounge,' Julie instructed.

The two teenagers walked into the lounge and Julie joined her husband in the family room.

'He used your aftershave,' she whispered. 'The nerve of him. He doesn't even shave.'

Peterson chuckled. 'I know,' he said and returned his attention to the paper.

Jim sat next to Chris on the couch. 'Now, tell me how certain you are as to the murderer's identity.'

She looked at him and took his hand. 'Before we get into that,' she began, 'let's start with this.' She leaned in towards him and, as their lips met, she wrapped her arms around him. He held her to him as he returned the kiss. Then, just as sudden as it had started the kiss had ended and Jim's arms lingered on holding her close.

'That's a strange way to uncover the identity of a murderer,' Julie whispered after the teenagers had parted.

'Will you sit down and leave them to their privacy?' Peterson remonstrated in a low tone.

Chris clasped her hands in her lap.

She was in the same clothes as she had been wearing while outside, Jim noticed. Her hair was different, though.

Chris looked at him. 'Two minus one leaves none,' she said quietly.

Jim blinked. 'What?'

'Two minus one leaves none,' she repeated.

'Okay,' he began. 'What has that got to do with anything?'

'Paul's body had been dragged into those bushes,' she began to explain. 'There was no syringe around, no nothing. If he had suicided – even accidentally – there would have been evidence of his shooting up.'

'Okay, I'll agree with you there. I know for a fact that the police did not find anything. They must already suspect murder. Do you really know who did it?' he asked softly.

'In school, you hear a lot of gossip …'

'I wouldn't know about that,' Jim mumbled. That wasn't what he wanted to hear. 'The problem is what you hear may not be the truth.'

'Don't let them kill me, Jim!' she suddenly blurted out.

The Gorgon held her close, comforting her. 'No-one's going to hurt you while I'm around.'

'Promise?'

'Of course, I promise,' Jim replied, worry starting to show in his eyes. What could she possibly have learnt about Paul's death – and how?

Chris glanced at Julie pottering about in the kitchen. She was certain that Julie may be listening in. 'Marlene's pregnant with Hank's baby!' Chris whispered. 'The rumour that's going around school is that she went out with Paul, following Hank's arrest. Marlene asked around about how the cops got onto Hank and found out that you lot were responsible and that you were tipped off by Paul. Then she started to go around with Paul. Now Paul's dead and Marlene's disappeared, and the cops can't find her. Jim, Marlene knows how I feel about you, and she will try to hurt you, somehow, and I'm so scared!'

'You reckon that Marlene will hurt you to get to me?' he asked.

Chris nodded. 'She saw us together before your exam that day. Marlene knows that I care about you … so much.' Her eyes dropped to her lap and the thought that there was someone out there that hated her so much that she was in peril because of her romantic choices. Her face whitened as the blood drained from her face and Chris's eyes found Jim's. 'I'm so frightened!'

Jim put his arms around her and held her tight. 'Don't be frightened,' he said. 'The police probably have her in custody now. They were tipped off earlier today that she may be hiding out at Andrews' place.'

Chris moved out of his embrace and looked him in the eye. 'She is.'

'How do you know that?' he asked.

'Because everyone knew that.'

'I didn't!'

Chris looked at him in confusion. 'How could you not know? It went around the school.'

'Because no-one told me,' Jim replied bitterly. So, it was true, the Gorgon Five were being ostracised by the rest of the school. How stupid of them all. One day, the student body will be glad that we exist!

'I better get back home,' Chris announced. 'Will ... will you walk me home?'

Jim looked at her. 'Yeah,' he said. 'Of course, I will. But what does two minus one leaves none mean? It makes no sense.'

'If Hank killed Paul ... or Marlene killed Paul, then that little baby has no parents. See? Two minus one leaves none.'

'Hank couldn't have killed Paul,' Jim mused, 'therefore that can only leave ...'

They both rose from the couch and Chris said her goodbyes and Jim explained that he would see her home. As they left, Peterson folded his paper and went over to the telephone. He dialled a number and waited.

'Hello, Sam?' he asked. 'I have a question for you ... No, I am not playing games like James! Have your officers succeeded in picking up the Manson girl?' He paused, listening to O'Reilly. It seems that Jim's girlfriend believes that this Manson girl murdered the boy that was found on Sunday ... No, I don't think that's a good idea. Just leave her out of it and question

Jim. She confided in him … Because I heard her … No, I was eavesdropping! … All right, I'll leave it with you. Good night.'

Jim returned, looking confused. He noticed Peterson moving away from the phone. 'So, you heard it all?' he asked.

Peterson returned to his seat. 'Yeah,' he said, grabbing the paper. 'I've told Sam. He wanted her brought in, but I suggested that he question you instead and leave Chris out of it.'

'Question me?' Jim demanded. 'Why? What Chris has said is only supposition! If Marlene killed Paul Matthews, there's really no true evidence! The moment I tell Sam that, he'll drag Chris into Police Central!'

'Calm down and think about what she told you,' Peterson advised.

'She said that Marlene and Hank had been an item,' Jim said, 'but the police had learnt that this morning. They'd been together for two years!' Jim sat down on the bean bag. 'It seemed the entire school knew that, except me! Hank's mum had been hiding Marlene until the police picked her up from there; they have her in custody now. She's a drug pusher, but that doesn't mean that she murdered Paul Matthews. Hell, he'd be her number one customer with Hank gone! Why kill him?'

Peterson lowered the paper. 'Why is Hank gone?'

'Because he was a drug pusher.'

'How did they come by that knowledge?'

Jim's eyes narrowed as he regarded his guardian. 'Because I told them.'

'How did you get the proof?'

'By questioning Paul Matthews.' Jim's eyes widened as he realised what happened throughout the school. 'The rumour mill must have started after the police picked up Hank! It spread through the school: our involvement, Paul's admission, the existence of drugs in the school. Marlene's boyfriend was carted off by the police and she was alone … and expecting! She would have felt abandoned, betrayed, and sought vengeance upon those that had caused this turn of events.'

'You got it,' Peterson said, unfolding his paper.

AUGUST 9. 9:30 PM, WESTERN AUSTRALIA TIME

Marlene Manson sat quietly at the table across from Senior Detective-Sergeant Sam O'Reilly. This time, she realised, the atmosphere had changed – a pin could have been heard dropping in the stillness of the room; the silence was deafening.

O'Reilly knew who Paul Matthews's murderer was but couldn't bring himself to ask for a confession. He had to get one from her, though, and he opened the file he had brought in with him. The news that Mark Peterson had relayed to him nearly two hours ago, was a hundred per cent circumstantial. At least James had gotten more out of that crazy Porter girl than they had! All they got from her were riddles! Oh well, O'Reilly decided, he'd just have to bluff …

'Marlene Manson,' he began grimly, 'you are to be charged with one count of premeditated murder! The murder of one Paul Matthews! I think it fair to warn you that anything that you may say, can – and will – be used against you in a court of law.'

'What?' cried Mrs. Manson, who'd been sitting beside her daughter quietly. 'Murder? You must be mad!'

O'Reilly turned his steel-like glare upon the mother. 'Mrs. Manson, we have a witness who is willing to testify, under oath, that they saw your daughter, wilfully and purposefully, kill Paul Matthews!'

Mrs. Manson regarded the girl sitting beside her. Marlene's face held no emotion, only her eyes betrayed anything. Oh no, she told herself, Marlene actually did do it. No. Her husband was already in prison, she can't lose her daughter – and grandchild – also. 'She killed him in a fit of madness,' she offered, desperately. 'He got her pregnant! He probably refused to accept responsibility for the child!'

'No!' Marlene cried. 'No, that's not the reason. He was a gutless little bastard! A useless, worthless bastard! He didn't deserve to live!' She stopped and gave the detective a defiant look. 'You're surprised? Yeah, I killed him – weird, isn't it? I don't feel nothing. No compassion. Nothing … just numbness! If it wasn't for Chris Porter and that idiot, Jim Saston—' She glared at the large mirror, knowing that Jim was standing on the other side '—no-one would know! The maggots would have eaten him just like he deserved!'

Her mother winced at the viciousness of her daughter's admission.

'Why?' O'Reilly asked softly. 'Did you hate him that much?'

She glared at O'Reilly. What was wrong with this f**ken pig? 'I was gonna marry Hank! He's my baby's dad. He said he was going to marry me. Make the baby legitimate, we weren't going to bring a bastard into this world! I joined him in selling drugs. We didn't have enough money. So, we sold that junk to the arseholes that took that shit. Then that bastard, Matthews, cried that he couldn't afford the price hike and went blabbing to those Gorgon mongrels! If it wasn't for all of them, I'd still have a father for my baby. Now it'll be born in prison a bastard!' She broke down into a fit of hysterical tears and her mother tried her best to console her, saying that all would work out in the end. All would be well.

O'Reilly looked away from the scene and regarded the mirror, behind him, where he knew that Hammer, Peterson, and James were looking in. He sighed. What compassion he'd had for this girl had died with the recital of her guilt. Before, he had hoped that James and the Porter girl had been wrong. But now, with a heavy heart and feeling like a proper louse, he realised he was the one who had been wrong all along. Damn this job! Has society reached the state that children now kill children? What hope was there left for civilisation when this becomes normal behaviour? He looked at mother and daughter. 'How did you kill him?'

'Really?' scolded Mrs. Manson. 'Haven't you upset her enough without hounding her?'

Marlene broke away from her mother's embrace, sniffling and wiping the tears from her eyes. 'No, it's okay. I want to tell you ... all of you,' she said. 'It was so simple, really. I found out everything from the school grapevine and learnt about the face-off between Hank and Paul. Then Hank was taken by you pigs and the goss[22] was that Paul had ratted out on him. Chris bloody Porter confirmed that the Gorgons had been involved somehow. So, I had to get the rest of the story from Paul. With Paul it was easy. I chatted him up, flirted. Then he asked me over to his house – his parents would be out. I told him I would meet him on the school oval. I grabbed some sugar from my stash—'

---

[22]Gossip (Australian slang).

Mrs. Manson gasped '—and I met Paul. He had some sugar left over from somewhere and I made out that I was desperate for it.' She smiled. 'He was pathetic! I only would get some if we f**ked – but not all of it. He wanted some so that we could trip together. We sat under the taps, near where you guys found him and prepared the stuff together. What went into that syringe was a big dose – a killer dose. I made him put it in his arm first, saying we would share it and, when he had injected half the stuff, I asked him what would happen if I pushed the plunger the rest of the way ...'

'What happened then?' O'Reilly asked, intrigued. The thought that capital punishment was no longer practised flashed through his mind. *This little bitch deserves the hangman's noose!*

'He knew then who I was – not his girlfriend – but Hank's avenging angel! It was weird watching the terror dawn in his eyes as I pushed the plunger all the way. A while later, he hit some kind of spasm and then I began to laugh. Later, when I stopped laughing, I realised he was dead. He had this weird look on his face ... and foam bubbling from his mouth ... and I giggled softly to myself as I pulled him along by his feet and shoved him under the bushes. I didn't think anyone would find him so soon. Before he took the dope, he was laughing at what had happened to Hank. He boasted that that's what should happen to dope pushers! I should've asked him what he'd do if there weren't any dope pushers left. He made me really mad – and that's when I decided to do what I did. He was just like a cowering animal before I knocked that sugar into him – like some snivelling dopey animal!' She kept looking from O'Reilly to her mother as she explained her actions on that Saturday night.

From his vantage point behind the two-way mirror, Jim shuddered as he saw the hatred and viciousness in her eyes. No wonder Chris was scared! Hell, he didn't think anyone could be that mad, insane, crazy to kill someone else because he hurt her real boyfriend. A boyfriend that most probably would have killed her, and the baby, in time, anyway.

O'Reilly looked at Mrs. Manson, she sat perfectly still as a single tear coursed its way down her cheek. He got up slowly like an old man and, closing the untouched file, he picked it up off the table, walked out of the interview room.

As he left, Marlene began to cry softly to herself – for Hank and her unborn child.

Chapter Thirteen
Ç'est La Guerre![23]

AUGUST 10. 10:03 AM, WESTERN AUSTRALIA TIME

For years, whether in the United States, the United Kingdom, or any other country, the policeman's job has been made easier by the unofficial help of the informer. These people, be they law-abiding citizens or the dregs of society who are – off the record – blackmailed by a detective, frequent the social circles and dives of known criminals and, basically, keep their ears to the ground in the hope of coming across an interesting piece of information which will appease the ambitious law-enforcer.

Bill Hammer was no different from any other detective and often depended on informers to get ahead in a case. A few hours before Marlene Manson's confession, Hammer had received a tip concerning the missing Slattery trucks, and their load of sugar-AKA-golf balls. Ever since the raid on the Slattery Enterprises' warehouse, on Saturday morning, the fleet of trucks – containing the contraband cargo – had gone to ground. Security was well organised when it came to Edmonds, mused Hammer. Not only had the trucks simply vanished, but there had been absolutely no news on the streets – that is, until this call. From an anonymous source, Hammer's most reliable informant learnt that the trucks were on the move again – from their hiding place, just out of

Bunbury – to Albany, where the cargo would be transferred to a ship, which was waiting for the trucks' arrival.

Hammer knew time was not on his side as he approached O'Reilly with this new development in the case. It wasn't hard to convince his superior and within an hour, Hammer and Turney were on their way – by private jet – to Albany.

AUGUST 10. 12:53 PM, WESTERN AUSTRALIA TIME

The brown Volvo, with the blue personal plates, pulled up behind the Mercedes-Benz. Alexander Simos, impeccably dressed, as always, and with briefcase in hand, trotted up to the door.

Barton opened the door and Simos couldn't help but wonder how much that man reminded him of the tall butler in that sitcom ... what was it called? Oh yes! *The Addams Family*. He had never seen a smile upon that square face. A ghost of a smile appeared on his own and was instantly gone as he reminded himself that the situation did not warrant any happiness. The news he had to convey to Edmonds would make the American shed more hair than he now possessed. He walked through the house, towards the patio and pool area.

'Ahhh ... good afternoon, Mr. Simos,' Edmonds greeted the lawyer, dropping his hand from the breast of the half-naked girl sitting on his lap.

Simos recognised the girl as the blonde from the pool on Saturday. *She still looked no older than sixteen!* he noted with disgust.

'What brings you here on such a lovely day?' Edmonds asked.

As if on cue, Simos sat opposite Edmonds and the blonde, placing his briefcase on his lap. 'A new development has occurred, sir, that I thought you should be made aware of – immediately,' he replied, keeping his eyes deliberately off Edmonds and the girl.

'It had better be important,' Edmonds snarled.

The girl's body tensed. She knew what was coming, Simos told himself. 'It concerns the trucks that were to rendezvous with the *Southern Star*.'

Edmonds dropped the girl, who made a hasty retreat into the house and promptly glared at Simos.

'"Were"? What the f**k's that supposed to mean?'

'The police stopped, searched, and proceeded to impound them and the "cargo", as each one entered Albany.'

'F**k! They took all of it?'

Simos nodded nervously and cast an envious eye in the direction of the girl's retreat. How he longed to be anywhere else than here also.

Edmonds rose from the reclining deck chair and went to stand at the edge of the pool, looking at the progression of the slight ripples in the water. 'It's those goddam kids!' he uttered suddenly to no-one in particular. 'I know it is! We haven't taken care of them, yet. So, it's about time we did. Barton, get me The Christian!'

Barton disappeared inside as Simos gave an audible sigh. More violence, the lawyer told himself. How he abhorred violence. It was so low class! Not only that, but it was economically unsound. Oh well, it couldn't be helped. Those kids had kept at it, and now it was 'time to pay the Piper', as they say. At least their deaths would discourage others from interfering in their business, ever again.

AUGUST 11. 11:58 AM, WESTERN AUSTRALIA TIME

The girl stopped next to Jim's desk. He regarded her quizzically until realising that she was waiting for his exam booklet. Jim handed it over with an apology.

Andrew leaned across his desk and tapped Jim on the shoulder. 'How'd you go?'

Before he could answer, a teacher, who had spied Andrew's breach of exam protocol, announced, 'No talking, please. Until the examination papers are all collected, we are still officially in an exam situation. Anyone caught talking will automatically fail.' He cast a reproachful glance at Andrew, who sat back and folded his arms, blushing. The murmurs died and the classroom returned to silence, but the pre-exam tension had completely disappeared.

This gave Jim time to mull over what O'Reilly had told him and Mark, the night before. Now with Hank and the other two pushers and Marlene in custody, things could return to normal at Tannen Heights High. Despite the policeman's not-so-subtle hint, Jim had already decided to step aside in favour of the police. With Callobar gone and the disagreements he'd had with Chris and Fab, Jim had no desire to take on Edmonds and Slattery Enterprises – just yet. But one day, when he was older and a proven trouble-shooter, he would cause Slattery to come crashing down and kill Edmonds for his own self-satisfaction!

With the papers in his possession, the teacher dismissed the class and beat the students out the door. One other classroom was pouring out students. Andrew and Jim were soon joined by Tet.

'Now you can answer my question,' Andrew stated. 'How'd you go?'

Jim started up the stairs. 'Let's just say I did good enough to pass, okay?'

'I can say the same,' Andrew replied, happy to conceal the fact that he had found the exam extremely difficult.

'Yeah, that was a hard exam,' Tet put in resignedly. 'You know, I'm curious to know how your guardian got us off on Monday. And, while we're at it, where were you the last few days?'

Oh no, not again! They'll never give up, not that he could blame them. After all, he hadn't given them even a possible excuse and, in their shoes, he wouldn't have let the matter rest either. But he couldn't tell them all of what he knew – that would be in violation of the Official Secrets Act – that he was an unofficial member of one of Australia's Security organisations, and that his involvement made it a federal matter. He knew this would have been told to Gardner, hence his change of heart. But, what could he tell his friends? All this passed through his mind as he formulated a flippant answer that would curb – hopefully – their curiosity. 'Who knows?' he finally answered. 'Maybe he offered to spay Gardner's wife for free!'

Andrew was at a loss. 'Isn't your guardian a vet?'

Jim nodded.

'You're not going to tell us, are you?' Tet challenged.

'What's to tell?'

'Well, at least come clean as to why you were at the cop shop[24] in the last couple of days.'

Jim sighed as he dropped his bag onto the bench, beneath his locker. 'When Chris was taken by the police the other day, it was to get a statement from her about discovering Paul's body. But it also seemed that she knew something about the murder as well and told them that we were also involved. That was the reason why they came round here and questioned you guys. I was informed of that when I got there, and they asked me what I knew. I replied that I knew absolutely nothing about it and then we listened to a tape recording.'

'You listened to a tape? All day?' Andrew queried in astonishment.

'*Ja*[25],' Jim replied. 'The police think that they may have the mobsters' top hit-man's voice on tape. I'm not supposed to be telling you this, but ... up to now, the police only know this guy as "The Christian". I've listened to the tape and, I have to admit, there's something familiar about that voice, but I still can't pinpoint what makes the voice familiar.'

Jim opened his locker and Tet moved to the one next to Fab's. Andrew's was under Mike's. Upon joining the Gorgon Five, he had moved his gear from the school-appointed one, outside Room Q, to the one outside Room W, with the rest of the Gorgons.

'So, what now?' Tet asked.

'I've just got to try to think and remember,' Jim replied, removing the maths file and textbook from his bag. The enormous blue biology journal, standing on its side in the bag, toppled over, and

---

[24]Police station (1970s 'Strine).

[25]Yes (Afrikaans).

he zipped the bag shut after straightening it. He shut his locker, placed the bag under the bench, and sat down.

'Larry was being very annoying while we were waiting in the office,' Tet said, trying to make conversation.

Jim smiled. 'So I've heard.'

Fab and Danny had just completed the Maths Two exam and were discussing the problems on the paper, as they headed for their lockers.

'How was the exam?' Andrew asked, being the first to notice their arrival.

Fab gave a thin smile. 'Don't ask.'

He lifted his bag onto the bench with some effort and produced his locker keys. Danny leaned against the railing, his bag next to his feet. 'It was f**ken hard. I don't think many people passed.'

'Thank God we do Maths One, instead of Two and Three,' Andrew stated.

'Fab,' Tet said quietly, a large grin spreading across his smooth features, 'have you heard that we have nothing to worry about, especially after practically killing De Boyz?'

'Yeah,' he replied, digging through the collection of files and textbooks in his bag. 'Jim parried my questions also.' He straightened up, looked at the Japanese boy, and said, 'I've known this f**ken shithead for three years and when he doesn't want to say something, there's not a f**ken thing on this Earth that's going to make him be f**ken honest with us! He assures us that we're not going to get into f**ken trouble for our little caper the other day, and as long as none of De Boyz die and my mum isn't stuck with the f**ken hospital bill, then she'll be right!'

'Yeah, but aren't you curious about how Jim was able to manage all that, just by phoning his guardian?' Tet closed his locker.

'Sure, I'm curious,' Fab admitted, depositing his Maths Two file into the open locker. 'I'm f**ken curious about a lot of things – like, who is Callobar? And what's really his involvement with Jim? How can he walk into a police station and belt up the person they're questioning and not be charged? But what's the point of being curious when you don't get any f**ken answers?'

Jim examined the concrete ledge under his feet and sighed. 'Tet,' Jim interrupted, 'there's no point in carrying on with this conversation. You'll learn nothing from Fab, as I didn't tell him very much – for the sole fact that I don't know much about it, myself.' He paused as Tony joined the group. 'But I do have my suspicions about what Mark said. As you know, my guardian is the director of the Animals' Haven Veterinary Hospital, and some very influential people are clients – some are even friends. Need I say more?'

The others shook their heads, including Tony who hadn't the faintest idea what they were all talking about. 'So, Jim's guardian's a vet, so what? Uncle Donald, in Sydney, is a vet and Tony never talks about him. Why should he? The bastard's a cheapskate, the one who had sent him, Tony, two dollars as a present for his sixteenth birthday!'

Fab shut the locker and after shoving his bag under the bench, dropped down next to Tet. 'What do we do now?' he demanded, directing the question past Tet to Jim. 'We've been instrumental in bringing four junior pushers to justice and sending a group of bullies to hospital. Do we track down any other pushers? Oh no, wait ... we're seasoned now. Let's find who's bringing that f**ken shit into the country and stop them! Then we can find the local communist and beat the f**k out of them!'

'What the hell is wrong with you?' Jim asked.

Tet decided to relocate.

'What's wrong with me?' Fab challenged. 'What the f**k is wrong with you? Why did you have to start all this bullshit now? Why not early next term? All this shitting around has interfered with my exams and grades! But you don't give a f**k about that, you want to play the hero pretending you're saving the world! Well, you know what? Those pushers will be replaced, and my grades will have suffered for nothing! How's that for playing the hero, Jim? Because of you, one kid's been murdered, there's been a brawl on the school grounds, and we've got a reputation we never wanted. Even Christine is starting to wonder about being seen near you. Tell me, after all that, what's the f**ken advantage of being in this group and associating with you?'

Jim looked Fab fully in the eyes. 'That's not for me to answer,' he said calmly. 'It's for you to answer.' He scanned each of the members present. 'If you don't, or can't, see an advantage in being in this group ... you're free to leave and never speak to me ever again. The one thing you can't deny is that we've had some fun times ... and we're pretty good friends who have always been there for each other when we've needed to be. But, hey, you know ... what the hell do I know? I spent the first twelve years of my life in a different country ...'

'So did I,' Tet admitted.

'I'm the same,' Andrew lied.

'We're out of the investigation,' Jim said. 'The police are pursuing their leads which have nothing to do with this school, at least. We're done with the whole thing. The mobsters who run this operation aren't going to come bothering us. We've simply been a minor irritation.'

The Gorgons looked at each other in silence as Jim's words sank in. For Fab, it simply wasn't enough. He wanted more ... an assurance – promise – from Jim that this was the end of any interference with police investigations. He voiced this and the others looked to Jim.

'Okay,' he promised. 'Never again will we involve ourselves in police investigations. It'll make life boring, but ... if that's what you want, then I promise never to drag you guys into anything like this ever again.'

The siren went and the tranquillity of a school in the throes of productivity exploded into the chaos of lunchtime. Studies could be forgotten, momentarily, over the twenty-minute break by the nine hundred-odd students and just over a hundred teachers.

For the Year 11s still on the school grounds, it would be a time for checking over notes and memorising formulae before entering the designated classroom for that afternoon's exam; for some of the Year 11s, but not the Gorgon Five. Biology, for Jim and Tony, needed little studying and Fab had successfully memorised his notes – word for word – during the term. Andrew and Danny had no exam that afternoon, but both had made the mistake of buying their lunch and had no choice but to stay and leave when the lunch break had ended.

Jim accompanied them to the canteen and, trading in the blue metal disc received a warm 'something' in a brown paper bag. He waited for the others and all three returned to Room Y. The four others doing the Diploma Course were also seated outside the history classroom eating and talking as usual.

Fab was holding a piece of paper and studying the drawing on it, with interest. Jim sat down next to him and noticed the Chinese dragon.

'Another Callahan masterpiece?' Jim commented idly, unwrapping the grease-proof package from the brown paper bag, removing half of a toasted sandwich.

'Yep,' Fab replied and handed it back to its owner.

'Have you seen it, Jim?' Harry asked.

'Yeah, Harry,' Jim said. 'They're getting better all the time ... you should add colour to it one day.'

'The next one,' he promised and returned it to his bag ... another piece to add to his already vast portfolio.

As he ate, Fab quietly mulled over what had been said earlier. 'I'm sorry I put you on the spot back there,' he said quietly, nodding towards where their lockers were. 'But I hope you can see where I'm coming from.'

'That's okay, Fab,' Jim replied, 'and I do understand. I'm sorry I got too involved in all this. You know me, I worry only about the current problem and forget about everything else.'

'Hey, has anyone thought about which movie we're going to see together?' Larry suddenly asked, spraying some food over the ledge of the balcony.

'That's actually slipped our minds,' Tony said, 'what with everything that's been happening. What's showing?'

'I don't know,' admitted Larry. 'I thought we had all been thinking about this.'

'Well, some of us do have exams,' Fab put in. 'So, no!'

'There's a Burt Reynolds movie on,' Harry put in.

'Yeah,' Danny said. '*Hooper*, I think.'

'It also stars *Batman* and *The Flying Nun*,' Larry said.

'Really?' Fab asked. He turned to Jim. 'That might be a good film to go and see.'

'Yeah, I guess so,' Jim agreed.

'Something wrong?'

'No,' Jim replied. 'Ever since *Smokey and the Bandit*, I haven't thought much of Burt Reynolds's acting ability.'

Fab shrugged. 'I don't see why.'

'Don't worry about me,' Jim said, smiling. 'I'm just fussy about films.'

The truth was that Jim was suddenly feeling a sense of foreboding. Something had happened and he couldn't shake the feeling that they all would be safer in their own homes, rather than being at school! He hadn't felt anything like this before. The feeling had come on just like the changing of wind direction. Jim smiled to himself. That thought had reminded him of a phrase from *The Christmas Carol* and he shrugged the feeling away and wrote it off as indigestion.

Jack Talbot screwed up his grease-proof papers with self-satisfaction, having enjoyed his double serving of lunch. The floor show was much to be desired, but the food was superb. Being the first in the group to decide to make a trip to the nearest bin, he collected up the rubbish of the other members.

Jim refused to hand over his unfinished lunch and said, 'Fab can throw it away. Besides, he hasn't finished yet. So, he'll have to go there, anyway.'

Jack shrugged and headed for the bin, at the top of the stairs beside the maths faculty office. Behind him, Fab was cursing Jim in a loud voice and, on Jack's return, he was still at it. Jack took his bag and wished the others a memorable lunchtime, and left for the school library, where the latest motor magazine awaited him.

Fab glanced at his watch between swear-words, and nudged Jim. It was time to head off for the Gorgons' Den. He rose from his seat and grabbed his bag.

Jim held up his brown paper bag with the grease-proof paper in it, for Fab to take.

Fab glared at his friend and snatched it from his hand before stomping off towards the stairs and the bin.

Mike left his bag with Andrew's and Danny's, under the bench outside Room W, and accompanied his brother Gorgons to the barricaded-off exam area.

The breezeway, allowing access to the Gorgons' Den, was two classrooms away to their right and the nine boys disappeared through it. When they had reached the small paved triangular area at the front of the school, they stood around and looked at each other, dumbly, before Danny took the initiative and started the discussion as to which film they should all go and see.

'Let's go and see *Hooper*,' Larry said with a sense of finality.

'Why?' Tony asked.

'Well, it's a good film,' Larry replied, defensively.

'How do you know that?' Harry wanted to know.

'Well, it's got Burt Reynolds in it,' offered Larry. 'He's a good actor.'

'Apart from *Smokey and the Bandit*,' Jim said. 'Name three other movies that he's been in to strengthen your argument.'

'Well, he was a regular on *Gunsmoke*,' Tet put in.

'Not a movie,' returned Jim.

'And he was the star of the police drama called *Hawk*,' Andrew said.

'Still not a movie,' Jim reiterated. 'You can't name a movie that he's been in that we're allowed to go see. So why should we spend the money to go ...' His voice trailed off as he noticed a foreign object on the tree. Stretching over the wooden rail, greyed from age, he plucked the rosary beads from the nail, on which they hung. He felt his stomach fall a thousand metres.

AUGUST 11. 12:30 PM, WESTERN AUSTRALIA TIME

In a maroon Holden Commodore, James Barton, with The Christian sitting beside him, watched the Gorgons' Den from their vantage point near the crest of the hill on Banksia Street. 'There they are.' Almost automatically the hand went to his mouth, the knuckle rubbing against his lower lip.

The Christian chanced a moment to look down at the Thompson M1921A submachine gun that lay on his lap. He checked the 100-round drum magazine and tested the gun's action. It was just over five kilograms and he patted it lovingly. Also, on his lap, was a woollen ski mask, which he put on his head and slipped over his face. The Christian hefted up the weapon and thought to himself that this was the favourite weapon of organised crime. Bonnie and Clyde had owned one each; it had been used at the St. Valentine's Day Massacre and had dispensed Mafia justice to many double-crossers! There couldn't be many of these babies in Australia. Soon these teenage bastards would hear her sing!

The two men watched the boys intently, not missing a single movement and a thin smile crept onto The Christian's face as he saw Jim reach over the railing and took the rosary beads. 'They found it,' he said. 'Let's go!' He stuck the barrel of the Thompson out of his open window.

AUGUST 11. 12:32 PM, WESTERN AUSTRALIA TIME

The sudden squeal of tyres drew Jim's attention from the rosary beads he held to the maroon car he had noticed parked at the top of the hill. He registered the muzzle of a gun sticking out of the passenger's window, in horror. It took him less than two seconds to react. He grabbed Andrew and threw him into Tet and Tony, the three collapsing to the ground with a unanimous grunt. 'Get down!' Jim shouted, pulling Danny, Fab, and Mike down, with him. 'Stay the f**k down!'

Any other warning was lost in the staccato cacophony of the submachine guns firing. Faintly through that sound, the Gorgons could hear the scream of the girls - seated on the southern lawn - and the shattering of glass. Then it was their turn. Bits of bark and plaster rendering and also large splinters from the railing rained down on them.

The guns' chattering ceased, another screech of tyres, and the car was gone. Jim was the first to glance up, warily, checking to see that the car had really gone and not just stopped to finish those off who got up. Clutching the switchblade more for reassurance than anything else, he got up to head towards the admin office. Mark needed to know about this ... even before Sam and those jokers called the police! The sight that met his eyes before taking a step made him utter a cry of despair. 'Oh my God!' Jim said, his voice a dry whisper as he fought to control the emotions that threatened to break free. 'Fab,' he croaked, 'get an ambulance!'

Fab, who had also regained his feet, didn't move. Instead, he stared dumbly at what was left of Harry Callahan. Unlike Larry Mitchell, he was dead ... having stopped three bullets across the chest. A fourth had removed the top of his head, plastering the pieces onto the splintered rendering of the school building.

The principal appeared with a group of teachers and stopped as they took in the sight of the carnage; no-one moved.

Suddenly, the barrier broke, and Jim succumbed to his emotions. With tears streaming down his cheeks, Jim shouted, 'What the f**k's wrong with you people? Somebody get a f**ken ambulance!' He fell to his knees beside Larry and felt for a pulse; faint, but it was there. 'He's still alive!' Jim said, his voice returned to a dry whisper.

Tony, who stood beside Fab, forced his eyes away from the horrible sight and regarded the front of the school. Glass lay everywhere, mainly just outside the admin office, but there were shards near where the teachers stood. Then he remembered the breezeway. The crunch of glass broke the spell and shock and he realised that behind the teachers were a crowd of students all competing for a better view. Suddenly, he was aware of his hatred for those students trying to gawk at the dead body of his friend.

The ranks of onlookers suddenly burst as a girl fought a way through. One of the teachers, who had managed to overcome her shock and was trying to push the crowd back and threatening to punish every one of them if they didn't leave, tried to stop the girl.

'Get your f**ken hands off me!' Christine Porter snarled and pushed past the teacher, who intended to write her up and have her suspended. Chris surveyed the scene for only a moment, trying to identify the still figures. Then she saw Jim, crouching next to and holding Larry's wrist. 'Jim!' she cried and rushed to him. Chris was so glad that he was alright. She felt guilty for feeling that way, but she didn't care.

He glanced up at her, dumbly. A tear sparkled in the corner of his eyes, tickling it. He stood, shakily, wrapped his arms around her and sobbed like a small child, burying his face in her shoulder.

AUGUST 11. 2:55 PM, WESTERN AUSTRALIA TIME

Hammer knocked and entered O'Reilly's office. He reached the desk in four short steps and handed the glass of water he carried to Jim.

The boy popped two aspirins into his mouth and washed them down. Across the desk, O'Reilly read Jim's handwritten statement, handed it back, and proffered a pen. Jim signed it, hoping that he would be able to go home and lie down or be sick. He wasn't sure which he felt more like doing.

It was a bad day. A day, he promised himself, he'd never forget … as long as Paul Edmonds and The Christian lived! One friend dead, the other seriously wounded, and another in a severe state of shock. Poor Fab! Seeing the remains of Harry's head splattered over a metre radius had been too much for him. Actually, Jim reflected, it hadn't exactly been calming for himself! The problem was that Fab had still not gotten over the death of his dad and being so close to death again had made him shut down. All this passed through his mind in the few seconds it took him to make up and scribble his new signature and return the statement to the detective. 'What happens now?' Jim asked, his voice still hoarse from what had occurred at school.

'The usual thing,' O'Reilly replied non-committally, 'we'll make inquiries and come up with nothing concrete. The car will probably be stolen and when – or if – it's found, it'll be wiped clean and the clues never to be seen ever again. I'm sorry if it sounds cold, but I'm giving you a clear and realistic idea of what we're faced with and what we're going to accomplish.'

Jim forced a thin smile. 'You didn't have to say that.' He stood up and regarded O'Reilly for a moment. 'Can I go home, now?'

O'Reilly nodded. 'By all means. Julie's waiting for you downstairs.' As the boy turned to go, the detective stopped him. 'I'm deeply sorry about your friends, James.'

'Ç'est la guerre,' Jim muttered with a shrug and walked out of the office, closing the door. His hand clasped the door handle tight. 'Oui[26], Monsieur[27] Edmonds, ç'est la guerre!'

Chapter Fourteen
The Pavement Artists

AUGUST 12. 9:15 AM, WESTERN AUSTRALIA TIME

The 'tweeting' of the digital alarm clock woke him. Feeling the familiar pins and needles sensation of being restricted under his pillow, his hand emerged and pressed the alarm button. The chirping instrument fell silent, and his hand shot back towards the welcoming warmth of the blankets. Jim uncovered his head and stared, bleary eyed, at the green digits of the clock for a minute or two. Quarter past nine? But he had set the alarm for half past eight. The clock had been tweeting for three-quarters of an hour until it, finally, penetrated Jim's dream.

He didn't get up straight away, but lay there, his hands resting between his head and pillow thinking of yesterday's tragic events. Poor Harry. The poor bastard hardly knew what was going on. Larry was still alive ... but for how long? He's seriously injured and – let's face it – he isn't one of the strongest people in the world!

Jim frowned as he noticed the growing darkness for the first time. Peering out the window, he saw the large blanket of grey rain clouds slowly covering the sky from one horizon to the next. He retrieved his jeans, from where he had thrown them the night before, and removed the rosary beads from one of the pockets.

Sitting at his student's desk, he held the beads in his hands and began speaking to them as if they were a phone to the man they represented. 'There's something familiar about you ... but what?' He briefly regarded the clouds and smiled as an idea formed. 'You don't have a criminal record ... what if you're not a crim? What if you're a spook – or used to be a spook? Maybe you resigned or were fired from the CIA, MI6, KGB, BOSS, ASIO ...' He paused as he realised what had been bothering him the past few days since listening to the tape of the suspected Christian's voice had suddenly come to light. 'Of course! BOSS! South Africa's Bureau of State Security. That's what had been familiar about the Christian ... he was a South African!' An Afrikaner, actually. The Free State accent was faint on those tapes – but nonetheless, it was there ... bleeding through certain inflections! His attempt to disguise his voice only worked for those not familiar with the Afrikaans accent! Jim rose from the seat. 'If the Christian's an ex-spook – and a South African spook, at that – it shouldn't be too difficult to identify him.' With a snap of his fingers, Jim decided to take a trip to ASIO regional headquarters and check out their records. He stripped off and walked, naked, to the shower.

Despite the late hour, it was still quite chilly, and Jim spent the next twenty minutes under a hot shower. Since the bathroom mirror was all misted up, he combed his hair in his room. He was dressed totally in brown, including a polo-neck jumper.

Removing the top drawer of his student desk, he produced a small identification card – with a colour photograph – from where it was taped at the underside of the drawer. Pocketing it, he returned the drawer to its proper place and left the room.

Shaka was lying in the family room near the kerosene heater, which was off and cold, two cats were cuddled up close to him. He opened his eyes and stared, lazily, at his master as Jim checked the sliding door. 'Watch the house, Shaka,' he said, and headed for the front door, marvelling at the optimistic behaviour of pets. Shaka was hoping he would turn the heater on.

Jim reached the bus stop before the green and white MTT bus. He selected a seat halfway down, on the driver's side and glanced around casually. There were four people on board, apart from him and the driver. A heavily made-up teenage girl in very tight jeans sat upfront, an octogenarian – who was knitting – was just in front of Jim, and a couple of tough-looking characters lounging across the back seat.

He sat back comfortably and imagined what Fab and the other Gorgons were doing. If yesterday hadn't occurred, they would be sitting for their chemistry exam today. But now, they were exempted from further exams and would be sitting special ones early in the third term. All this had been arranged by Mark.

He had been given a good talking to last night. Julie had urged him to drop the matter and leave it all to the police. But Jim had assured her that he and the Gorgon Five were already out of it. Evidently, the mobsters thought differently … that wasn't his fault. Of course, if he hadn't pursued the case those two and Callobar would still be alive now. He reminded Julie that Larry wasn't dead … yet. Well, saying that wouldn't bring any of them back! Maybe not, but in the future leave police work to the police! When Mark had gotten home and, after a conference with his wife, he had ordered Jim - as regional director of ASIO, WA - off this drug case.

The bus turned onto Fitzgerald Street and headed south, towards the Perth CBD. Crossing Roe Street, it entered the private access to the bus terminal on the corner of Wellington and William Streets, next to the Horseshoe Bridge. Jim walked along William Street crossing both Murray and Hay streets and finally turned west on St. Georges Terrace. Passing several minor streets, he finally entered a five-storey, red-brick building bearing an unobtrusive name in the shadow of the Barracks Arch.

Peterson's office was on the third floor and a few doors away from the elevator. Jim's guardian was sitting behind a deeply stained oak desk, a set of filing cabinets flanked him on either side - one set crowned with a small potted cactus. Three paintings decorated the walls: an imitation Rembrandt hung behind him; a copy of the Mona Lisa was above the cactus. The third painting looked more like a photograph rather than a painting, depicting the panorama of Perth as seen from Kings Park near the wishing well. Peterson looked up from the memoranda he was reading as Jim entered.

Jim smiled as he shut the door. 'I can see by the expression on your face that reading doesn't agree with you,' he remarked and pulled up a chair for himself.

'No-one ever warned me that there would be so much paperwork to go through as regional director,' Peterson commented and placed the paper in his OUT tray for his secretary to collect and got up, coming around his desk. 'Now, what do you want?' He sounded suspicious but pulled up a chair and sat beside Jim.

'I just had a brainwave,' Jim explained. 'The police are searching for the Christian among the police records of Interpol.'

Peterson's eyes narrowed. 'You were ordered off this police case.'

'I know,' Jim replied. 'But as a law-abiding citizen of this country, it is my duty to volunteer all information concerning a case of interest. That is unless you're prepared to pass over official ASIO files over to the West Australian Police Force.'

Peterson looked bewildered. 'What are you talking about?'

'Didn't I say?' Jim asked innocently. 'I've identified the Christian's true ethnicity. He's a South African. Not only that … he's also either an active, or rogue, intelligence operative!'

Peterson remained quiet as he regarded the teenager. The Christian an intelligence operative? Hardly likely, he thought, but not impossible. Why would an intelligence organisation send an operative to act as a hitman? A thought dawned in his administrative mind. There had been a CIA operation in the early 1970s. A CIA operative went rogue in Europe and, eventually, it was discovered that he had been suffering from amnesia and the only identity his mind had been clinging to was that which had been created for him and their operation. His eyes focused on Jim. 'Intelligence operatives do not go around killing people for mobsters!'

'Well, what if he was fired … or resigned?' Jim persisted. 'He'd still have to live … and with the training he's received, a job like that would be a cinch. After all, some combat veterans do become mercenaries!'

Peterson's eyebrows shot up in surprise. That was the first – and most probably, the last – time he would ever hear Jim use the word 'cinch'. 'So, what you want to do is check what records we have,' Peterson mused aloud. Jim nodded. Bingo! 'Well, the answer's no. Last night you forced me to order you to desist—'

Jim sat forward. 'I said I would no longer take an active part in the case. Your order repeated that fact! I am not taking active participation, I'll leave it all to the police, as per your orders ... Sir! All I want to do is sift through our files that are not accessible to the police. I won't be endangering anybody's life ... and what I learn – if anything – will be passed on to them.'

The regional director of the Western Australian Division of ASIO regarded the boy, his ward, not sure whether he should believe him or not. Peterson had a nagging feeling that he should not. What Jim was saying was convincing, flimsy, but convincing, nonetheless. Like any other operative, Jim would obey orders, Peterson knew that already, was sure of that. But just in case ... 'All right, Jim, you've sold me on the idea. But whatever you discover is handed straight to me and I'll pass it on to Sam, that's an order. Mind you, anything that is not a national secret and in no way endangers the security of this nation will be up to my discretion to pass on to the Western Australian Police Force.' He smiled. Jim was a good kid, really. Mixed up, but then who wouldn't be after going through what he had? No, Peterson told himself, Jim's alright. That training had done the world of good; he had never regretted organising it for him. Unfortunately, he now wanted to be given assignments like any other operative. Not at sixteen years of age, mate ... sorry. Besides, there was more training, still to be done, before being released into the field. 'We put in computers, Jim, to save space and time. All our records and files are stored in the main computer bank in Canberra. We're trialling a system developed by the Americans during the Vietnam War. The system allows a computer to talk to another one, the signal bouncing off a satellite. You'll have the information you ask for, at your fingertips in seconds, despite the four-thousand-kilometre distance between us and Canberra. So, the Records Room is now full of terminals. When using it, all you do is feed in your serial number ... you do know it, don't you?'

Jim nodded.

'It'll respond after it's checked out the ID and the files are open to you ... but only the ones you are cleared to view.'

'Okay, thanks,' Jim replied, rising, and turning to go.

'Jim.'

The teenager stopped at the closed door. 'Yeah?'

'The equipment is expensive ... don't break it.' A grin appeared on Peterson's face.

Jim scowled and left the office, slamming the door to sound his reply to Peterson's comment.

RECORDS was on the fifth floor and took up about half of that area. Along one wall was a line of visual display units, one in each cubicle, of which three were occupied. The others, filling the large room, were new and still inoperative. Those against the wall must be the test equipment. Jim chose a cubicle on the far end, away from the other personnel, and regarded the VDU. On the screen was written, in bright green script against a black background:

HI, I AM FRED

A thin smile appeared on Jim's face as he typed:

BIG DEAL

A line of question marks appeared underneath Jim's response, then:

INSUFFICIENT DATA

Jim burst out laughing. Suddenly, he remembered where he was and forced himself to stop, then looked around, sheepishly. No-one had heard, or cared … With a shrug, he typed in:

680

In a blink of an eye Jim's dossier appeared. Curious, he read it.

(EF2/1AS5/1)

NAME	**SASTON, JAMES ANDREW**
CODE	**AQUARIUS.**
SERIAL NUMBER	**680.**
STATUS	**NU.**
COVER	**HIGH SCHOOL STUDENT.**
NATIONALITY	**AUSTRALIAN (CAUCASIAN).**
BORN	**21-01-1962.**
EYES	**BROWN.**
HAIR	**BLACK.**
HEIGHT	**165.10CM (5'5").**
WEIGHT	**63.56KG (139.83LB).**
SCARS	**NA**
EXPERIENCE	**BORN IN THE EPWORTH FREEMASONS HOSPITAL, EAST MELBOURNE, VICTORIA, COMMONWEALTH OF AUSTRALIA, AND COMPLETED PRIMARY EDUCATION IN THE REPUBLIC OF SOUTH AFRICA, AND IS CURRENTLY ATTENDING**

**TANNEN HEIGHTS SENIOR HIGH
SCHOOL, TANNEN HEIGHTS,
WESTERN AUSTRALIA. FOLLOWING
THE DISPLACEMENT (22-05-
1975) OF HIS FATHER, JOHN
GREGORY SASTON, WAS PLACED
IN THE CUSTODY (25-05-1975) OF
MARK ANTHONY PETERSON
(EF2/AS5/8), WHO MADE
THE DECISION THAT SUBJECT WAS TO
BE TRAINED AS AN OPERATIVE, UPON
THE ADVICE OF THE DEPARTMENT'S
PSYCHIATRIC DEPARTMENT.
TRAINING PROVED BENEFICIAL
AS THE RIGORS OF TRAINING HAD
MINIMISED THE EFFECTS OF THE
POST-TRAUMATIC STRESS OF LOSING
HIS LAST SURVIVING PARENT. UPON
COMPLETION, SUBJECT RESUMED
HIS NORMAL TEENAGE LIFE.**

Jim removed the dossier from the screen and typed in:

ESPIONAGE FILE ELEVEN

Another blink and the menu appeared. Jim studied the list.

1. **BOSS: BUREAU OF STATE SECURITY**
2. **SPECIAL BRANCH**

He chose the first one, having decided that he would leave the second one for last. Blink and another list appeared. Jim scrolled down and chose:

PERSONNEL
Another menu appeared and he chose the second listing:

INACTIVE
This section, once it opened fully, consisted of some three hundred-odd operatives who had either died, retired, were gaoled, dismissed, or had resigned. With a sigh, Jim began the arduous task of searching through each dossier until he found what he believed to be in the files. An hour – and a hundred and five dossiers – later, Jim took a break, stretching while combatting the headache which had crept into his forehead. He regarded the notepad, upon which he had hastily scribbled two names.

It would be interesting to find out where these two were today, and what they are up to. Jim glanced at his watch; it was 12:30. No wonder he felt hungry. But he had no time for eating, he had to finish with these dossiers. Completing another hundred, Jim paused once again and regarded the notepad. At least the list was growing; there was now a total of seven names on it.

He held back on the next dossier. It belonged to Marty Torino. 'Well, what do you know,' Jim murmured to himself. He knew that Marty was a South African ex-pat; after all, he spoke with a strong Afrikaans accent. But what was surprising was that Marty was once an operative of BOSS. Jim wondered if Mark knew. Curious, he decided to give Marty's dossier the once over.

(EF11/1RSAS79/1) (RESIGNED)

NAME	**TORINO, MARTINO ALPHONSE**
CODE	**NA**
SERIAL NUMBER	46211100.
STATUS	**BETA.**

COVER	OWNER OF *TORINO LIBRARIES* (SPECIALISING IN RELIGIOUS BOOKS).
NATIONALITY	SOUTH AFRICAN (CAUCASIAN).
BORN	01-05-1948.
EYES	BLUE.
HAIR	BLACK.
HEIGHT	195.58CM (6'5").
WEIGHT	108.51KG (238.72LB).
SCARS	NA
EXPERIENCE	BORN AND RAISED IN BLOEMFONTEIN, ORANGE FREE STATE, UNION OF SOUTH AFRICA, AND STARTED NATIONAL SERVICE (03-09-1966) IN THE SOUTH AFRICAN DEFENCE FORCE, SERVING ON THE ANGOLAN- SOUTH WEST AFRICAN BORDER. DUE TO ACQUIRED ADVANCED SKILLS IN SILENT KILLING, SUBJECT WAS RECRUITED (05-12-1968) BY MILITARY INTELLIGENCE, LATER (13-03-1970) TO THE BUREAU OF STATE SECURITY. SERVED EFFICIENTLY UNTIL THE DEATH (10-11-1974) OF HIS BROTHER AND PARTNER, GUILIO VITTORIO TORINO (PENDING), WHOM HE HAD RECRUITED. SUBMITTED HIS RESIGNATION AND LEFT THE COUNTRY.

QUALIFICATIONS	**EXPERT DRIVER AND ADEPT IN CRYPTOGRAPHY. TRAINED IN THE HANDLING OF EXPLOSIVES AND MASTER OF DISGUISE. ELECTRONICS EXPERT AND MARKSMAN WITH THE PREFERENCE OF USING A SMITH & WESSON M42. DEXTEROUS LOCKPICK AND CRACKSMAN. SKILLED INTERROGATOR.**
NOTE	**IN ALL OPERATIONS UNDERTAKEN BY THE SUBJECT, EACH WET OPERATION CARRIED OUT HAD A RELIGIOUS EMBLEM LEFT BEHIND (EG. SMALL CRUCIFIX, ROSARY BEADS, PENDANTS OF CATHOLIC SAINTS, ETC.), EARNING HIM THE SOBRIQUET: *THE CHRISTIAN*. DUE TO RESIGNATION, FILE ON MARTINO TORINO HAS BEEN CLOSED.**

Jim stared at the **NOTE** section, dumbly. No! That wasn't possible! Marty Torino? No. He knew Marty, they had always been friends ... well, acquaintances, at the very least. Jim pressed the 'clear' button dejectedly. Torino's dossier vanished from the screen only to be replaced by a solitary, almost pathetic:

GOOD-BYE
Then:

HI, I AM FRED

Jim sat there and thought over what he had just learnt. There had been a few things in the dossier that Jim had positively not known about Torino, such as being a former BOSS assassin. This is crazy! Marty had taught him some hand-to-hand combat moves and how to handle various weapons. Jim had always thought of him as more of a mentor, rather than just a friend. Why would Marty fall in with mobsters? Jim asked himself. No. No, it couldn't be. He trusted Marty ... he had told him all about his friends. About their likes, their interests, where they spent most of their school breaks ...

Torino knew about the Gorgons' Den, knew that they would all be there when that f**ken thug, in the hood ... Jim had insisted on having Torino help him and Callobar break into Slattery's warehouse, that night ... Jim stopped his train of thought and suddenly realised that this explained their welcoming committee ...

Jim rose and tore the page from the notepad, screwed it up, and headed to the door. As he passed the wastepaper basket, he lobbed the paper ball into it. Walking slowly along the corridor, he realised that he had learnt practically nothing. Okay, so Marty Torino had the nickname of 'The Christian' ... big deal! One guy at school was known as 'the Saint' but that hardly made him Simon Templar! There was no real, concrete, evidence to tie Marty in with Edmonds or Slattery ... or was there? What exactly did Jim know? The late Craig St. James was visited by an unidentified person and murdered. The unknown person had attempted to disguise his ethnicity but to no avail ... His Afrikaans accent had still bled through.

Marty Torino, on the other hand, spoke with a strong Afrikaans accent because he had grown up in the Orange Free State. No-one would ever believe that he was of Italian ancestry.

The elevator doors were open, and Jim pressed for the third floor. He knocked on Peterson's office door and entered. But Peterson was not there. It was all for the best, Jim decided. At least he wouldn't have to lie to his guardian about what he had discovered.

It was raining when Jim left the building, and since he refused to run, for fear of slipping and getting embarrassed, he walked deliberately to the bus terminal. Despite the jumper, Jim was shaking from the cold when the bus arrived twenty minutes later.

During the journey back to Tannen Heights, Jim's doubts slowly disappeared. The internal debate was just as slowly breaking down the excuses that defended Torino. By the time he had arrived at his stop, the logical accusations had nullified the illogical defences. Thinking about Harry Callahan and Larry Mitchell, and the way they had been brutally gunned down had created the hatred that he now felt for the man, whom he once regarded as a friend.

Stepping back into the rain, Jim wondered how much Torino knew about the Mafia? He knew that the Mafia – and certain races – left little calling cards on their victims-to-be. That's where Torino must have gotten his idea. Was it Robert Louis Stevenson who wrote about pirates sending each other 'black spots'? He knew that the Bushman of South West Africa sent *pangas*[28] covered in dried blood, to their intended victims. But the Mafia was different. Their 'cards' were either carefully worded phrases, a white feather, or a cross of dried blood on a page ... torn from the Bible. Jim chuckled. Highly effective.

---

[28]African bush knife, like a machete.

As Jim approached his home, he wondered if he should send Torino a similar calling card. But what? He didn't know where to get a *panga* in Perth, besides, there was no blood with which to cover it! The white feather was useless as he knew no-one with chickens. He couldn't speak Italian let alone write the blasted language and though he was not a practicing Catholic, he was reluctant to tear up a Bible. It would be rather idiotic to send Torino a black dot on a piece of paper. 'Oh, forget it,' he told himself as he fumbled for his key. 'This isn't a "B" grade film, so let's cut out the theatrics.'

Julie still wasn't home but Shaka, tail wagging, greeted his master. Jim patted the German shepherd and let him out in the backyard, remembering that he hadn't taken his dog for a walk since Paul Matthews's body had been discovered. 'After tomorrow, boy,' he promised his dog, who was lapping up water, 'we'll go for a walk.'

The ginger tabby was curled up on Jim's unmade bed. She opened her eyes momentarily, as he sauntered in, and casually returned to sleep having detected no food odour. Jim patted the cat gently and then remembered that he hadn't checked the letterbox on his way in. He was still awaiting a letter from Wally Bryant in America. It had stopped raining and Jim stepped up to the letterbox. There were a few letters in the box, but none for him. He glanced up and down the road but failed to see the postman. At first, he didn't pay much attention to the green and white station wagon, not until he noticed the tall man step out and watch him intently. Jim was horrified as he recognised the man. He was one of the thugs at the warehouse. The man raised his right hand to his mouth and began rubbing it against his lips.

AUGUST 12. 2:05 PM, WESTERN AUSTRALIA TIME

James Barton sneered as he watched the kid rush back to the house. He was still amazed at how one school punk could cause a multi-million-dollar business so much trouble. Since he and that nigger visited the warehouse, Slattery's trucks were being stopped, searched, and impounded by the pigs! None of the pigs, however, seemed to know anything about the bloodbath those two had left behind, at the warehouse. Strange that. The cargo ... lost! Thirty million dollars' worth of heroin and cocaine, not to mention the lesser drugs ... all lost! And all because of a bored kid!

He got back into the car and looked at the driver. Subconsciously, Barton scratched his right hand, a habit that resulted from orders denying him the pleasure of killing ... and to kill this little bastard, he sorely craved! Very few people ever survived his attempts on their lives, and he now regarded this kid as something of a challenge.

AUGUST 12. 2:09 PM, WESTERN AUSTRALIA TIME

Jim peered out the window, in the lounge, in time to see Barton climbing back into the car. Turning from the window, he nearly fell over Shaka, who had gotten back into the house by pushing open the flyscreen door. He beat the Alsatian to the family room and switched on the TV. An Australian police show, concerning murderous drug racketeers, kept him enthralled for the next hour.

Through the show, he couldn't help but think how further away from the truth could the makers of this show really go? In less than an hour, the police had managed to arrest four members of the gang, killed one, and saved the hostage by shooting the leader. And what made it worse was the fact that the police had not even lost one man! Whereas in real-life Australia, the mobsters can shoot up two teenage boys and the police are powerless to apprehend the criminals because the people of this country continually tie up their hands.

Glancing at his watch, as the cuckoo of the clock, above the set, announced four o'clock, he switched off the TV and made for the telephone. Fab was home, and Jim hoped, in a good enough state to answer the phone.

Fab's mother answered it, instead, in her pidgin English. 'Hallo?'

'Is Fabrizio home?' he inquired. 'It's me, Jim.'

'Jim? Jim? Aaahhhh ... Jim! Hokay.' She all but put the receiver down and Jim could hear her shuffle away. In the background, she was yelling and as he approached the phone, Fab's replying yell made Jim hold the receiver away from his ear.

'Yeah, Jim?' Fab said into the mouthpiece rather flatly.

Jim smiled; at least Fab's voice displayed his renewed inner strength. That was one thing about Fab, no matter what happened, he was always the first one to bounce back but to listen to him now, for some reason, made one doubt that. 'I just called to see how you were,' Jim replied.

'Apart from being groggy ... I'm fine.'

'Groggy?'

'Yeah,' he replied. 'After the cops brought me home yesterday, Mum shoved a couple of sleeping pills down my throat ... I only woke up half an hour ago.'

'I see,' Jim said politely. 'Listen, you remember how we planned to go to the *bio—* ... pictures, well, I thought it'd do us a lot of good if we went within the next few days.'

'You're not serious?'

'Of course, I'm serious.'

Fab hesitated. How should he put it? 'Well, I don't know, Jim. What do the others think about it?'

'I haven't talked to them, yet.'

'Well, talk to them first, then phone me back.'

'Fab, what's wrong?'

'Oh, Jim, don't you think it's a bit premature going to the pictures after ... Well, anyway, I think it's morbid!'

'Morbid? It may be,' Jim answered. 'But I think we need it. Go to a movie and escape from the world for a couple of hours. We're all tense after the happenings of the last two weeks, we need a bit of relaxation.'

'Yeah, I know, but—'

'Look,' Jim said. He was angry now. 'Sitting at home brooding isn't going to bring Harry back, man. So, are you coming or aren't you?'

Fab hesitated. No matter what Jim said it still felt wrong. What would people think? Their friend dies one day and the next day they all go to the pictures pretending nothing had happened.

'Well?' Jim persisted.

'Okay, Jim. If the others agree, I'll go. Bye.'

Jim lowered the receiver. What was wrong with him? Was it so bad to want to forget what had happened, for a few hours, at least? Hell, we are going to have to live with it for the rest of our lives. Can't we spare just a couple of hours?

He returned to the lounge and glanced out the window, but the pavement artists were nowhere to be found. Opening the front door and ordering Shaka to stay seated, Jim went to inspect the letterbox once more. This time he glanced up and down the street in search of Edmonds's men. The station wagon was parked a few houses away on the opposite side of the road, having made a U-turn.

Shaka never moved from where he sat, obeying Jim's orders to the letter. And since his master had not told him to move, he remained seated, harassing Jim's efforts to close the door. 'Would it be too much to ask if you moved?'

With a wag of his tail, the Alsatian walked in.

Jim returned to the phone and dialled Andrew's number.

Chapter Fifteen
The Liquidator, Liquidated

AUGUST 13. 12:27 PM, WESTERN AUSTRALIA TIME

The clouds crept up on a sleeping Perth after a clear and quiet evening; the rain started, drizzling at first and, gradually, it fell faster, harder, and louder. Then suddenly it stopped. The wind, the clouds' ally, continuously moving, brought another cloud bursting with rain, and it was to this storm that the city awoke.

It was a dismal day. Fitting atmosphere for a dismal job, Jim reflected, peering out the lounge window. All the sky he could see was dark grey, instead of its comforting blue. Directly opposite was the green and white station wagon containing the two Edmonds cronies. From Mark's quadrophonic hi-fi came an ABBA song. Jim returned to the family room and flopped into a bean bag, listening to the song. He liked their song, 'Waterloo'; it was an inspiring piece of music. 'Fernando' was another. Jim was alone in the house, save for his trusted Shaka and the cats; Julie was at the veterinary hospital where she worked.

The cuckoo clock announced half-past twelve and Jim realised he wasn't hungry. Nerves, he told himself ... And why should he not have them? Good God! He was going to go out and kill a man! Yeah, he had killed that night watchman and those mobsters that night, but that was different. It wasn't on a one-to-one basis as Torino's execution would be. Jim preferred to call it an execution than just killing ... for the sake of his conscience.

Just him and me ... no-one else. After today, this sugar case was closed as far as he was concerned. Jim no longer wanted to hear about sugar and drugs and 'Cats' and 'Christians' and sporting gear and ... and ... The *shwoop shwoop*, from the hi-fi, told him that the record was finished. Instead of playing another LP, he switched it off.

Placing the switchblade in his black leather jacket, Jim locked the sliding door and, when the rain had stopped, hopped over the fence into the yard behind the Petersons' property. Nobody was in the backyard. The lady of the house was probably watching the soapies on TV, he mused, and turned onto the street, heading for the bus stop. Jim reached it on time to catch the bus and avoid the rain. As he found a seat down the back, he tried to settle the conflict within him.

Why was he going to Marty's flat? Did he really intend to go through with the course of action that he had decided upon and kill him? Murder him in cold blood? Premeditated homicide? Yes! For f**k's sake, yes! Jim decided. He had every intention of killing Marty Torino! But why? Because! Because? Because what?

'Just because!'

Jim looked around sheepishly at the people staring at him. He gave a weak smile and sat low in the seat and crossed his arms. Because, he told himself. The Christian had an Afrikaans accent. Marty was raised in the Orange Free State and has an Afrikaans accent. Marty had worked for BOSS and was known as 'The Christian'. The Christian left little calling cards with his victims; Torino's dossier stated that he did the same. For BOSS, Torino was a professional assassin. So is The Christian! Now Marty and The Christian were both in the country ... at the same time! It couldn't be coincidental! Maybe so, but that reasoning is only circumstantial. I know that! Do you think I haven't already thought of that? I've got to find out if he is The Christian I'm looking for, for my friends' sake! Only their sake? No! Not just for their sake ... but also for my own sake and to renew my trust in people! He betrayed me ... and purposefully killed Callobar ... and Harry! If he is – and I believe he is – The Christian, I am going to kill him! Images of Callobar and Harry Callahan dominated his thoughts for the remainder of the trip to the central business district of the state capital.

Torino's apartment was in Highgate, and from the bus terminal, Jim walked to Barrack Street. On the corner of Murray and Barrack streets, he stopped and gazed east along Murray Street. A thought had crept into his troubled deliberations and the kernel of an idea formed. He crossed Murray Street, Passing the Cinecentre on his right and walked leisurely down towards Royal Perth Hospital. At Pier Street, he passed Miss Maud's Swedish Restaurant and the Perth Fire Station. Murray Street, at the hospital, formed a round-about with the Roman Catholic Cathedral, St. Mary's, in the centre. Jim crossed the road and entered the cathedral. Five minutes later, after making a purchase, he left St. Mary's Cathedral and retraced his steps.

Once back at Barrack Street, he caught another bus. As this one headed north along Beaufort Street, past the Family and Children's Courts and the WA Museum, Jim's thoughts changed from what he had intended to do to what he had found out, yesterday. Jim was still shaken by Fab's curt attitude as much as

Andrew and Tony were. Both had called Fab, and both had been coldly brushed off. But they had decided to go to the pictures with him, despite the way he was treating everyone. There had been no answer at Mike's or Jack's, they could've been out of town. Tet would be going as well as Danny. Jim had asked Chris, and after much deliberation, she agreed to go. Later, that evening he had phoned, Fab relented and after being told the others' decisions, Fab agreed to go as well.

Jim suddenly realised that his stop was coming up and pressed the bell strip. He got off just before Vincent Street and crossed Beaufort Street. Jim headed up towards Harold Street, and along to the Catholic school, on the corner of Harold and Stirling Streets. Looking south, from that corner, Jim could see the six top floors of the Great Lakes Apartments. The Great Lakes was a ten-storey apartment building situated on Stirling Street, one of the quieter streets of Highgate.

Jim turned down Stirling Street, heading towards this white building. On reaching the lavish entrance to the place, Jim glanced around the carpark and spotted Marty's Fiat in the shade of a carport. The lift was on the ground, he entered and pressed the button for Marty's floor. A few moments later, the doors opened on a quiet, carpeted, corridor.

He approached apartment 1005, Torino's, and Jim admitted to himself that he felt a twinge of excitement bordering on fear, and this feeling was slowly growing, becoming more difficult to subdue. Again, his conscience questioned his motives, and he wished it were a cricket and that he could crush it beneath the heel of his shoe! He removed a picklock, but before inserting it, he found that his hand was shaking. The other grasped the switchblade – his only weapon – tightly. Jim willed his hand to stop shaking and it, eventually, obeyed. The bolt clicked back and slowly, oh so slowly, he turned the door handle.

'Come in, Jim,' a thickly accented voice said, invitingly. 'I've been expecting you.'

Jim scowled and closed the door behind him. He glanced around but failed to discover the whereabouts of the owner of the voice.

'Really, Jim, you must be slipping, man. It took you three days to discover my alias.'

'So, you don't deny it?' Jim inquired sadly.

'Deny it? What *blêrrie* reason would I have to deny it, man? Denials are for *blêrrie* detective books!'

'Do you mind making an appearance, Marty? I feel like a character from *The Invisible Man*.'

There was a chuckle and Marty Torino's two-metre-tall frame emerged, warily, from the bedroom on Jim's right. Jim regarded him coolly, pretending not to notice the automatic that the South African held.

Torino's green eyes drilled into the teenager. With a wave of the gun, he indicated to Jim to move to the centre of the room. 'Now, if I'm not mistaken,' he said in Afrikaans, 'you've come here to kill me. So, I will have to demand that you empty your pockets.'

Jim didn't move.

'*Asseblief*[29]!'

Damn, Jim swore. After all that training and he had to go and blunder straight into an ambush! Now he was left with no choice but to hand over his only weapon. There must be a better way to ...

---

[29]Please (Afrikaans).

'I'm getting tired, *jong*[30]. Throw what you've got towards the balcony. I will not be asking again! The first bullet will be non-lethal, but it will hurt like a *kaffir*.'

Jim glared at the ex-BOSS operative. But, after a while, decided to comply with the bastard's demands; there would be plenty of time later to dispose of *Meneer*[31] Marty Torino. Still, the present situation was unforgivable ... because of his eagerness to complete this task, and driven by his impetuous bloodlust, he now, unwillingly, had to wait and rely upon an alternative plan ... which, at this precise moment, did not exist!

He emptied his jeans' pockets first, leaving his wallet and loose change on the coffee table. From the jacket, came his set of keys and the switchblade. He threw the switchblade over the couch towards the balcony. It bounced on the carpet, but stopped short of the balcony and lay still.

Torino regarded it with the utmost curiosity then returned his eyes to the teenager. Jim stood quietly, giving Torino a defiant stare.

'Is that it?' he demanded in disbelief. Jim nodded. Torino's top lip curled in his arrogance. 'That's about right. The same old over-confident Jim Saston.' He moved towards the exit to the balcony and picked up the black-handled weapon. 'Did you honestly believe that you could take me down with this little thing? I'm insulted, man! You, above all people – I believed – would have had enough foresight to think that it would take more than a simple knife ...' He stared at Jim, intently, then studied the switchblade. Keeping Jim covered, Torino stepped out onto the balcony and rested against the railing.

---

[30] Young (Afrikaans).

[31] Mister (Afrikaans).

A flock of turtledoves were settled on the railing of an adjoining balcony. Torino smiled wickedly, aimed, and pressed to release the blade. The piece of metal shot from the handle and passed right through the neck of an unsuspecting dove, decapitating it. The startled doves abandoned their resting place and flew away in panic. Pressing the release button a few more times, Torino found it harmless and threw it back into the apartment.

Jim watched it fall onto the coffee table.

'That's a *lekker* toy, man!' Torino announced. 'Where'd you get it?'

'I made it,' Jim croaked. Torino's eyebrows shot up. 'Why, Marty?'

'"Why" what?'

'Why fall in with a bunch of mobsters – it couldn't be for the money ...'

'*Nie*[32], not for the money. At least, not all the reasons.'

'Then why?'

'Because I like the job I do, man.'

'You mean killing?'

'*Ja*, I mean killing! Let's just say it's an aphrodisiac, okay, man? I found, during my time in the SADF, that I had a knack, a talent for killing. You know what I mean, man. After your first kill, it is so much easier, and it gives you such a rush. It's *lekker*, man!'

Jim glared at him. 'You call killing people *lekker*? You're as much a hairy-back as the Afrikaners, you worthless *scaapa*! You're sick, Torino!'

'Am I ... or are you?' He was enjoying the confrontation. It had been a long time coming.

---

[32]No (Afrikaans).

'You bastard!' Jim spat in Afrikaans. 'A proper white *kaffir*!' He stopped, for a moment, and contemplated Torino's comment. 'How can I be sick? I'm not the *blêrrie* sadist who nails people to walls – actually violating a religious symbol! Only a truly sick mind would do something like that!'

Torino shrugged. 'I had to get you here somehow.'

Jim frowned. 'Why?'

'Because you're a Saston, man! To kill you!' It was Torino's turn to spit out words. He did it with undisguised venom.

'To kill me ... Why?'

'You saw my file at headquarters – not the ASIO one, but BOSS.' He waited for confirmation, but none came from Jim. 'Your father worked in South Africa. What was he doing?'

Jim sat on the sofa. 'Okay, let's play this game,' he said. 'My dad was working at the Australian Embassy in Pretoria.'

'That's *kaffir*'s *kak*, man, and you know it!' Torino exploded, taking a step closer. 'He was operating under the codename "Bluebird". He was spying for your government and this country of convicts and prostitutes!'

Jim sat forward. 'That may be so, but—'

'At BOSS,' Torino interrupted Jim, 'we didn't know who Bluebird's identity was for a long time. But through a stroke of good luck, my partner stumbled across his identity. Your father killed my partner. *Ja*, killed my partner ... my brother!' He regarded the teenager intently; disgust was evident in his eyes. 'By the time we discovered that your dad and you had returned to Australia. When I had the money, I resigned from BOSS – unofficially, of course – and came here, to this benighted country. I went through the farce of changing my nationality and joined ASIO. That's when I learnt that your dad was dead.'

'So, you're a double agent, then?'

A thin smile appeared on the South African's face. '*Ja*, I'm a double agent. I've been spying on this hypocrite country for *Die Vaderland*[33]. I've only got one unfinished job to do and then I can return to where I belong.'

'What job is that?' Jim asked, he had slowly brought his hands under his jacket and behind his back, momentarily, long enough to withdraw a blade from his pouch of spare blades. He knew what was coming and glanced at the switchblade, committing its position to memory.

'You see, man, I'm still an Italian, although I sound like an Afrikaner, and we live by a code of vendetta.' Jim already knew this, having read up about the methods employed by the Mafia during his training. Therefore, he only listened with half his mind while the other half devised a plan for arming the switchblade and killing the enemy before Torino could fire his gun. 'Your father killed my brother and now, I'm going to kill you!' From his trousers' pocket, Torino produced a silencer and slowly, but deliberately, fastened it to the automatic. Stepping just inside the apartment, he raised the gun. '*Tot siens*, Jim Saston!' Torino squeezed the trigger.

You waited too long, you fool! Jim dived onto the floor, between the sofa and the coffee table, narrowly missing the bullet that embedded itself into the sofa. He made a grab for the switchblade. Frantically, he shoved the blade home and leapt up.

Torino had taken a few more steps towards the sofa, watching warily for any sign of the teenager. He could have shot, blindly, through the wood of the table ... but where was the fun in

---

[33]The Fatherland (Afrikaans).

that? With Jim's sudden appearance, he raised the automatic; however, before he could squeeze the trigger, Jim had pressed the switchblade's release.

The blade shot across the distance and hit Torino low in the forehead. The force of the impact sent him staggering back out onto the balcony and the railing. His body hit the railing and tumbled over.

Jim rushed forward, loading another blade into the switchblade, and saw that Torino's hand had stopped his fall by latching onto the railing. Jim stared fascinated while the fingers slowly relaxed their hold upon the railing. As each nerve impulse ceased, and the fingers died, they loosened the grip on the railing. Torino's lifeless body plummeted down the ten stories to the carpark below, transforming Torino's remains into a large red stain on the bitumen.

Jim walked out onto the balcony and looked down at the mess that once was Marty Torino, alias 'The Christian'. '*Tot siens, wit*[34] *kaffir!*' he spat out, devoid of all emotion, and pocketed his switchblade. Jim returned inside and gathered up his belongings, replacing them in his pockets. Then he remembered what he had purchased at the cathedral. Jim removed the white paper bag and, from it, took out a set of rosary beads. He placed them on the coffee table and turned to go, then stopped. No! Fingerprints! Get rid of the fingerprints. With one of Torino's handkerchiefs, Jim wiped all the surfaces that he remembered touching. The rosary beads were the last items that he wiped down. Once he had closed the apartment door, he wiped the handle and headed for the stairs.

---

[34]White (Afrikaans).

By the time Jim reached the ground, via the stairs, quite a large crowd had already gathered around the grisly sight. He stopped in the foyer, momentarily, and looked at the rear entrance, leading towards the pool. Jim slipped out that way and circled the pool and, after assuring himself that no-one was watching, climbed the fence into the backyard of the house/shop combination and headed towards a side gate and out onto Beaufort Street. He closed the gate behind him and began to walk towards the Perth city centre. His hands began to shake, and he slipped them into his jeans' pockets.

The green and white station wagon was parked directly opposite the Petersons' house and its two occupants were taken aback when they noticed their target approaching from the bus stop. They exchanged looks and received a pleasant wave of the hand from the teenager.

Shaka met his master at the front door and followed him into the bedroom and licked him, excitedly. Jim wiped his face and glared at the dog who moved back a few paces and sat obediently. 'Do you mind? I want to sleep.' And that is what he did; he slept the sleep of the innocent.

AUGUST 13. 6:05 PM, WESTERN AUSTRALIA TIME

Chris was waiting for Jim that evening. He had already given Shaka his food and was now in the cat shed with the cats. She smiled as she heard them meowing anxiously lest they get no food. When they eventually stopped, she knew that Jim's chore was finished.

Jim walked out and, without looking at her, said, 'Hello, Chris.'

'How did you know I was here?' she bridled. Her surprise had been spoiled.

'Because,' he said, stepping up onto the small stack of bricks and bringing his face closer to hers, 'girls have a larger chest and lungs, so it stands to reason that they breathe louder than guys.'

'Oh yeah,' she replied sarcastically, 'I so believe that one!'

Jim looked into her bright blue eyes. 'You do?' he asked in feigned surprise. 'My lying must be getting better.'

Their lips came together in a light simple kiss and, as they drew apart, Chris asked, 'How was your day?'

Jim pictured the burst mess that had been Marty Torino and raised his eyebrows. 'Enlightening,' he replied. 'I went hunting vermin.'

Chris looked puzzled. 'What's that supposed to mean? Were you hunting rats, foxes, or rabbits? What kind of vermin?' she pestered him. 'You could have asked Mum to remove them. They just come to her, and she takes them elsewhere ... depending on the kind of vermin that they are.'

'Really? Do they just come to your mum? No, never mind ... forget it. You haven't forgotten that we're going to the *bioscope* tomorrow?'

The teenage girl sighed, shaking her head slightly. 'Jim, the word is "pictures", "movies", or even "cinemas", not *bio*—whatever you said.'

'I don't like calling it the "pictures",' Jim admitted, 'it sounds like we're going to the art gallery.'

'Well, it's better than what you call it. That sounds like a science lecture.' She shuddered at the thought. It was the August holidays, two free weeks of no science, no maths, or anything else. 'What time are we leaving?'

'I checked the papers, and the session starts at eleven, so we'll leave about half-past nine. You can come round here at about eight.'

'What time will Fab, and the others, turn up?' she asked suspiciously.

'Half-past nine,' he replied matter-of-factly.

She eyed him for a moment, a mischievous smile appearing on her pretty face. 'What are you planning?'

'Me?' Jim asked, giving a pained expression. 'Nothing. What makes you think I'm planning something? I just thought that, since we are going to be with the rest of the guys at the … pictures … we should have some time to ourselves before they turn up. That's all.'

Chris arched her right eyebrow. 'I could spend some extra time getting ready. Or I could get to yours at eight-ish and you could help me with my nails or makeup.'

Jim looked at her. 'Makeup? Nails? We're just going to sit in the dark and watch a film. Why all the fuss?'

AUGUST 13. 6:20 PM, WESTERN AUSTRALIA TIME

James Barton grabbed the CB mike. 'Yeah?' he said in a flat, bored voice, making no attempt to disguise his annoyance.

'The Man wants you here – pronto!'

'Okay,' he said, a little puzzled, 'On our way.' He threw the mike onto the dash. 'Let's go,' he told the driver. As the driver guided the station wagon from the kerb, Barton wondered as to the reason for their being called back. Edmonds rarely called for him. Something more important must have come up. Maybe, big boss Slattery had been breathing down his neck. After all, didn't they lose something like thirty million dollars' worth of product? That is enough to make Slattery do a rain dance! The end of his mouth curled at the thought of Slattery dressed as a Red Indian – complete with warpaint and loincloth – doing a classical rain dance. They could use the rain, he quipped to himself silently. Whatever happened, it must've been serious. Billing sounded nervous – and he hardly ever did. Maybe that bastard kid did something! God knows how long he had been gone. Barton's pride was still seething at receiving that kid's wave.

Twenty minutes later, the driver turned the car onto Stirling Highway and headed southwest towards Peppermint Grove. The station wagon halted behind Simos's car, and the two men marched to the front door.

Arthur Billing, tall, bald, and Australian, opened it in answer to Barton's authoritative knock. 'Good, you're here,' Billing said in a low voice. 'All hell's blown up and he's been waiting for you … and getting madder every minute!'

'What happened?' Barton asked as he stepped into the house.

'What happened? Is that what you want to know? The Christian's dead!' Edmonds bellowed as he approached the front door, a neat scotch in his hand. 'While you and Morris have been doing f**king knows what, that little bastard, you are supposed to be watching, went and killed The Christian!' Edmonds's face was very red.

Barton's mouth fell open. So that's where he had been, the little … 'You're kidding—'

'Kidding! Kidding? Is that all you have to say?' Edmonds bellowed. 'Where were you two, anyway?'

'We were outside that kid's house—'

'Doing what? Sleeping!'

'He must've sneaked out the back, 'cause he walked home from the bus stop at about four o'clock. We would've followed him if he had walked out the front door.'

Edmonds turned to look at Simos, who had joined the group in the foyer. 'It makes you wonder how we got this far, without police interference, with such incompetence. That kid is dangerous! That's why he had to be watched. Now he's gone too far!' Edmonds stepped up to Barton. 'If you can possibly manage it, I want him stopped … soon … permanently!'

Barton gritted his teeth and glared at his boss but refrained from saying anything. At all costs, he needed this job. Just a few thousand bucks more and Barton's five-year-old daughter, stateside, could continue her therapy and sessions in dialysis.

Simos gave a thin smile and raised his own scotch and soda to his thin lips, while Edmonds continued.

'Barton, you're a good man,' the chief mobster said. 'You've done a lot of work for me and because of your kid, I'm going to give you another chance. I just hope you – and him – can do it right.' He motioned to Simos.

The Greek lowered his drink and moved closer to the two men, nobody else need know what was going down, he told himself. As he briefed them, Edmonds disappeared upstairs with the redhead who had been sitting in the corner. She looked no older than sixteen.

AUGUST 13. 7:15 PM, WESTERN AUSTRALIA TIME

Peterson stopped Jim on the patio. 'Let's sit,' he said. 'I'd like to talk to you.' Peterson sounded solemn.

'What about?'

'Marty Torino.'

Jim's eyebrows lifted in calm surprise as his Adam's apple dropped into his stomach. 'What about him?'

'He's dead!'

Jim sounded stunned. 'Dead? How? Why?'

'That's what we're trying to ascertain. He was stabbed, by the way.' Peterson eyed his ward carefully, but the teenager betrayed absolutely nothing. Good, he told himself. He'll make a great operative one day.

Jim lowered himself into a patio chair shakily. Fairly good acting, he thought. 'I can't believe it,' he said aloud. 'Marty was a very adept agent; he would never allow somebody close enough to stab him.'

'Well, it happened. He must've struggled, though there were no signs of it in the flat. Apart from a bullet hole. We found the blade in him but the handle's missing. The occupants of the flat next door complained about a decapitated bird on their balcony.'

'You found a bullet hole?'

Peterson nodded. 'The bullet buried itself low into the wall after passing through the couch. It was fired from his gun. His body fell from the balcony.'

Jim grimaced as he remembered the sight of a one-time friend after a ten-storey fall. 'Poor Marty,' he said and felt the hypocrite for it.

'You knew him better than anyone else,' Peterson began, 'Did he ever tell you about anybody who wanted to kill him?'

The Gorgon thought for a moment. 'No,' Jim said after a while. 'No. Marty, Callobar, and I usually just chatted about what we had done .... or been doing.'

'Damn!' Peterson stated. 'Then it must've been our friends from behind the Curtain. He always was active against their shenanigans. But how did they get that close to Marty?'

Jim shrugged and headed for the sliding door. *If you only knew, Mark*, he said to himself. *If you only knew.*

But unknown to the teenager, Peterson did know.

Chapter Sixteen
The Farm Of Death

AUGUST 14. 9:35 AM, WESTERN AUSTRALIA TIME

The bell interrupted them. Drawing away from each other, Jim, reluctantly, rose and went to answer the door, cursing under his breath. Meanwhile, Chris straightened up her top, after re-hooking her bra and buttoning up her blouse.

The door opened and Fab stood there looking rather sheepish.

Jim noticed that the sky, behind Fab, had gone to blue. The sun was even shining down, chasing the shadows away. The grey day was becoming nicer. 'You could've been a few minutes later than what you already are,' Jim commented flatly, letting his friend pass him while looking around for any others. 'Never mind, you're the first of the late arrivals. Chris was the only one who arrived on time,' he said, with a gleam in his eye. He soon discovered that he had only wasted his breath in mentioning Christine's early arrival as Fab had already made his way into the family room and was busy admiring the girl in her white jeans and pink blouse. Jim stood behind his friend and admired Chris, who was blushing. Her clothes, Jim decided, complimented her figure. *Who'd ever believe that she's only fifteen?* He asked himself. To Fab, he said, 'Would you like something to drink?'

But Fab didn't answer. Instead, he looked past Chris at a point on the wall which, subconsciously, he didn't seem to see.

Jim repeated the question and his friend snapped out of from wherever he had been.

'No,' he replied. 'No thanks, Jim,' and he sat on the settee, away from Christine.

Jim and Chris exchanged looks and, sitting on the coffee table, he asked, 'Fab, are you okay?'

Fab gave a weak smile. 'Yeah. Yeah, Jim, I'm all right. It's just I keep seeing Harry lying on the ... in the ...' He shook his head, trying to shake that vision from his mind.

'I know how it is,' Jim replied. 'Sometimes I see him, too. Look, Fab, what's done is done—'

Fab's eyes focused on Jim's. 'What?' he cried. '"What's done is done"? That's a f**ked up way of looking at things! A mate of ours died ... because of what we did! So, we just shrug our shoulders and carry on as if it didn't matter? Just another soldier that has fallen in the mud of the battlefield! He doesn't matter, just baggage that's now lost! F**k, Jim! He was a mate! He had a life, a voice, a mother that weeps for him, an angry dad who feels helpless ... And all you can say is "what's done is done"!'

'I know that sounds callous, but whatever we do, it isn't going to bring him back. I wish it could, but it can't. All we can do is remember him the way he would want us to: a bloody great guy who was crazy about horse racing, always flush with money, and our high school's sideline bookie.'

Jim rose from the coffee table and went through the kitchen to the dining room and glanced over the wooden balustrade, through the large windows of the lounge which looked out onto the street. The familiar station wagon was nowhere to be found.

'Besides,' he said, returning to his guests, 'the bloke who took credit for it won't ever do so again!' He checked his watch. 'We've waited long enough; I suggest we get a move on.'

'What about the others?' Chris asked.

'That's their problem. They should learn to be on time, especially Andrew. He's so proud of German punctuality, he should practice it. Besides, Danny and Tet will be meeting us in town.' What he didn't tell them, however, was the fact that he wanted to be long gone before Edmonds's pavement artists arrived for their daily vigil.

After ordering Shaka to guard the house, the small group walked out, Jim locked the front door, and they headed towards the bus stop, the two boys on either side of Christine.

Immediately a shout attracted their attention and, looking back, they saw Andrew Bremenh and Tony Waters, only a block away. Fab shouted back that they would await their arrival at the bus stop, so Andrew and Tony continued at their leisurely pace.

'Well, you seem to have snapped out of it,' Jim commented.

Fab remained quiet for a bit, then said, 'I've been thinking of leaving the group.'

Jim stopped and looked at him. 'What?'

Chris looked at the footpath, remembering a game from early childhood, and watched the cracks between the concrete slabs attempting to avoid stepping on them, lest she falls in.

A blue car sped past, and Andrew admired the Mercedes-Benz as it pulled up almost abreast with the three, up ahead. 'Are my eyes deceiving me,' he asked Tony, 'or are they actually getting into that beautiful Mercedes?'

Tony, whose eyes were keener, noted the distressed expression on Fab's face as he disappeared into the car, which then sped off with a squeal of tyres. 'No, your eyes were not deceiving you, and yes, they were getting into that car – but not willingly! Come on, we've got to find a phone.'

AUGUST 14. 9:48 AM, WESTERN AUSTRALIA TIME

'I just think I need to leave,' Fab said.

'Why?'

'This whole thing has been way too serious, Jim,' he said. 'Don't you see that? A boy is murdered, one of Chris's friends is accused of being a drug pusher and another turns out to be the pusher and a murderer to boot; you break into warehouses—'

Chris looked up. 'What?' She looked at Fab, then at Jim, who pulled his eyes away from hers.

'—Only to steal those guys' drugs to give to the police,' Fab continued. 'Then that drive-by and Harry's dead and Larry's in the hospital, fighting for his life. I don't care what you say … I want, no, I need to get out and keep away from you. We'll go see this film and then, we're no longer friends … and I'm no longer in this group.'

'Fab,' Jim said. 'I think you're over-reacting.'

'No, I'm not,' Fab snapped back. 'That's the problem. You always think you know better. Well, you don't. Not all your decisions work without affecting every one of us. We get affected badly. You are the only one who keeps marching on unaffected. Why is that?'

'I don't know,' Jim lied. He glanced back towards Andrew and Tony, and noticed a blue Mercedes-Benz heading towards them, but thought little of it.

The Mercedes-Benz braked a few metres ahead and the passenger's window was wound down. A revolver appeared, held in a hand that possessed an extra-large knuckle. The back door opened, and Barton ordered them to get in. The three teenagers hesitated, thinking of running. Barton aimed his revolver at Chris. 'Get in – or she dies. Right here, right now!'

Jim sighed. Shit, he thought. They changed cars, the bastards! 'We better do as he says,' Jim conceded. He entered the car first, just in case the mobster tried something with the first one in. Fab closed the door behind him. 'I know it sounds like a well-used cliché, but where are you taking us?'

'To Mr. Edmonds. He wants to see you!' Barton's eyes surveyed Chris and noticed that the girl shuddered as she felt his eyes linger upon her.

Jim could feel Chris shaking next to him and he grabbed her hand, gently squeezing it.

'How sweet,' Barton sneered and transferred the revolver to his left hand, leaving the right free to rub the knuckle against his bottom lip.

'What does Edmonds want with us?' Fab asked suddenly, forcing his voice to sound braver than he felt.

'With you – nothing. It's your friend here he's interested in.' Barton glared at Jim. 'He wants to know how a stupid teenager, helping the police, can commit murder so easily!'

Chris turned to look at Jim, her eyes wide with the shock of the casual announcement. She didn't ask anything, but her eyes wanted to know what was going on.

Jim could feel Fab's eyes on him as well and returned an apologetic glance. Taking a deep breath and staring out the side window, at nothing special, he said, 'It's not difficult.'

The driver was controlling the vehicle, casually taking extra care to remain within the speed limit. Being overcautious cost him numerous delays at the traffic lights. The three extra passengers remained silent with Barton keeping his gun in view and steady while smothering his knuckle. The Mercedes stopped at the lights before entering the Mitchell Freeway. An RTA[35] patrol car was beside them, both officers were smoking.

Jim regarded them for a moment, wishing them to look his way.

As if reading the teenager's mind, Barton softly warned, 'Don't try it.'

Chris suddenly squeezed Jim's hand. He turned from the glass to see the revolver pointing directly where her navel was. Barton held the gun low and slightly closer to his target, the driver's bulk hiding it from the RTA men. The lights changed and the Mercedes pulled away slowly, allowing the patrol car to overtake them. Twenty minutes later, they turned onto the Canning Highway off-ramp and headed west along the highway.

My God! Jim said to himself. *Where are they taking us?*

For most of the trip, Chris had remained silent – from fear, Jim mused – but she was visibly shaking. Though she was still squeezing Jim's hand, she wasn't comforted. Jim couldn't feel his fingertips; she was squeezing them so tightly.

Jim had properly met her at the beginning of the year, though he had 'spied' on her through the gaps in the wooden fence – separating the two properties – weeks before and, even though they talked practically every night, he realised now – in this very real time of danger – that he hardly knew her, at all. She wasn't

---

[35]Road Traffic Authority (now defunct).

crying hysterically, as – he believed – most girls would. She was one strong lady to fight the mental battle that must be raging inside her at this moment. Apart from the shaking, she was winning the struggle with her fear. Jim glanced at her, once more, and noticed a tear trail, slowly, down her pale cheek. The walls have been breached and the turning point – the moment that decides victory or defeat – is close, he told himself, preparing to comfort her. But surprisingly, no hysterics occurred.

After ten minutes, Jim noticed that they were now on a secondary road and heading south, fast. No fear of police here. There were very few houses to be seen and were becoming less and further apart every kilometre. Large areas of open pastures flanked the road on either side. Now, where were they? Bibra Lake? South Lake? Yangebup? Banjup? He didn't know.

The driver turned off and headed west along a dirt track.

Looking out the window, Jim saw several horses in large paddocks. The black and brown mares and stallions enjoyed the lukewarm sun while eating the clover that carpeted the ground in abundance. They passed four paddocks each divided by log fences. On Fab's side, the dirt track was lined with trees, mostly eucalypts.

The Mercedes passed through a gateway, which was crowned by a semi-circular plaque informing that they had arrived at Meadow Fields Stud Farm. A cobblestone driveway led to the single-storey hacienda-style house.

Barton holstered his weapon and gave a toothy grin. 'End of the line. I trust you've enjoyed your trip and hope you'll travel with us again.' He began to laugh, and the driver joined in with a high nasal laugh of his own. Barton opened the back door and the teenagers climbed out in silence. Three other men, all holding revolvers, were standing behind the Mercedes-Benz. Barton pushed Jim towards the house and the teenager resisted and turned. The safeties of the revolvers were flicked off noisily.

Jim hesitated and glared at Barton. 'I swear on all the gods of Olympus, I'll kill you before the sun sets today,' he vowed quietly. 'Keep your hands off us, you lackey!'

Barton didn't answer; he simply smashed Jim across the face with the back of his hand, then pushed him – savagely – towards the front door. Jim staggered on the step and Chris grabbed his arm to steady him. The door was opened from inside and the teenagers were led into a spacious living room. Though the sun was out, the temperature was still cold, and a roaring fire blazed in the stone fireplace. A pair of two-metre bookcases flanked the fireplace on both sides and each shelf was crammed with hardcover books. Three full-length windows let in enough light to make every corner of the room absent of shadow. The floor was covered in a thick cream pile carpet.

Leaning on the mantelpiece, directly in front of the fire, was the man from the warehouse, a half-filled glass in his hand. He drained the glass, swallowing the liquid noisily, then regarded the new arrivals with a distinct lack of interest. 'Well,' he said to Barton, 'you finally got here. I thought you had failed – again!' He surveyed the three teenagers, once more, and seemed to notice Chris and Fab for the first time. 'Why are there three instead of only the one?'

'They were with him at the time, and we had to take them also, Mr. Edmonds,' Barton replied humbly.

So, this was Edmonds, Jim said to himself. A bald, blimp of a man in a grey suit. Why did mobsters always dress in suits? They probably think it displays a sense of class. Born a peasant, die a peasant, Jim sneered to himself.

'Unfortunately, you've arrived late,' Edmonds stated, dismissing the existence of the extra two teenagers. 'Mr. Long will be here in a few minutes.' He stared at Jim as he spoke. 'Do you know who Hun Long is?' Not waiting for an answer, he said, 'Of course you don't – even the cops don't know who he is. He—'

'He is an operative of the Qong-Ho Brigade, a minor directorate of the Ministry of State Security,' Jim announced coolly. 'We have him on file. We also keep an eye out for him and follow him everywhere he goes.' Jim gave an overconfident smile.

Edmonds squinted. Suddenly, he felt that he no longer had total control of the situation. 'Why? "We"?'

'The Australian Security Intelligence Organisation!' Jim replied proudly. 'Better known to you lot as ASIO.' He noticed the change of expression on Edmonds's face, the blood draining away from it, leaving a sickly pallor. 'That's right, Edmonds,' he said in a low voice, 'ASIO! Your stinking little setup here has irritated more than just the Western Australian Police Force. By murdering an ASIO operative, you've put yourself onto ASIO's radar! Just like Torino – The Christian! That's how I identified him, he wasn't very good at imitating an American ... let's face it, a South African is very noticeable!'

Edmonds grinned as he watched the expressions of the other teenagers. 'So, you're not going to deny that you murdered him yesterday?'

Jim stared at Edmonds, forgetting everyone else. 'Are you going to deny you ordered The Christian to kill my friends?'

Edmonds's mouth broke into a wide grin. This kid was really something else. The tension and fear had dissipated with his grin. Edmonds was regaining control of the situation. *'Touché!'* He looked at Chris and Fab. 'He was meant to kill you only; your friends were only collateral damage.'

Simos entered the room and marched over to the mobster. 'Mr. Long has arrived, sir,' he said. Simos paid no attention to the teenagers.

Edmonds's eye never left Jim's as he issued his orders. 'Barton and Morris, put them in one of the back bedrooms … and put a guard on the door. Also, make sure they don't climb out the window.' As Barton and Morris herded them into the side hallway, Edmonds turned to the Greek. 'Show Long into my den.' As Simos hurried off to carry out the order, Edmonds went to his own bedroom to change out of the grey suit which, suddenly, reeked of sweat and fear, and exchanged it for an expensive tailored navy-blue pin-striped suit. Then, when he thought that his guest had been waiting long enough, Edmonds made his way, leisurely, to the den.

AUGUST 14. 10:20 AM, WESTERN AUSTRALIA TIME

Jim checked the door. It was locked.

Chris and Fab watched him as Jim searched the room. It was just a bedroom, he told himself. Bed and bedhead; small side tables with lamps on them; large wardrobe, with an in-built mirror, and a small writing desk and padded seat. A couple of cheap paintings hung on the wall; one was a portrait of Grigori Rasputin! Jim recognised him from a photo from his history textbook. He looked out the window and surveyed the scene: a large pasture with a couple of horses. There were some outbuildings to his left. Must be stables ... or a barn. He wondered if there would be some farm vehicles in there. He pictured a steam-powered tractor and shook his head to clear the image from his mind. Come on, Saston ... It's not just your life on the line. There must be a way out of this predicament. He noticed the shadow of the guard, posted outside, to stop them from climbing out the window. He slid open the doors of the wardrobe. There were a few coat hangers, some wire ones, hanging from a solid thick dowel. Jim tested it but couldn't remove the dowel. He sighed and joined his companions on the double bed.

'What was that bullshit you were spouting out there?' Fab demanded angrily.

Jim sighed again. 'That wasn't bullshit.'

'You mean that was true?' Chris asked uncertainly.

'Every word of it,' Jim replied.

Fab stood and squared off in front of Jim. 'So, you killed someone?'

Jim remained quiet.

'Well?'

Jim looked up at Fab's face. An idea crept into his mind. It might just work, Saston, he convinced himself. Silently, with slow deliberate movements, as if he were measuring out distances, he stood and circled Fab and stopped facing both of his friends. 'Since this all began, I've killed five people.' It was the calm and callous manner, not the fact, that surprised Chris. Jim's admission simply made Fab angry.

'What are you saying?' Chris cried in disbelief.

Jim focused on Fab. His friend was approaching boiling point. 'It's true,' he said. 'The first time was in the Slattery warehouse.

I hit the nightwatchman too hard, by mistake.' He paused as he remembered that night, the day before Callobar's murder! He was so ashamed of that. 'Then Edmonds and his stooges surprised Callobar and me; we had to fight our way out. The next day the Christian killed Callobar, hoping the act would scare me off. They were wrong. We were at Police Central questioning Hank when they hit him. When that newsagent, St. James, was murdered by the Christian, I was at Police Central and listening to a recording from inside St. James's house. We heard the Christian's voice. I, eventually, identified his accent as South African and I went to ASIO to search through the files there. I identified him and, yesterday, I went to his flat ... and ... killed him.'

Chris visibly shuddered. 'But ... how...?'

Jim tried his best to answer the questions Chris couldn't ask. 'My dad was an ASIO operative, seconded to ASIS. When he was gunned down, the Petersons took me in. Mark is the regional director of ASIO for this state and he managed to get me trained as an operative – as part of the psychiatric therapy I was undergoing.' He stopped and regarded his friends.

'The Christian was responsible for Harry's death. That's why I killed him.'

'The Christian killed Harry,' Fab said, 'and you killed the Christian in retaliation. It doesn't change the fact that you refused to stop all of this!'

'I suppose,' Jim admitted, stepping back and away from Fab.

Fab stepped closer to him. 'You "suppose"?' Fab demanded. 'Is that all? You "suppose"? Harry didn't mean much, then, did he? F**k! I bet none of us mean anything to you! We're just going to be collateral damage like that Yankee f**kwit said!'

Jim had been backing away, as Fab, subconsciously, moved forward. Now Jim was where he wanted them both to be. 'Collateral damage is unavoidable!' Jim yelled back. 'Paul Matthews was collateral damage! So was Marlene Manson's unborn baby! There will always be collateral damage. That's the way of the world. Maybe you should try living in it, instead of bleating on about tests, exams, and your stupid marks and grades, because no-one – least of all me – gives a f**ken shit!' That was the right amount of prodding.

Fab pushed Jim into the wardrobe. He bounced off it and was falling forward towards Fab's right cross. Jim evaded the punch and Fab's fist hit the mirror with such force that the glass cracked. Jim pushed Fab away and put his heel into the mirror, causing the whole thing to shatter.

AUGUST 14. 10:44 AM, WESTERN AUSTRALIA TIME

In the corridor, near the bedroom, two of Edmonds's men sat on wooden chairs, smoking. The smaller of the two, with tiny black eyes and a crew cut, crushed the life out of the butt and threw it into the copper ashtray on the small, varnished table between them. This was Peter Morris. As an incurable chain smoker, Morris had already lit the next cigarette and taken his first drag. The other was a small-time thug named Arthur Billing.

Billing regarded the oil painting that hung opposite them. The semi-nude girl in it looked no older than sixteen, he thought lasciviously. But, hell, she was a real looker! He wondered if the artist had had the privilege to sleep with the model. His mouth fell open at the thought and realised that it was dry and that he needed a drink. He turned to his companion. 'You want some coffee, Mo?'

Morris took a long luxurious last drag of his cigarette before crushing the life out of it. It had been his second cigarette in the last fifteen minutes. He turned, lethargically, and blew the smoke out between pursed lips in the direction of the other man. 'Okay, Art.'

Billing left and Morris lit another cigarette. *That girl's pretty,* he told himself as he regarded the door to the teenager's prison. *Must be really good in the sack, maybe a bit frigid – just like I like 'em. You could always belt warmth an' feelin' into the frigid ones. Think I'll grab a bit while the boss is busy. If the others talk, I c'n tell the big boy they're makin' it all up. Besides, Edmonds likes 'em young too.* Billing found his sexual experiences with children and young adolescents, more rewarding than that with mature women ... or even men! The positions he could devise with that girl ... Then it occurred to him that those kids were making a hell of a row and decided he'd tell them to shut the f**k up ... after his smoke, at least.

A shattering of glass suddenly came from the room, forcing Morris to decapitate his cigarette with his fingers. Revolver in hand, he opened the bedroom door and stood back as it swung open, revealing the girl sitting on the edge of the bed, staring at him with wide frightened eyes. He couldn't see the boys. Where were they? Morris glanced at the window and saw that it was intact. All sexual fantasies forgotten, Morris kicked the door viciously; it swung around and collided against the wall with a loud bang, it started to swing back slowly. He put his foot against the moving door, stopping its movement, and took a wary step into the room. The two boys were facing each other, angrily. The Ding[36] boy had his fists up and he was breathing heavily; the other was backed up against the wardrobe, his fists were down by his side. At a time like this, these f**kwits were fighting!

'What the f**k's goin' on in 'ere?' Morris barked.

Fab stepped away as Morris approached them. 'Ask him,' he spat, indicating Jim. 'He f**ken always has all the answers!'

Morris turned to Jim. 'Well?'

'A bat escaped from your belfry and was flying around hysterically trying to get out. So, I tried to break the window but misjudged and hit the mirror instead!' Jim gave the thug an idiot grin.

Morris stepped forward the revolver held low and pointing at Jim. 'You think I'm stupid or somethin'? You were tryin' to escape.'

'No,' Jim admitted, sweetly, 'I don't think you're stupid at all. I think you're dead!' He brought his right fist up; the switchblade held tight in the fist and released the blade while his left fist hit Morris's gun hand.

The thug's legs buckled from under him as the flying blade passed through his forehead and exited from the back of his head to embed itself in the brick wall, near the bedhead. Jim stepped over Morris's body and closed the bedroom door after removing the key.

'You killed him!' Fab stated incredulously, not believing what he had seen before his eyes. He moved over to Chris and placed his hand over her mouth. She was staring at the grisly

---

[36]Western Australian slang name for people of Italian descent.

sight in disbelief. Her senses telling her to let out the shock by screaming.

'I sincerely hope so,' Jim replied, removing another blade from the pouch he carried. 'Now, listen up, we haven't much time.' He went over to the wall where the end of his blade was sticking out of the exposed brick wall, pieces of plaster littering the carpeted floor. Jim removed the slippery blade and checked it for any defects. It looked okay and wiped it clean on the bedspread, then replaced it in his pouch. He moved over to the girl who stared down, at the dead body, with wide frightened eyes, Fab's hand still over her mouth. Jim knelt in front of her, breaking her line of sight to the cadaver. 'Listen to me,' he said gently. 'Chris, listen carefully. I'll get you out of this nightmare safely. I promise. What I need you to do is stay calm and – more importantly – quiet, no matter what you see, or hear. Can you do that for me?'

Chris looked into his eyes as he talked to her. She could see his normal confidence in his eyes and knew that what he said was true, at least for him. Something told her inside that Jim Saston was her only hope of staying alive in this defective rollercoaster ride from hell. Chris bit Fab's hand.

Fab yelped and pulled his hand away, shaking it. 'For f**k's sake!' He looked at Jim and shook his head. 'When were you going to tell us about that weapon?'

Jim regarded Fab. 'It was need to know,' he said, 'and you didn't need to know.' He picked up Morris's revolver, broke it, and checked that the cylinder was full. Happy, he closed it and looked at Fab. 'Now, are we going to stand here and argue?' Jim stated. 'Or are we leaving? The choice is yours!' He couldn't stop the vitriolic way he sounded. 'Okay,' he said. 'Keep quiet, no matter what.'

Jim turned the door handle, slowly, and checked the corridor. There were no signs of life and activity, so he led the way along until faint voices and laughter reached his ears. It came from one room up ahead. As they neared it, the odours emanating from that room proved it to be the kitchen, and not an exceptionally clean one at that, Jim mused as he crept closer. There was no door, but an archway, and Jim stopped his friends.

'We have to cross in front of that opening,' Jim explained in a whisper, 'without making a sound or being heard.' He peered around the corner into the kitchen. Two men were sitting at the table, a pot of coffee between them. Neither of them was facing the archway, but any sudden movement in that direction would surely be noticed by their peripheral vision. Oh well, they had to take that chance.

'Fab,' Jim instructed in a whisper, 'you go first, I'll cover.' He watched the mobsters and waved his friend on. Jim glanced across and found Fab already on the other side of the archway. He turned to Chris. 'You're next,' he whispered.

She gave a thin, frightened, smile.

Jim watched the mobsters once more and beckoned Chris to join Fab with his right hand. Before reaching the safety of the other side, her shoe slipped on the hall rug, but she managed to regain her balance after uttering a cry of surprise.

Billing turned and regarded the archway. 'Did you hear something?' he asked, suddenly alert.

The other man lowered his cup and listened. 'Hear what?'

'I dunno. A sound.' Billing rose and started for the archway, withdrawing his Walther from its shoulder holster.

Jim indicated to his friends that he wanted them to get away – now! The girl shook her head, refusing to leave him there alone, but finally surrendered to Jim's insistence. Fab led the way to the door at the end of the corridor.

Jim tightened his grip on the gun, then remembered what he had been taught during his training. He made a conscious effort to loosen his grip on the revolver. Jim could hear the loud beating of his heart as if that muscle had lodged itself, permanently, between his ears.

Billing rounded the corner and Jim fired twice at point-blank range. The force of the bullets lifted the mobster off his feet and deposited him in an untidy heap where Fab and Chris had been standing, some seconds earlier. Jim scowled at the ringing of the gunshots that echoed through the corridor and kitchen. The other mobster had risen from his chair and stared in disbelief at the perforated remains of Arthur Billing. Jim didn't hesitate but swung around and fired. The man was propelled against the refrigerator and, slowly, slid to the floor, leaving a fresh red streak on the white door of that appliance.

Urgent voices came from the dining room on the far side of the kitchen and Jim ran for the exit. Outside, Fab sat on one of the three Suzuki motorcycles that were parked just near the door. Chris stood beside him.

'What are you two still doing here?'

'We were waiting for you,' Fab stated.

'All hell's about to break loose,' Jim replied. 'Take one of the bikes and get out of here!'

'I'm not going!' Chris said with finality.

'Oh, yes you are!' Jim replied sternly. 'Now, get on the bike behind Fab.'

'What about you?' she demanded.

'I'll be fine,' Jim replied. 'I'll draw them away from you. Chris, this is what I'm trained to do.'

Reluctantly, Chris climbed on the Suzuki behind Fab.

'Now, Fab,' Jim swore, 'f**k off!'

A mischievous gleam sparkled in Chris's eyes as she wrapped her arms around Fab's waist and gave Jim an angelic smile as she rested a cheek against Fab's back. With satisfaction, she noticed the jealousy momentarily flare in Jim's eyes. 'Let's go,' she whispered to Fab in a husky voice.

Jim watched them go and, when they were speeding down the cobblestone path, got on one of the remaining bikes and waited. Almost half a minute later, a group of men – with Barton in the lead – burst through that back door. Jim pulled away from the other Suzuki – but in the opposite direction taken by Fab and Chris – towards the marked bridlepath.

Barton was the first to react and he raised his revolver and fired. Jim and the motorbike seemed to rise slightly, tilting over to the right. Barton's lips parted in a satisfied grin as Jim sprawled on the ground near the scrub between two gum trees. He walked casually towards the teenager's unmoving body, his grin growing broader with each step.

Chapter Seventeen
Pain Will Not Stop Them

AUGUST 14. 10:50 AM, WESTERN AUSTRALIA TIME

Fab and Chris had sped along the cobblestone driveway; he was proud of the fact that he had reached a speed of nearly seventy kilometres even on the dirt track, when all of a sudden, he felt Chris tap him on the shoulder.

'What?' he said, irritated.

'Stop!' Chris yelled.

They had reached the road and he stopped just off the property and under the cover of some bushes and an old rusty car. They started to argue.

'Why have we stopped?' Fab demanded.

'Because I'm going to help Jim,' Chris stated.

'But, Chris,' pleaded Fab, 'Jim said—'

'I don't care what Jim said!' Chris shot back.

'But—'

'Listen, Fab, I said I don't care. I'm not a member of your stupid gang, so I don't have to obey Mr. Jim bloody Saston! Just—'

'Jim said he was trained to deal with all of this,' groaned Fab, trying to stifle a grin. Normally that was just a figure of speech, but now Jim Saston just might be telling the truth!

'Listen,' Chris stated. 'I'll go back … just to make sure he's okay. You go and find a place to call the cops, and I'll just hang around here with Jim, okay? Fine? Good!' she ordered.

They both turned toward the sound of a gunshot, then exchanged looks.

'Go!' she said.

Burt Hammond and Sarah, he mused. 'Well, can I have a kiss for luck?' Fab asked. 'Just in case …!'

'Okay,' Chris replied, feeling naughty, but turned her cheek towards him.

With an offended glance, Fab turned her face towards him and kissed her on the lips hard.

Despite being surprised by the kiss, she waved Fab farewell with a smile and turned back towards the buildings.

Blushing, Fab revved, loudly, up the road. *Why the devil did he suddenly feel shy and embarrassed?* he asked himself as he sped along the gravel track, kicking up rubble and creating a large cloud of dust. He felt light enough to float. The bike fishtailed on the loose gravel but Fab was able to correct it in time.

Chris got off the cobbled road and took advantage of the short scrub between it and the electrified fence of the horse pasture. Her progress was slow as her sandals kept catching on the dried-out and prickly ends of the scrub. Muttering a curse as these sandals got caught, for the umpteenth time, in the scrub, Chris came to a final decision. They might be her one and only best sandals and one of the most flattened pairs she owned, but right now, they were a hindrance at this moment. Removing them, she mentally noted the bush's position and texture. The bright lemony-green one she was behind was unique among the other brown dead colours.

Staying low, she moved along slowly and then discovered a discarded horseshoe. Chris pocketed it and moved on. It might bring good luck, she told herself. She needed all the good luck she could get. In comparison to Jim Saston, she was a rank amateur basing what she was doing on the films and television shows she had seen! Her good luck was paying off as Chris spied a forgotten and rusty hammer in the dirt ahead.

Glancing around, she suddenly stiffened as she spotted a man's shadow just over to one side of her cover. Moving back slowly, her bare foot bumped into something, and she gave an involuntary squeal as the cactus's barbs slid effortlessly into her heel.

The man had heard it but was unaware as to the exact location of the sound. He moved down and began searching the scrub.

Later, Christine Porter would remember how slowly things seemed to move. The man's head appeared over the low scrub, and she had pushed forward, grabbing the hammer and, in one fluid movement, raised it as she twisted and hit him as hard as she could on the side of the man's head.

The man's limp body fell heavily, onto the small, prickly cactus. Blood flowed freely from an open gash into his open eye along his nose and poured into the soil.

Chris gasped in horror at what she had done and then shook his body vigorously, desperately. 'Are you alive?' she whispered in his ear. His head moved limply from side to side as she sought reassurance. Numbly, she dropped the lifeless head to the ground and scurried away from what she had done. Her heel throbbed and she brought her foot up to see the damage. Her heel was bleeding, and a few fine barbs were protruding from it. 'Damn!' she groaned, and began pulling the barbs, she could see, from her heel. Then, allowing her foot to heal itself, she moved on still clutching her precious hammer. She was a seasoned killer now, she told herself, just like Jim. She hadn't seen the foot at first, then it was too late. Chris's eyes followed the shoe up and it joined a jean-clad leg which, unfortunately, had a body attached!

The man, holding a small Bowie knife, didn't seem at all surprised to see her. 'Come on, girly, out from behind the bushes,' he ordered, licking his lips in anticipation.

Chris hid her arms behind her back and obeyed, struggling to get to her feet. She held her injured heel off the soil.

'What you got there, girly?' he asked suspiciously.

'Something to kill you with,' she muttered under her breath.

Immediately the knife was at her throat. 'Drop it!' he ordered.

Chris reluctantly obeyed, wondering why it had worked for Jim.

The hand, holding the knife, relaxed slightly, but remained at her throat.

Christine saw her chance as she realised that the perve's eyes were wandering over her body – undressing her, evaluating her. As he moved closer, she raised her knee and buried it with extreme force into his groin, just as her mother had taught her, and jumped back, reaching down for the hammer. As the thug dropped, reaction made him toss his knife, to lose itself in the pasture. Unfortunately, the keen blade sliced into Chris's upper arm in its trajectory. She yelled at the sudden pain and instinct took over. She struck the groaning man savagely with her illegal weapon again and again, until his head was a spongy mess! Chris then dropped to her knees and felt the wounded area on her arm. It was throbbing quite violently now as her adrenaline rush wore off. She could see that the wound wasn't very deep, but hell, was it bleeding lots! *Would it need stitches?* she wondered. Ripping her soiled blouse, she bandaged her arm up as best she could. Jim was right. Killing is easier the second time around!

She dragged herself into the concealment of the scrub, each movement sending shooting pain down her arm and up her leg from her heel. Suddenly, unable to stop the tears from flowing, she felt alone, hopeless, and frightened. She hated this feeling that quickly washed over her, and wished that Jim – sure-of-himself Jim – were with her right now comforting her, protecting her. Chris shook her head to clear it. They were going to die! Jim and her! At least Fab had gotten away. He would tell the cops what had happened here, today. Looking back, she saw that she had only traversed nearly a hundred-odd metres. At this rate, she mused, she'd reach Jim in time to die of old age! Jim? I wonder where he is ... 'Jim.' *I hope he's okay.* With the thought of Jim's welfare as motivation, Chris forced herself on. 'I'll just ... just go and ... see ...'

Pulling herself along to the nearest bit of sunlight, Chris raised herself slightly and peered through the scrub for him. There he was, lying face down in the dirt! That horrible man with the knuckle was walking towards him! She had to warn him, call to him – somehow, attract his attention. 'Jim!' she cried, and then wondered if she had cried aloud or in her mind? But her mind would not think anymore, and darkness came with a sense of defeat, prematurely to a world that knew no pain, giving her the peace she needed for the moment.

AUGUST 14. 10:53 AM, WESTERN AUSTRALIA TIME

Laying prostrate in the dirt of the bridlepath, with his left hand under him, Jim could hear 'Knuckle' approaching. He already held his switchblade that had tasted blood once today and would taste it again – soon! Jim could imagine the satisfying grin on that killer's face as he slowly strutted over to his still body. Kick the dog when he's down, eh? You'll learn that this dog can bite in more ways than one.

Barton stopped beside the still form and scanned for any sign of blood. There was none! Using his foot, he turned the teenager over.

Jim's hand was raised in an instant and the blade was released. Barton screamed as the blade bit through his left eye, performing an immediate lobotomy. The fluid drained from the dissected eyeball, some of it falling on the young Gorgon.

Jim shuddered and moved before Barton's body collapsed on him.

Meanwhile, the other mobsters had been searching for Chris and Fab and had failed to hear Barton's scream. Taking the dead man's revolver and retrieving the one he had dropped, Jim decided to head back towards the house, behind the cover of the cypress pines that lined the path. Pictures of Harry Callahan, Callobar, and Larry Mitchell flashed through his mind. The man directly – or indirectly – responsible for their present state of health was in that house and desperately awaiting to meet his Maker!

One of the stables was on Jim's side of the bridlepath.

Most of the men were searching around the house for the other two teenagers, thinking Jim slain, but, unknown to him, one of the thugs was searching through the stables. He registered the boy standing over Barton, with disbelief.

Jim heard only the singing of the bullet as it passed his ear. He dived to one side and hit the ground hard, using Barton's body as cover. Two bullets hit the still warm cadaver. He paused for a second or two to regain his breath and then fired at the man in the stables.

Attracted by the shots, the other mobsters fired at the Gorgon as he suddenly dashed from the bullet-ridden corpse towards the cover of the stables. Some bullets buried themselves in the woodwork around him.

Recalling the last few seconds, Jim calculated that he had roughly three or four bullets left between the two revolvers in his possession. Had Chris and Fab made it all right? Have they got in touch with the police, yet? No telling how long he can hold out with only two guns, against God only knows how many mobsters. He registered the silence. What's happening now?

Jim chanced a look and dived back for cover as a bullet dug into the side of a stall. Apart from that single shot, they weren't firing. Why not? What's going on? He suddenly felt horribly cold. Those mobsters were up to something, and Jim could feel the fear of the unknown creeping up his spine. He had to fight it, otherwise he would be of no use to himself. Trying valiantly to contain the growing fear, Jim moved to a vantage point where he could see three mobsters discussing what they should do. But before he could attempt anything against them, he heard another shot – from behind him – and felt the hot, searing pain bite into his lower back. The force of the projectile flung him around. He shot wildly in the direction from which, he believed, the shot had come until Barton's revolver was empty. What remained of the mobster fell to the ground.

Jim reached round in a bid to stop the pain and stared at the blood on his hand! His blood! He'd been shot! How bad was it? Would he live? Except for the pain from the wound in his back, he felt fine, maybe a little nervous, but fine. He discarded Barton's gun and took that of the recently deceased assailant. The guy who had shot him had come through a back door. Do stables have back doors? Keeping low, he moved to the far side and found the door ajar. So that's how he got in. From where he stood, Jim could see two of the three remaining men taking cover behind a bunch of cypress trees. Had they seen him? Jim hoped not. He whistled a well-known signal and one of the thugs exposed himself. Jim greeted him with a bullet between the eyes! The second one returned fire.

Jim dived for cover into the side of one of the stalls, with a groan and felt weak and dizzy. The hot sensation returned and with every gulp of air, came a stabbing pain. *If he was going to die, it wouldn't happen before killing Edmonds!* he decided stubbornly. There was still one mobster behind the cypress trees, he reminded himself, and the other covering the front of the stables. Taking careful aim at the dark patches visible through the thick foliage, Jim emptied the four remaining bullets of the third gun, into the line of trees. A cry of pain erupted from there and no other sound was heard.

Jim threw the empty gun away and transferred the other one to his right hand. One shot left, this had better count. Aiming the gun, the way Grosvenor had taught him, where he knew the last mobster was, he yelled in a voice, 'It's okay, mate, I got 'im!' Thank the gods for dropped balls!

The last mobster straightened, lowering his weapon as he got up from his crouching position. Jim's bullet hit him in the throat!

Casually, Jim walked over to where the terminally wounded man lay, blowing red frothy bubbles out of his mouth and picking up the mobster's revolver. He gave the scene the once-over and with a morbid smile, Jim pointed the revolver at the man and squeezed the trigger. The report echoed around the cypress trees. 'Ngadla[37]!' he said with finality, then moved towards the main house. For the first time, he felt the wetness of the shirt, which his blood had soaked. How much blood had he lost? Hell, he felt so tired! Jim heard a car door close as he reached the back door and entered the house. By the time he had reached the lounge, Jim saw the man called Simos speed off in the Mercedes which had brought him and his friends here. Jim swore to himself for letting one get away. But voices filtering through a darkly stained door on his right attracted his attention. Resting against the wall, trying to regain some lost strength, and fighting a bout of nausea, Jim listened to the voices.

'The shooting seems to have stopped,' one said. Jim didn't recognise it.

'Yeah, Mr. Long,' replied Edmonds. 'Hopefully, they've gotten rid of those pesky foxes.'

'Why are foxes such a problem?'

'They have no natural predators,' Edmonds explained, 'on this continent. The Limeys brought these damned animals here to

---

[37]'I have eaten!' (Zulu).

give officers and gentlemen something to hunt. You know, this was once a British penal colony.'

Penal colony maybe, Jim said to himself, wishing Edmonds could hear him. *But at least we still have a Queen, unlike your traitorous country!* He stopped that train of thought immediately. If it hadn't been for the American Rebellion, then Australia would never have been settled by the British. In truth, Australia owed the USA a very big thank you.

'I am well aware of this country's history, Mr. Edmonds,' Long said curtly. 'Let me make it quite clear that my people are not pleased that we must change the method of exporting our ... merchandise.'

Edmonds shrugged. 'It can't be helped. The police have gotten wise to our operation. Up to now, we've been able to cover our tracks ... so to speak.'

Long, you've wasted your ... people's time and money by coming here, Jim said to himself as he twisted the door handle. It wasn't locked and Jim stepped in, wearing a mask of calmness, hiding the effect of the wound in his back. Somewhere, in the distance, Jim could hear sirens. Sirens? No, imagination playing tricks!

Edmonds stopped talking and looked at Jim with an expression of surprise on his face. 'Where's Barton?'

The sirens got louder.

Long followed his host's stare and took in the teenager, armed with a revolver, standing in the open doorway. 'What is this?'

'I'm the fox!' Jim said, looking the Chinese operative in the eye before shooting him. Long fell back into the chair and Jim trained the gun on Edmonds, whose eyes widened in terror. Jim leaned against the door jamb. Damn those sirens!

Even though he seemed frozen from fright, Edmonds's hand had reached the desk drawer and his fingers were only centimetres from his concealed automatic pistol.

'Surprised, Edmonds?' Jim asked in defiance. The sirens kept getting louder. Damn it, they're worse than the usual ringing caused by air pressure! Sirens? The police? Chris and Fab had succeeded in contacting them! Damn! He'd have to do what he had planned without delay. Steadying the gun with both hands, Jim said, '*Tot siens*, Edmonds! Barton's waiting for you!'

The bullet blew Edmonds's expression away. His office chair tilted back and fell with a crash. Jim viewed it all as if it were in slow motion.

The sirens got louder still as the cars approached Meadow Fields Stud Farm.

The throbbing pain began, accompanied by conquering waves of nausea.

The sirens stopped their mournful song as the police cars halted outside. There was a shout of triumph and sudden discovery.

A part of Jim's mind was still working. It wouldn't be long before the police entered the study and he unsteadily turned to face the front door. After what seemed an abysmally long time the front door opened and a couple of police officers appeared, with Fab a little way behind. Jim's vision became wavy, blurred, and he wondered, somewhere in a mind once healthy, where Chris was. Suddenly, Chris's tired face appeared. Pushing past the policemen, she rushed as fast as her wounded foot would allow over to where Jim stood and threw her arms around him.

Jim stared in horror at the blood on Chris's arm, unable to distinguish whether it was his ... or hers. He winced as she placed her arms, unaware, on the wound on his back. The pain grew more intense as it overwhelmed him, his legs surrendered to his weight, and the darkness, mercifully, flooded over him.

Chris looked at the fresh blood on her hand in disbelief and screamed.

Epilogue

AUGUST 16. 9:00 AM, WESTERN AUSTRALIA TIME

Somewhere, in the distance of this pitch-black tunnel, he could hear the murmuring of voices. The odour of antiseptic reached his nostrils and though his vision, when he opened his eyes, was blurred, he could distinguish the white ceiling. With total consciousness, Jim realised he was lying on a hospital bed. A nurse was checking his pulse on his right wrist. Mark Peterson stood beside her.

'Chris?' Jim croaked drily.

Peterson looked down at him, his face was still a blur to the teenager.

'Chris!' Jim cried, trying to sit up. He grabbed the nurse's arms. 'Christine! Is she okay?'

'Hey, hold it,' Peterson said calmly and prised Jim's fingers from the nurse's person. The nurse moved away. 'Christine is fine. A bit groggy, but fine. How are you feeling?'

Jim surveyed his surroundings, unsure as to how he had gotten there and mentally feeling every part of his body. He hadn't fallen, like in his dreams, he was all right. Not a bone broken. 'Okay, I guess,' he replied. He was surprised at the rasping feeling of his throat and the dry croakiness of his voice.

Peterson waited until the nurse left the room with the kidney-shaped dish she had walked in with. 'You've been unconscious for two days. The doctors removed the bullet. It was lodged in front of your spine and had nicked your right kidney. You lost a lot of blood.' He glanced at the bag of blood hanging from the post attached to the bed, as proof.

'What happened to Chris? Why was there blood on her arm?' Jim demanded, trying to control the growing hysteria in his voice.

'Calm down,' Peterson said. He pushed Jim, gently, back into the bed. 'Seems like she got rid of two of our friends. She reckoned you couldn't handle them by yourself even though you had to publicise your status. So, she went back and helped. The guy she came across with had a knife which ended up slicing her arm open after Christine caved in his head with a hammer. Also, she backed into a cactus. Christine's more dangerous to herself than to anyone else. Anyway, she's got nine stitches for the knife wound and a tetanus shot.' Peterson chuckled. 'They had to give her tranquilisers as well because she was going mental since no-one had told her about you.'

Jim tried to hide a smile. At least Chris wasn't too banged up. He'd find out more from Mark later. Right now, as he could feel his mind clearing, it was time to debrief. But instead, he inquired about Fab.

'Fab's okay. A little shaken after what he's been through. He's tough, he'll get over it. Oh, Christine gave me this to give to you.' Peterson removed a blue envelope from his jacket pocket and handed it to Jim. 'Do you know what I had to go through to get you off a murder charge? Practically three-quarters of the Perth police force know you're an ASIO operative. At least we were able to keep you out of the papers and the news services.'

Jim smiled but said nothing. Instead, he examined the envelope. It was just an ordinary envelope with nothing but 'Jamie' written on it. He moved with the surprise of finding that version of his name there, winced, and fell back into the pillow.

'Are you okay?' Peterson asked, his voice laced with genuine concern.

'Yeah. Yeah. I'm okay, I moved too suddenly, and this thing didn't like it one bit,' indicating the cannula taped to his left hand.

'Okay, since you're all right,' Peterson began, 'we have some business to discuss. Firstly, concerning a unique switchblade that was used in killing Marty Torino and one James Barton! I'm not happy when operatives go around killing other operatives—'

'Torino was a double agent.'

'You think we didn't know that? He passed only what we wanted him to. What did surprise me, though, was that he hired himself out as a contract killer.'

'He was a sadist,' Jim spat out. 'Torino enjoyed killing. You know, he was a BOSS killer and came here to hunt down my dad. Klostek got dad before Torino arrived. This entire thing was simply a matter of the sins of the father ...' Jim frowned and scanned Peterson's face. 'But why do I get the feeling that you already knew that?'

Peterson smiled knowingly. 'Where did you get that switchblade?'

'There's an army surplus store in the city,' Jim said. 'They sell pocketknives and replica weapons. No *ixwa*[38], unfortunately. I bought it and modified it myself.'

'You did?'

'Yeah, my dad showed me how to make and repair all sorts of things.'

'Well, you have a talent for it, mate. Frank Laurence has been examining and testing it and reckons it's one of the finest handiworks he's seen in a long time.'

Jim laughed and winced at the pain caused by the sudden movement. 'Just tell him it's patented,' he said, once the pain lessened. 'I also want it back.'

Peterson chuckled, then became serious again. 'There are some developments that you need to be aware of. All four pushers in the school have been formally charged with peddling and using illicit drugs. It seems Graeme Madden's family possesses an influential relative who's trying to get the charge dropped or expunged totally. Because of your involvement, however, ASIO now has a vested interest and will make sure the charge will stick and not go away.' Peterson stopped and looked hesitant. 'Jim,' he began, 'that psychopath – Marlene Manson – well, she hanged herself with her blanket in the detention centre. She ... and the baby ... didn't make it. Your friend, Larry Mitchell, went into a coma early yesterday morning and crashed about two hours ago. The doctors and nurses tried everything, but he didn't respond. He died an hour ago.' Peterson felt awkward delivering the news. More could have been said but now, he couldn't think of anything else to say.

---

[38] Zulu stabbing spear. Named after the sucking sound it makes when withdrawn from a human body (Zulu).

Jim lay quiet, taking in all that Peterson had just said. It didn't seem real, somehow. Larry's dead. It's surreal. Too many innocent people have died because of this escapade! He didn't care for Marlene or any of the criminals that have gone to their maker, but the night watchman was accidentally killed by him, and that guy was only doing his job! Callobar knew the risks, being an operative, but Harry and Larry were collateral damage … so were Hank and Marlene's baby! 'Talk about something else,' Jim said suddenly, fighting back the tears of sorrow and guilt.

'Why did you kill Hun Long?'

'Because he was there!' Jim snapped back. What the f**k? Hun Long was a known Red China operative. 'He had no right to be in Australia! His organisation has been supplying the Slattery mob. At the cost of Australians' lives and happiness … and you have the audacity to ask me why?'

'His liquidation had not been sanctioned,' Peterson said softly.

'I don't care!' Jim spat back. 'He was there, and I wasn't going to leave any witnesses behind!'

Peterson checked the door to the private room. It was closed. 'ASIO wanted him alive. Do you know how long we've been after Long?'

Jim's lips creased into a smile. 'It doesn't matter how long you guys were after Long,' Jim began, 'the fact of the matter was that while ASIO sat back and played the long game, Long kept entering this country and organising an illicit drug trade that supplied his organisation with funding to carry out other activities around the world! Perhaps you guys shouldn't have been playing ping pong with Long. After all, we all know that Long was not a member of a Chinese tong! Even though it was a long shot, Long ended up at

Meadow Fields Stud and I terminated Long, not with a long shot, but a close shot! Meeting me was his swan song!'

'Droll.'

Jim closed his eyes. He felt exhausted. Poor Larry, Jim ruminated. Poor everyone! Thank God it was over. Now he could go back to being just another normal teenage school kid ... and, maybe, even going around[39] with Christine, if she'd have him. She might not want to, after learning the truth about James Andrew Saston and the danger he had brought to her normal life. All their lives! He opened his eyes, suddenly, and focused on Peterson. 'The other guys, Andrew and Tony, are they okay?'

'Yeah,' Peterson replied. 'Worried about you, though. They were the ones that contacted me right after the three of you were taken. We knew where Edmonds's getaway was and informed the police. They met Fab on their way there.'

Jim frowned. 'How come you knew that much about Edmonds?'

Peterson grinned. '"Trade secret", I think, is what you always tell your friends. Well, that's all you're entitled to know. The rest is far above your clearance level.'

'Now wait a minute ...' Jim sat up and the cannula refused to be a party to the motion, and he winced. Jim lay back.

The door opened and Peterson remained silent.

'Look who wanted to visit you,' Julie said as she guided a wheelchair into the room. She wheeled Christine up to Jim's bed. 'How are you feeling?' she asked, a mother's concern and fear betrayed in her words.

Jim smiled. 'I'm fine. A bit sore, but okay.'

---

[39]'Going around with' (Australian teenage slang for 'dating').

'Well, don't you ever do something as stupid as that again,' she barked suddenly. Julie turned to Peterson. 'And you ... don't you ever let him risk his life again!'

Peterson glanced at Chris, then turned back to his wife. 'I think we need to discuss this calmly, and softly, away from anyone.' He guided Julie to the door, and they left, closing it behind them.

'So, she knows, as well?' Chris asked.

'That was their "plausible deniability" act,' Jim commented. 'Yeah. She knows what her husband is. Otherwise, they'd be living a life of true lies.'

Chris leant forward in her wheelchair, looking defiant. 'Now that I know, what are you going to do?'

'Nothing,' he replied. 'What do you expect me to do?'

'Be honest, from now on.'

Jim smiled. 'I can do that. Up to a point.'

'No,' she demanded. 'There are no limits. What you know, I get to know.'

'Suddenly, you sound like a foreign spy.'

'Why shouldn't I?' she replied, rising from the wheelchair. Chris winced as she brought weight to her bandaged heel. 'After all, my boyfriend is a spy!' She hugged him, shifting her weight off the injured heel, and transferring it to him.

'Ow! Ow! Ow! Ow!'

Chris moved away. 'What's wrong?'

'You're leaning on the drip hose and the needle in my hand doesn't like it, one bit!'

'Oh. Sorry.' She got off his arm.

Jim lifted his arm, taking the strain off the hose. He sighed with relief, his hand stinging. 'Thank you. Now, you can't tell anyone about what I am. It must remain a secret. Besides, I'm not a spy ... I'm more of a secret agent.'

Chris looked him in the eyes. 'What's the difference?'

'A lot,' Jim said with a laugh. 'Spies, saboteurs, and secret agents all differ in skill sets. Spies gather information which is passed on to analysts who process that information and, in turn, hand it off to those in charge of operations. They, in turn, organise operations that are carried out by secret agents, saboteurs, or assassins! I don't want to be a spy.'

'Why not?' Chris whispered.

'Because they plant bugs to listen to what is said, hoping for valuable information. More often than not, they spend their time hearing people go to the toilet or having sex!'

'Lucky them,' Chris said laughing. 'But isn't being a secret agent more dangerous?'

'Yeah,' Jim admitted. 'But it's more fulfilling, as well. Listen, Chris, I've already decided what I want to devote my career to.'

'Hunting down Russian spies?' she asked seriously, 'and killing Chinese ones?' Chris tried to pull away, but Jim's hands stopped her.

'No,' he said. 'The Cold War is nearly over; everyone is behaving themselves. There's a new enemy. Six years ago, the Olympic Games were disrupted by terrorists that took the male Israeli team hostage. They murdered them! After that, Europe re-evaluated its security forces and created units to specifically target terrorist actions. Because of that, terrorists hijacked a French passenger plane and re-routed it into North Africa. They landed in Uganda and that pig, Amin, used the plight of the victims to bolster his international popularity! An Israeli strike force covertly landed at Entebbe and killed all the terrorists and Ugandan soldiers, ordered to protect the terrorists!'

'What's that got to do with being a spy ... sorry ... secret agent?'

'I'm getting to that,' Jim said. 'In March of this year, the Italian Red Brigade kidnapped Aldo Moro. The terrorists made demands that were not met, and they murdered Moro in May! There's a war coming ... against terrorism. A new international alliance is being formed and I intend to be a part of it!'

'How do you know all this?'

'I have access to more information than the world press will ever know. That's how I know these things.'

'Well, you're not doing anything without me,' Chris stated flatly.

He smiled. 'Then we'll spend our lives without true lies.'

'You better believe it. I sent you a note.'

'I know. Mark gave it to me.' Jim picked up the blue envelope. 'I'll read it now.'

'No,' she said. 'Read it when I've left. It'd be embarrassing if you read it in front of me.'

Jim was surprised. 'All right, I'll wait.'

The door opened and the nurse looked in. 'What are you doing here?' she asked Chris. 'Back to your room, my girl.' The nurse placed her hands on the handles of the wheelchair. 'Come on, let him go. He needs his rest ... and so do you. Honestly, you'd think he was a Bay City Roller, the way you've draped yourself over him!'

'Okay, nurse,' Chris said huffily, getting back into the wheelchair. She gave Jim a mischievous smile. 'See you later, lover!'

The nurse guided the wheelchair from the room, lecturing Chris on decorum and behaviour.

As the door shut, Jim ripped the envelope apart. From it came a single sheet of paper with a few lines of writing on it. As usual, instead of writing a straightforward letter, Chris had put her thoughts into a cryptic poem:

Jim,
Stars are shining through the gap
leaving out the pain and lies.
I can live through life
and die a death a thousand times,
as long as you're somewhere around.
I love you,
Christine.
XXX

Jim read it and then returned it to what was left of the envelope and held it up, studying the 'Jamie' written on it. It always took him some time to decipher what she had to say in these poems. Her phraseology was worse than some of the most difficult cyphers he'd had to study! But, as the mud began to clear, a smile grew on his face. She liked him! Him! James Andrew Saston was liked by a girl! No! Loved by a girl!

'I love you, too, Chris,' he said, calming down. Jim placed the letter on the bedside table and was soon asleep.

In the corridor, Mark and Julie watched the nurse wheel Chris away. They exchanged knowing glances.

'Do you think my performance worked?' Julie asked.

Peterson grinned. 'Not on Jim. Hopefully, on Chris.'

Julie looked serious. 'Problem is I wasn't acting. I warn you. Nothing had better happen to him. There will be no missions important enough to concern him. From now on,' she said, 'Jim has the lowest security clearance possible, and can't get his hands on any ongoing operations.'

'That's fine, Julie,' Peterson stated. 'As of now, Jim Saston's off the Active List.'

"Good!'

They turned to go, but Julie had a quick peek into Jim's room and saw that he was resting or sleeping. With a smile, she took Peterson's offered arm and walked towards the waiting elevators.

Peterson's left hand was in his trouser pocket handling the modified switchblade. He knew that the moment Jim left the hospital the teenager would expect it back. Peterson would return it to him, of course. Better to have him armed rather than unarmed! Jim had passed the initiation he had set for himself. This little weapon had killed quite a few people and Peterson knew, as they crossed the road towards the Catholic Cathedral, that now Jim couldn't be stopped!

THE END

BUT THE LEAGUE OF THE GORGON FIVE WILL RETURN!